MOTORCYCLE

BOOK

Second Edition

W9-CAO-542

THE COMPLETE

MOTORCYCLE

BOOK

A CONSUMER'S GUIDE

Second Edition

Jim Bennett

☑® Checkmark Books™
An imprint of Facts On File, Inc.

By the Same Author

*Cheap Wheels: The Complete Guide to Buying,
Selling, and Enjoying Used Cars*

The Complete Motorcycle Book: A Consumer's Guide, Second Edition

Copyright © 1995, 1999 by Jim Bennett
First edition 1995
Second edition 1999
Artwork by Susan Toler and Marlys Weber

Checkmark Books
An Imprint of Facts On File, Inc.
11 Penn Plaza
New York NY 10001

Library of Congress Cataloging-in-Publication Data

Bennett, Jim (James S.)
   The complete motorcycle book : a consumer's guide / James Bennett.
  —2nd ed.
    p. cm.
  Includes index.
  ISBN 0-8160-3853-8. — ISBN 0-8160-3854-6 (pbk.)
   1. Motorcycles—Maintenance and repair. 2. Motorcycles—Purchasing.
  3. Motorcycling. I. Title.
  TL444.B46 1999
  629.227'5—dc21   98-30311

Checkmark Books are available at special discounts when purchased in bulk
quantities for businesses, associations, institutions or sales promotions. Please call
our Special Sales Department in New York at 212/967-8800 or 800/322-8755.

You can find Facts On File on the World Wide Web at http://www.factsonfile.com.
And visit the Complete Motorcycle Book web page at http://www.dogwork.com/
motorcyclebook.

Text design by Catherine Rincon
Cover design by Semadar Megged

Printed in the United States of America

RRD FOF 10 9 8 7 6 5 4 3 2 1

This book is printed on acid-free paper.

CONTENTS

ACKNOWLEDGMENTS

The following people provided their knowledge and energy toward the production of this book, and I thank them for their indispensable help:

Mr. Sammy White, Kawasaki City, Irving, TX
Mr. Ron Seidner, Bert's Motorcycle Mall, Azusa, CA
Mr. Tom Blake, No Five Trails, Santa Maria, CA
Ms. Diana Pierce, Linder Cycle, New Canaan, CT
Mr. Robert Maxant, Illinois Harley-Davidson, Berwyn, IL
Mr. Joe Bromley, Bromley Motorcycle Sales, Trevous, PA
Mr. Mike Reynolds, Mike's Cycle Center, Belleview, FL
Mr. Bill Vickery, Vickery Motorsports, Denver, CO
Mr. Brad Niehaus, Niehaus Cycle Sales, Litchfield, IL
Mr. Kary Krahel, Portland Off-Road Center, Portland, OR
Ms. Robyn Figueroa, *Cycle World Motorcycle Magazine*
Mr. Spiros Gabrilis, Velocita Italiana, Portland, OR
Mr. Jim Woods, Simi Valley Honda, Simi Valley, CA
Ms. Jo Ellen Shires, Common Sense Computing
Ms. Leslie Breed
Ms. Alice LaChapelle
Mr. and Mrs. Robert Medley
Ms. Meegan Kelly
Ms. Elizabeth A. Smith
Mom Jean Bennett
Uncle Harry Swanson

The following companies and organizations were extremely helpful in providing research and photographs:

Motorcycle Industry Council
Motorcycle Safety Foundation
BMW of North America, Inc.
Harley-Davidson Motor Company, Inc.
American Honda Motor Company, Inc.
Kawasaki Motors Corporation, USA
American Suzuki Motor Corporation
Yamaha Motor Corporation, USA
Cagiva North America, Inc.
KTM Sportmotorcycle USA
Triumph Motorcycles, Ltd.
Yuasa Exide Battery Corp.
Amsoil
U.S. Tsubaki
Metzeler Motorcycle Tire North America
Spectro Oils of America
Cycle World Magazine
AAA Foundation for Traffic Safety

American Motorcyclist Association
ATK America, Inc.
Big Dog Motorcycle Company
Buell Motorcycle Company
California Motorcycle Company
Chrome Plated Hearts Motorcycle Club
Drysdale Motorcycle Co., Victoria, Australia
Ducati North America
Motorcycle Consumer News Magazine
Motorcycle Heritage Museum
Portland Sport Touring Center
Polaris Industries
Spokes-Women Motorcycle Club
Ural American, Inc.

With special thanks to Roy Marvin and the Tillamook Burn.

THE COMPLETE

MOTORCYCLE

BOOK

Second Edition

WHEN SOMEONE YOU LOVE WANTS TO RIDE A MOTORCYCLE

The allure of the motorcycle is unique and powerful. The motorcycle is a cerebral machine, appealing to the intellect, employing technology any technophile can appreciate. It symbolizes cultures in a way any social anthropologist can appreciate. The motorcycle is a romantic machine. It evokes deep, bittersweet, nostalgic longings. It is the tool of the lone wolf, the predator and the free and independent spirit. Cultures idolize these traits.

But most of all, the motorcycle is a visceral machine. It appeals to the carnal, the instinctual and the physical senses. It puts before you a challenge and an opportunity to prove yourself. No other 20th-century machine has the appeal, charm and attraction of the motorcycle.

The motorcycle's intellectual, romantic and physical appeal makes its image enduring and makes it a sought-after possession. This appeal explains why owning and riding a motorcycle is such a deeply satisfying experience. But motorcycles are not for everyone.

THE DECISION TO RIDE

The most fundamental question about motorcycles is, "to ride or not to ride?" The decision to ride a motorcycle, whether it is a decision made by you or by someone you care about, should be an informed one. The author of this book is an avid motorcycle rider, experienced in the art and science of motorcycle riding, safety, mechanics and care. I experienced a bountiful youth comprised of many motorcycle-related episodes. However, as much as I love motorcycles, they are not for everyone.

The goal of this chapter is not to convert the masses and spread the gospel of motorcycle riding to every lost soul. On the contrary, although I greatly enjoy the sport, I hope to dissuade many people from riding. If you are dealing with a loved one who is hell-bent on buying a motorcycle, and you are not sure it is in his or her best interest, this book will assist you.

Let us look at a common example: Your 14-year-old son has just informed you that he must have a motorcycle. The acquisition of a two-wheeled vehicle possessing the same horsepower as your sport utility vehicle has suddenly become his only priority. Surprisingly, he has done his homework on this subject. He has become friends with several people who own motorcycles. He has smuggled fringe-group motorcycle magazines into the house. He has memorized the horsepower, displacement, features and popular paint schemes of every motorcycle produced on the planet today. He is fanatically driven and ready to purchase a motorcycle. He wants, perhaps needs, your okay.

If you are like many parents, the thought of your child racing virtually unprotected down Route 50 at Bonneville Salt Flat speeds fills

YAMAHA GTS1000

Class: sports.
Engine: liquid-cooled, in-line four 4-stroke.
Displacement: 1003cc.
Valve Arrangement: DOHC 5.
Transmission: 5-speed.
Final Drive: chain.
Brakes: single disc front & rear.
Weight: 637 lbs.

(Art courtesy of Yamaha Motor Corporation, USA.)

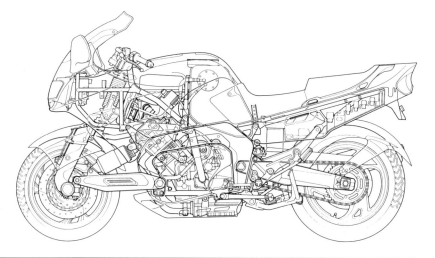

you with horror. You have spent time, love and money raising him, and he is perhaps only now beginning to show a redeeming quality or two. After all, he is so soft, and all those things on the road are so hard . . . so unforgiving. You have a responsibility to protect him from death, protect your family from the current dysfunctional trauma, and, depending on the situation, protect society from your child.

What should you do?

There are four basic courses of action. The first choice is to "just say no." The second alternative is to talk the prospective rider out of riding through superior logic and practical reasoning. The third position is to offer a better option to the prospective rider. The final course of action, when the others fail to produce the desired result, is to accept the fact that there is a new motorcycle rider in the family. (This last option may not sound great, but it is realistic.)

JUST SAY NO

Back to our scenario. Your 14-year-old son has just informed you that he must have a motorcycle. You are in a quandary: What to do? First, let us discuss what not to do. Based on personal experience, you should not trust this decision to any of the off-the-shelf methodologies parents often employ in times of conflict with their young. For example, do not:

- Deliver the one-two punch that jabs with "NO!" and crosses with "not as long as you're under my roof." More likely than not, if he is ready for a motorcycle he is also ready for his own roof. If he is really determined to own a motorcycle, this will only compound your problems.
- Refuse to talk with him further on the subject. He doesn't really want to talk to you about it anyway. He wants you to sign the paperwork, maybe loan him a few bucks, etc.
- Tell him that you rode a motorcycle in the old days, and that you know all about them. Motorcycles these days bear about as much resemblance to the motorcycles of 20 years ago as a bottle rocket does to a space shuttle.
- Think that this is only a phase which will pass quickly. The particular mind set that compels people to ride motorcycles (one-part thrill seeker, one-part exhibitionist and one-part death wish) is often a lifelong condition.
- Threaten to write him out of your will, spend his college fund on a trip to the Bahamas or deliver him bound and gagged to a U.S. Army recruiter. Chances are these things don't matter to him or don't scare him at all. Besides, basic training is not nearly as scary as a high speed turn on a motorcycle.

You may have already made a mistake by taking one of these precipitous courses of action. Do not worry; the damage is not irreparable. You can gain your son's respect (and gain credibility in future discussions) by learning some things about motorcycles that he does not know. The next step is to use logic and common sense to dissuade your young lad.

THE LOGICAL DISCUSSION

If you tried the "just-say-no" option, perhaps a little growth on your part is required. Face the fact that you have raised a child who likes shiny things that go fast. He is drawn by the urge to skillfully pilot potent, exotic machinery. He may even be afflicted by the most virulent form of the disease: the uncontrollable desire to see the overtaken adversary (amidst clouds of dust) in his rearview mirror. Lament if you must, spend sleepless nights wondering where you went wrong, but do not confuse the issue. To deal intelligently with your child about motorcycles, you must know something about them!

This course of action rests on two important questions. One is, "Should your loved-one ride?" Does he have the mental, physical, spiritual and financial resources to responsibly operate a motorcycle? Does he have the knowledge to combine these resources into a smooth, error-free ride?

The other question is, "What should he ride?" Will this bike enhance or degrade his resources? Both questions have profound consequences if not fully explored and rationally answered. Since the decision to ride is the most fundamental of the two questions, that question is examined here. Later chapters examine what to ride, should the situation come to that.

So, does your son have the mental, physical, spiritual and financial resources to responsibly operate a motorcycle? Does he know what motorcycle riding is about? Discuss the following topics in an honest and fair conversation with your son.

Mental Resources

Does your loved one possess the mental faculties to handle a motorcycle? Riding takes composure, maturity, respect and a continuous attentiveness that is unique to the sport. Motorcycle riding is defensive driving in the extreme. The slings and arrows of outrageous fortune happen, and it is the motorcycle rider's personal imperative to prevent catastrophe. (Other drivers may have the legal imperative, but if you find yourself arguing over who has the legal imperative, something very bad has probably happened to the motorcycle and possibly to the rider.)

Even if your son is a good motorist (a.k.a. car driver), he does not necessarily possess these faculties.

To ride a motorcycle safely, a motorcyclist must perform many crucial tasks, most of which are not applicable to automobile travel. Not only must he follow the rules of the road like all other drivers, he must also:

- Take full responsibility for being seen by other motorists. The most common explanation offered by motorists at the scene of an auto-motorcycle accident is "I never saw him 'til I hit him."
- Pay special and constant attention to the road surface. A pothole that wouldn't even ripple your coffee inside a Cadillac Seville can send a motorcyclist head over heels (known as an "endo").
- Maintain a constant and intense level of scrutiny on a variety of objects and situations on or near the road that are of little or no concern or danger to motorists. Is that loose muffler on the Studebaker Lark two cars ahead going to fall off onto the road? Is that raven, picking away at road kill, going to fly into my path? Is the wind burst from that Freightliner going to blast me out of my lane? Is that a shiny tar spot in my path or wet pavement? Is the bee that just flew up my shirt going to sting me so badly that I lose control of the bike?

A motorcycle rider must anticipate, recognize, evaluate and act upon the smallest clues about many aspects of driving that are inconsequential to the automobile driver. And he must do these things quickly—often very, very quickly. It takes acute mental skill and practice to learn to evaluate the road and its drivers. It is a process that will include mistakes and errors in judgment, many of which can put the motorcyclist in harm's way.

ACTION: Anyone who rides should demonstrate good mental skills. How has your potential rider shown these skills? Take your young rider for a drive in your car. Ask an experienced motorcycle rider to ride along. During the trip, ask both to keep a list of potential motorcycle hazards. After about a mile drive, the experienced rider will probably have a list of 30 or 40 different hazards. If your son does not come close, give him two weeks to read up on motorcycles and offer a re-test. If the second test brings poor results, shut the book on motorcycle riding for now—your young rider is just not ready.

Physical Resources

A motorcyclist must be a healthy, physically fit, fully functioning person. Here are some examples why:

- In an emergency, an average motorcycle traveling 60 m.p.h. needs approximately five seconds (220 feet) to come to a full stop on good road. The first half second is reaction time, or the amount of time it takes the rider to recognize a need to brake and then activate the brake lever and pedal. During that time, the bike will travel 22 feet. The remaining distance is consumed by applying pressure to the brakes. A rider with poor, or drug inhibited, eyesight, reflexes or hearing may not identify a braking situation fast enough or apply the proper braking force to safely stop.
- When the rider cannot brake his way out of a situation, an emergency maneuver may need to be performed. Often this entails countersteering, an action where the bike is steered in one direction while the rider leans to the other. This maneuver takes strong leg, arm and upper torso muscles, along with a very good sense of balance.
- When a rear tire blows out on a motorcycle, the survival response is to grip the handlebars firmly and keep the bike on a straight course while the rear fishtails wildly behind. This takes a great deal of upper body, arm and hand strength. (By the way, the rider shouldn't brake. Braking changes the suspension telemetry and reduces the rider's grip on the handlebars, neither of which is desired.)

In other words, riding a motorcycle takes a fit, strong, agile body with all senses working fully. Does your potential rider display these physical skills?

Spiritual Resources

This is simple. Does your son have a spiritual understanding that will allow him to appreciate the honor, privilege and responsibility vested in him whenever he is on the road? Does he have the respect for life required of someone who has the potential to take life? Does he have respect for his own life? These are often difficult concepts for a teenager, filled with immortality and life, to understand. (Many people never achieve this understanding, but that is beside the point.) Do not let this child ride without this respect for life! A spiritual grounding can offer more protection than a full face helmet and leather chaps.

Financial Resources

Somehow motorcycling has a reputation as a fun and inexpensive sport. It is fun. It is not inexpensive. A safe and reliable machine can cost anywhere from $1,000 (if you look long and hard at the used bike market) to $20,000—and more if you finance the purchase. In addition, there are the costs of licensing, taxes, insurance, protective wear, gas, maintenance, tags and a host of accessories. In the final analysis, a motorcycle may not be as inexpensive as a used automobile.

Here are some costs of riding: Insurance (if he can get it) can cost anywhere from $400 to $2,600 a year. Insurance is a must, not just for the rider, but for the innocent bystander that may be injured.

Maintenance will average about $300 a year over the life of an average motorcycle. Maintenance will be more if the bike is raced, not garaged or otherwise abused. Motorcycle parts, often made out of rare materials, are very expensive. Using a Yamaha Virago as an example, good tires cost about $100 each; a battery costs $75; the air filter costs $26; a complete tune-up costs $186; non-competition muffler replacements cost $150.

Your son might mention that he can get a job if he has a motorcycle. He may propose doing yard work for Mrs. Jones three miles away, flipping patties at the burger joint or working as a motorcycle courier in the city. You will need to weigh the relative practicality of this claim. If he makes a deal that depends on the motorcycle for transportation, he will need backup transportation for those days when the weather prohibits two-wheeled travel. [Note: My advice is not to let your son become a motorcycle courier in a city. It is bad, dangerous work.]

ACTION: List the costs and savings of motorcycle ownership. Do not forget to have your son call around for insurance quotes.

ACTION: Your son may not understand the significance of riding without insurance. May I suggest that, with some finesse, you take something he values, perhaps his favorite CD or guitar. Hold on to it and refuse to replace it when he really needs it. This may seem to you to be a shallow, materialistic gesture only simulating about a hundredth of the agony suffered by a victim of an uninsured motorcycle accident. You are right. But do not underestimate the shallowness and materialism of a young male.

Knowledge Base for Riding

Does your young rider really know what he is getting into? Motorcycling involves more than just owning a motorcycle. Even with the individual mental, physical, spiritual and financial resources, he must have the knowledge that brings these skills together. This book is part of that knowledge base. But since this chapter is about the question of whether or not to ride, here are some discouraging ideas few novices think about.

Safety—An old motorcycler's adage goes, "There are old motorcycle riders, and bold motorcycle riders, but there are no old, bold motorcycle riders." On average, there are 100,000 reported motorcycle accidents resulting in 3,200 deaths each year. But these statistics do not tell the whole story.

One of the most influential research studies on motorcycle safety was produced by H.L. Hurt of the University of Southern California Traffic Safety Center in 1981. It is required reading for anyone wanting a motorcycle. A few of its findings are especially relevant here.

Not unexpectedly, it is the inexperienced or incapable riders who get hurt most often:

- More than half the motorcycle riders having reportable accidents had less than five months' experience on that vehicle.
- Ninety-two percent of riders in reportable accidents were essentially without training.
- Almost half the motorcycle accidents involving fatalities show alcohol involvement. Although the percentage of motorcycle riders who drive under the influence of alcohol is no higher than that of car drivers, a motorcycle rider driving while intoxicated (DWI) is two-and-a-half times more likely to be seriously injured than is a motorist DWI.

Inexperience is the most common contributor to motorcycle accidents. Alcohol use is the most common factor in serious injury accidents. Combined, these two conditions are deadly.

Why? When on a motorcycle the rider must protect himself not only from his own mistakes, but from those of other drivers. And other drivers make many mistakes. Multivehicle accidents make up 75% of all motorcycle accidents. Sixty-six percent of these (i.e., 50% of all motorcycle accidents) are caused by a motorist's failure to see the motorcycle. Out of the 25% of accidents that are single-vehicle motorcycle accidents, a car forced the motorcycle out of the rider's lane two-fifths of the time. In other words, nearly 60% of all accidents are the fault of a car driver!

The failure rate of car drivers apparently shows the dismal lack of attention they pay to the task of driving. It also suggests that the remaining 40% of motorcycle accidents are caused by motorcycle rider error. Many motorcycle accidents are totally within the power of a motorcycle rider to avoid.

In the final analysis, a new rider like your son is more likely to be involved in an accident and much more likely to be involved in a fatal accident than an experienced rider. Clearly, the trick is to stay out of an accident. This is something inexperienced riders do not do as well as seasoned riders. The statistics show that there are a large number of trained motorcycle riders whose risk of a fatal accident is almost negligible. There is a small number of immature, untrained or inexperienced riders racking up some frightening fatality statistics.

There are several myths about motorcycle riding that the Hurt report dispels:

- Myth: Motorists attack motorcyclists. Fact: Deliberate hostile action by a motorist against a motorcycle rider is a rare accident cause.
- Myth: Bad weather causes many accidents. Fact: Weather is not a factor in 98% of motorcycle accidents.
- Myth: Road defects cause many accidents. Fact: Road defects (pavement ridges, potholes, etc.) are the cause of 2% of accidents; animal involvement is responsible for 1% of accidents.
- Myth: Helmets make riding less safe. Fact: Wearing a helmet does not increase the probability of an accident. It also does not reduce vision or hearing. Wearing a helmet does not increase the probability of neck injury in an accident. If the only thing you or your son learn from this book is WEAR A HELMET, WEAR A HELMET, WEAR A HELMET, you have your money's worth. There is an old motorcycle adage that goes "If you have a cheap head, get a cheap helmet." Better advice was never given.

The Hurt report is available through the University of Southern California Traffic Safety Center or through the National Technical Information Service in Springfield, Virginia.

ACTION: Alcohol plays a major role in half the motorcycle accidents. Discuss the implications of driving while intoxicated with your son. Even at 14, he has access.

ACTION: Ask your son to put on shorts and a tee shirt, go out in the driveway, and get down on his knees and elbows. Now tell him to crawl the length of the driveway three times. Chances are that he will explain to you how that would leave his elbows and knees raw and sore. Query him about how pleasant cascading down 150 yards of asphalt at 50 m.p.h. would be.

ACTION: Take your son to talk to an emergency room doctor. One I knew, who worked at a U.S. Air Force emergency room, said that motorcycle accidents rival airplane crashes for the kinds and amounts of damage done to human beings.

Clothing—Proper motorcycle attire is essential. No matter how sunny the day, how pretty the girl, how light the traffic, how compelling all the reasons to ride less than properly clothed, the rider must be properly swathed in case of a fall.

The best protection comes from those items that are rigid, padded, tear and abrasion resistant or some combination of the three. The list of mandatory clothing is expensive. Take your son to the local motorcycle shop or get a parts and accessories catalog and price the clothing. Here is a representative list of what the rider must have, with modest current prices:

Full Face Helmet	$250
Thick Leather Jacket	$250
Leather Chaps	$150
Leather Boots	$150
Boot Socks	$12
Leather Summer Gloves	$35
Leather Winter Gloves	$55
Optic Yellow Rainsuit	$85

These clothing items total almost $1,000. Note that saving a few bucks on motorcycle clothing usually buys you an inferior product and a reduced margin of safety.

Motorcycle clothing is different from the clothing required by most other sports. Motorcycle clothing should be chosen with protection, not fashion, in mind. Also note that denim jeans and jackets are not on the list. Although denim is the material of choice for many motorcycle riders, and is preferable in an accident to being nude, it affords little protection in case of a hard fall. Denim—and we're talking about the industrial grade, ditch digging kind—offers good protection against small airborne rocks, bugs and wind. It offers almost no protection against concrete or asphalt at 60 m.p.h.

We are not talking about fashion leather, either, which is not heavy enough to provide the abrasion protection motorcycle riders need in a wipe out. For leather protection, go to a motorcycle dealership or to the local leather smith and buy a jacket or chaps made for motorcycle riding. These will have special features to make riding safe, warm and enjoyable. Fashion leather does not have these features, although it probably costs as much or more.

The temptation to shed any or all of these items on a sunny day is great. It is indescribably pleasant to zip down a windy country road clad only in shorts and flip-flops. It is also indescribably stupid. Because the laws of physics are not suspended on sunny days, some kind of compromise between comfort, protection and enjoyment must be reached. In practice, smart riders wear the most and best clothing they can stand to have on. Smart riders never ride barefoot, shirtless, in shorts or without a helmet. At a minimum, total body coverage must be maintained.

Weather—Only an Arctic explorer knows more about cold than an experienced motorcycle rider. Most new riders do not consider or understand the physiological implications of riding at 55 m.p.h. on a chilly day. Unless you live in Southern California or along the Gulf Coast South, you can build a very compelling argument against motorcycle riding by getting a wind-chill chart and doing a little math.

ACTION: Go to the library and get some rain and temperature statistics for your area. There are going to be some very cold and wet days every year. Using the wind chill chart found in the chapter on Safety, calculate the average wind chill for each month in your area. Explain to your son how cold this will make him when he rides. Tell him that at calculated temperatures below about 30°F, no amount of clothing will help. If your area has cold weather, have your son ride his 21 speed bicycle in the cold and rain. Any trip of more than five minutes will be agony.

ACTION: To prove your point, have your son dress as warmly as he can and hose him down with the garden hose for 10 minutes. Be sure to get a good soaking spray over his face to simulate the low visibility he will have when driving in a downpour.

Sex—While teenage girls have an affinity for motorcycles, they are not as compatible as one might think. Dating on a motorcycle is difficult and limited. Besides not having a back seat, motorcycles have other serious drawbacks when it comes to dating.

Here are two facts that might impress your son:

- In the entire history of the world, no parents have knowingly let their teenage daughter go out on a date on a motorcycle. Ever! Having a motorcycle can, then, be the same as going to an all boys' school.
- Girls cannot safely wear high fashion clothes on a motorcycle. They will melt their boots on the muffler, get oil on their dresses, burn their legs on the engine and get bugs in their hair. They know this, and frequently will not be willing to subject their fashion statement du jour to the buffeting effects of a motorcycle trip.

ACTION: Have him call around for a few dates. Be sure the girl's parents know that there is a motorcycle involved.

Horror Stories—No other mode of transportation or recreational pastime has a vocabulary as lethal as motorcycle riding. The lexicon of motorcycle wrecks includes names such as "T-bones," "low-sides," "high-sides," "flips" and "endos." These names are more than colorful phrases. They are shorthand jargon describing the more common motorcycle mishaps.

The most frequent accident, according to the Hurt report, is an automobile making a left turn in front of an oncoming motorcycle. If the motorcycle proceeds at roughly a 90° angle into the side of the car, the rider has just executed the classic "T-bone." That is, the longitudinal axes of the vehicles form a "T."

When a motorcycle is turned too sharply and loses traction, you have what is known as a "low side." In a low-side accident, the bike slides along the pavement on its side, with the rider on top. Thus, the bike is on the "low-side" of the rider. The proper rider response to a low-side is to sit on top of the bike and ride it out until the bike comes to rest, being sure that no legs or arms are pinned between the motorcycle and the road.

Should the rapidly decelerating motorcycle hit an obstacle or a patch of pavement having high traction, a low-side may turn instantaneously into a "high-side." A high-side is one of the most dangerous motorcycle accidents. During a high-side, the downed and sliding motorcycle snags, rotates on its longitudinal axis and begins to roll. The unsuspecting rider can be launched with considerable velocity off the island of safety afforded by the top of the motorcycle while it is grinding to a halt. This happens very quickly, and usually results in the rider being tossed some distance.

A "flip" is just that. Flipping a motorcycle involves having the front wheel raise straight up past vertical, continuing its arc until the motorcycle is upside down, with its rear wheel in the front.

An "endo" is not named for the fact that it might end your life, but it might. An endo is the mirror image of a flip. That is, the rear wheel rises past vertical, and continues its arc until it is the leading wheel. Again the motorcycle is upside down.

These terms refer only to how a motorcycle accident is started, or to the way in which control of the vehicle is lost. The variety of motions and the unlimited number of obstacles into which the out-of-control motorcycle rider may impact defy cataloging. In retrospect, each accident warrants, and will undoubtedly receive, individual description. For example, "I swung left to avoid T-boning the bus, tried a low-side to avoid the guard rail, high-sided on the curb, and cracked my skull on the median 25 feet away."

You can surely find a motorcycle rider (or ex-rider) who is willing to talk to your son about the hazards of riding. Just ask around at the office. Everyone knows someone who has given up riding because of some horrendous accident. One relative smashed up my Honda SL125 jumping a deep rut along a fire road in the Siskiyou mountains of Oregon. The bike leaped into the air in "Hi-Ho Silver" fashion as he gunned the motor, hopelessly out of control. The entire bike landed on his knee. It ended any chance of his going to Vietnam (he was rated 4F), and ended any chance of his playing professional football. Damage to the bike was $350, or 40% of the cost of a new SL125.

ACTION: It is possible in many communities to arrange for your son to ride along with a law enforcement officer or paramedic crew for an evening. He might see the lump of human flesh that is the aftermath of a T-bone, low-side or high-side.

FALLBACK COURSE: BRIBE HIM WITH A CAR

After you have exhausted the advice and strategies already detailed, and tranquility in the family has vanished, you may have to reassess the situation. It is quite likely that your son has displayed a single-mindedness that you have never seen before. If he has held true to form, he has told you that he can muster the resources to buy that motorcycle himself. He may or may not purchase insurance and protective gear. He may or may not take a safety course.

He may startle you with his resolve to work nights and weekends pumping gas or frying hot dogs. His plans may include forgoing school, sports, girls and family until he has managed to purchase a motorcycle. Peace in the family may never exist again unless this issue is successfully resolved.

If you are dead set against him having a motorcycle, consider helping him buy a car. If he is not mature enough for a car, sacrifice peace in the family: For his sake and for that of other motorists, KEEP HIM OFF THE ROAD!

DEFAULT COURSE: MAKE RIDING AS SAFE AS POSSIBLE

Your son may buy a bike anyway, without your approval or support. Or, all your fine logic notwithstanding and against your better judgment, you may capitulate and let him have a motorcycle just to bring serenity back to your household. If either of these situations should happen, try to remember that your position about motorcycles was based on your concern for his safety. Hold that thought, and take the steps that are available to you to ensure that he rides as safely as possible. Like it or not, your son now rides a motorcycle.

You can help him ride more safely by giving him a copy of this book to read. You can help him ride more safely by reading this book yourself, especially the sections of the book on how to buy, maintain and ride a motorcycle. You can help by participating in the decision-making process. You can help by finding the right motorcycle for him. If he plans to buy a new bike, read Chapters 2, 4 and 5. If he wants to buy a used bike, read Chapters 2, 6 and 7. If he buys a used bike without the benefit of the knowledge in this book, offer to take it through the inspections described. If the bike does not measure up, consider helping him get something better. No matter what he wants or buys, read Chapter 9 on safe riding and quiz your son on its contents.

When someone makes the decision to ride, the best thing you can do is make it as safe a ride as possible. A friend went through this process with his parents. He finally got the motorcycle against his parents' protests. The next day his father bought him a $300 Vanson leather jacket. There is good sense in that. There are only so many things you can do to protect someone from their craziness in a democracy. Those things you can do, you do.

Make sure he gets insurance, especially catastrophic health insurance (required for motorcycle drivers in some states). Make sure he enrolls in a safe driving course through your local police department or community college. Make sure he buys some protective riding gear so he can make it through the first year of ownership. If he does, his odds of not being involved in an accident dramatically improve.

TO RIDE OR NOT TO RIDE?

Motorlife with a teenager is often a series of Richter Scale increases in intensity and drama. This is nothing new for parents. You are not a bad parent for incurring your son's wrath when trying to save his life.

Not everyone has a 14-year-old son to look after. Perhaps it is your daughter who has just announced that she needs the money to buy a bike, or your 22-year-old boyfriend, 45-year-old husband or good friend. Or maybe you are thinking about a motorcycle. No matter. We all share that same fever of the 14-year-old (albeit with less hormonal discord). We all have some deep primal craving to satisfy. Everyone should have the benefit of the knowledge in this book, whether they read the book themselves or you read the book and tell them about it. The point is this: It is everyone's business to be sure that the best decisions are made.

TYPES AND STYLES OF MOTORCYCLES

Motorcycle terminology is not precise. What one manufacturer refers to as an enduro another may call an off-road. What one calls a cruiser another may call a street bike. And so on. For clarity, this chapter breaks down motorcycles into street bikes, trail bikes and dual purpose bikes. Street bikes can be divided into touring, cruisers, sports, sports touring, customs, choppers, standards and Harley-Davidsons. Trail bikes include off-road, motocross, trials and cross-countries. Dual-purpose bikes are simply that, bikes that serve the needs for both street and trail.

In addition, motorcycles may transcend their category if they become valuable enough and rare enough to merit collecting. These bikes are classified as either collectible or vintage. There are also enough modified bikes to merit separate classification as sidecars and trikes. Finally, there are the imitators and wanna-bees: mopeds, scooters and minibikes.

STREET BIKES

Street bikes range in size from 50cc (cubic centimeters) to over 1600cc. Each is built to serve as transportation on macadam or asphalt rather than on unpaved dirt. A street bike is a bike designed solely for use on paved surfaces.

The term "street bike" is used by some to refer to any bike that is legally capable of being licensed for the street. To be "street legal" a machine must have lights, brakes on at least one wheel and a rearview mirror. Most states require the rider to wear a helmet and have eye protection. Many states require additional street equipment such as turn signals, a speedometer, passenger seat and buddy pegs. A motorcycle must also be approved by the federal Department of Transportation (DOT), the Environmental Protection Agency and possibly your local bureaucracy responsible for vehicle regulation or environmental quality.

However, the ability to license a bike for the street does not in itself make the bike safe to operate on the street. For example, an off-road motorcycle is not a street bike because of the compromises made to allow it to operate optimally in the dirt, even though an off-road bike can be street legal. The high fenders do not provide protection from tire spray should you cross a wet surface. The knobs on the tires will make for a bumpy ride at low speeds and are nothing short of treacherous at highway speeds. The transmission is geared for low speed and high torque. A rider would have trouble keeping up with traffic on the freeway with such a bike.

Other bikes, such as 50cc minibikes or professional cafe racers, are also not street bikes even if street licensed. The first is too gutless and the other too brawny to be safely operated on the road. A street bike is one that can be legally licensed to operate on the street and is designed for riding on the street.

A true street bike has street legal equipment and street tires, street suspension, street riding position, street instrumentation and street mufflers. These are very distinguishing features. These features not only mark a true street bike, they make it virtually impossible to use off-road. Street bikes are usually characterized by the following features and attributes:

- Engine
  - ☐ Single cylinder if less than 250cc
  - ☐ Multicylinder if more than 250cc
  - ☐ Low-slung exhaust systems
  - ☐ Five- or six-speed gear box
  - ☐ Relatively low power-to-weight ratio
  - ☐ Key ignition switch

- Frame, suspension and steering
  - ☐ Seating capacity for two
  - ☐ Smooth suspension
  - ☐ Short travel suspension

- □ Center and side stands (kickstands)
- □ Low fenders
- □ Relatively narrow and swept back handlebars
- □ Moderate to extreme steering rake

- Wheels and tires
  - □ Relatively small diameter wheels
  - □ Relatively weak wheels
  - □ Wide radius tires
  - □ Shallow tread patterns

- Controls and gauges
  - □ Speedometer
  - □ Tachometer
  - □ Turn signal indicator
  - □ Neutral light (gear indicator on large machines)
  - □ High beam indicator
  - □ Gas gauge (on larger bikes)
  - □ Oil pressure or level lamp

- Electrical system
  - □ Large, high-powered headlights
  - □ Large, conspicuous blinkers and taillights
  - □ Loud horn
  - □ Electric start
  - □ Relatively large and high-capacity battery

Obviously, there are exceptions to these generalizations. For example, a 125cc bike, be it street or off-road, is not going to have elaborate controls or need an electric start.

Street bikes come in the following variations: touring, cruisers, sports, sports touring, customs, choppers, standards and Harley-Davidsons.

Touring Bikes

Also called full dressers, touring bikes are designed to make you virtually self-contained, independent of anyone and anything except the gas station. Long range riding is the purpose of touring bikes. Riders are surrounded with creature comforts. The ride is extremely smooth, quiet and plush. Modern touring bikes offer plenty of performance, too. Some common features of a touring class motorcycle include:

TOURING BIKE

KAWASAKI VOYAGER

Class: touring.
Engine: liquid-cooled in-line
4-cylinder 4-stroke.
Displacement: 1196cc.
Valve Arrangement: DOHC
4 valves per cylinder.
Transmission: 5-speed.
Final Drive: shaft.
Brakes: dual disc front, single
disc rear.
Weight: 729 lbs.

(Photo courtesy of Kawasaki Motors Corp., USA.)

CRUISERS

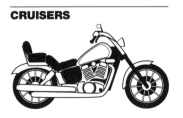

- Large fairings to provide excellent protection from wind and rain
- Broad seats with back support
- Plenty of cargo space incorporated into the bike's design
- Radios, tape decks, CBs, intercoms, shortwaves, etc.
- Trip computers, cruise control, digital displays
- Air compressors and easily adjustable suspensions
- High visibility "Freightliner" lighting
- Trailer towing capacity
- Shaft or belt final drive

Cruisers

Cruisers are large displacement, long distance machines. A cruiser is designed for a comfortable full-day ride. Cruisers are not cluttered with all the motorhome accoutrements of a full dresser. Power comes from raw, brutal displacement. Enjoyment comes from the fundamental blending of man, machine and road. Features of a basic cruiser include:

- Massive displacement
- Enough power to scorch young punks

POLARIS VICTORY

Class: cruiser.
Engine: oil-cooled, 50° V-twin 4-stroke
Displacement: 1507cc.
Valve Arrangement: SOHC 4 valves per cylinder, hydraulic tappets.
Transmission: 5-speed.
Final Drive: belt.
Brakes: single disc front and rear.
Weight: 600 lbs.
Horsepower: 75

(Photo courtesy of Polaris Industries.)

- Heavy, but who cares
- Relatively easy to ride, if you're going straight
- Relatively easy to maintain
- Comfort for a long day's ride
- Mellow, satisfying exhaust note
- Room for two

Cruisers have developed into two distinct variations in recent years. The first is the standard cruiser where form follows function. Competent execution of riding fundamentals takes precedence over style.

KAWASAKI NOMAD

Class: retro cruiser.
Engine: liquid-cooled 50° V-twin, 4-stroke.
Displacement: 1470cc.
Valve Arrangement: SOHC 4 valves per cylinder.
Transmission: 5-speed.
Final Drive: shaft.
Brakes: dual disc front, single disc rear.
Weight: 660 lbs.

(Photo courtesy of Kawasaki Motors Corp., USA.)

With the outrageous success of the Harley-Davidson and its influence on the world market, all manufacturers seem to be producing a "retro" cruiser, the second type of cruiser. These versions borrow heavily from Harley and Indian designs of the 1940s and 1950s. The elements imitated include flared, skirted, valenced fenders; wide white wall tires; V-twin or V-four engines; displacements from 500cc to 1600cc; front light bar with spotlights; two-tone paint jobs; big chrome; shrouded forks and spoked wheels.

Sports

Modern sports bikes right off the showroom floor are just a step shy of what competes on the cafe racing circuit. The technology of racing bikes combined with the creature comforts folks require for a day of swift canyon blasting is the basic formula for a sports bike. The look of the bike is that of a race bike, with plenty of aerodynamic fiberglass molded around the engine and rider. Features include:

- High-tech designs and materials
- Low "sport" riding position
- High-performance suspension, engine, brakes and tires
- High ground clearances for steep leaning in turns
- Enough off-the-line power to beat all but the most specialized drag bikes
- Enough top end to beat all but the most specialized race bikes
- Abbreviated fairings
- Rear set footpegs
- Clip-on handlebars

SPORTS

BUELL WHITE LIGHTNING SPORTS BIKE

Class: sports.
Engine: air-cooled, V-twin 4-stroke.
Displacement: 1203cc.
Valve Arrangement: OHV 2 valves per cylinder, hydraulic adjusters.
Transmission: 5-speed.
Final Drive: Kevlar belt.
Brakes: single disc front & rear.
Weight: 425 lbs.
Torque: 90 lb.ft.
Horsepower: 101.

(Photo courtesy of Buell Motorcycle Company.)

SUZUKI TL1000 SUPERSPORT

Class: supersport.
Engine: liquid-cooled, 90°
V-twin 4-stroke.
Displacement: 996cc.
Valve Arrangement: DOHC
4 valves per cylinder.
Transmission: 6-speed.
Final Drive: chain.
Brakes: dual disc front, single
disc rear.
Weight: 411 lbs.
Horsepower: 109.

*(Photo courtesy of American Suzuki
Motor Corp.)*

Within the sports bike category are three distinct classifications: sports bikes, supersports and superbikes. The distinction between the three is in the level of technology each delivers.

Sports bikes are the lowest level, but this does not mean that they are low tech. Even though these bikes are at the bottom end of the category, they still deliver far more speed, power and performance than the average street rider could ever put to the test. Sometimes called "crotch rockets," these bikes are known in hospital emergency rooms as "donor-mobiles."

Simple modifications to a sports bike can increase horsepower by 20–25% and raise top speeds by 20–30 m.p.h. These bikes are known as supersports. For an extra few thousand dollars, knowledgeable, sophisticated enthusiasts can get a near cutting-edge speed machine.

The superbike, a variation of the sports bike, has found its own significant niche in the market. Superbikes are top-of-the-line sports bikes with one basic goal: sidereal speed, 180 m.p.h. speed. As such, every component must be optimized for this goal. Hot-looking plastic shrouds and other fancy features that the marketing department puts on the wish list for a sports bike have no place on a superbike unless they add m.p.h. Purchasers of a superbike are the most serious of the speed freaks. Additional features include:

- The stiffest of rigid suspensions
- Wide-open, free flowing, sinuous exhaust systems
- Large rotor, multipiston caliper disc brakes front and rear
- Big bore, short stroke pistons
- Straight port cylinder heads
- Wide power bands
- Gobs of low-end torque

DUCATI 916 SUPERBIKE

Class: superbike.
Engine: liquid-cooled, 90°
V-twin 4-stroke.
Displacement: 916cc.
Valve Arrangement: DOHC,
Desmodronic, 4 valves per
cylinder.
Transmission: 6-speed.
Final Drive: chain.
Brakes: dual disc front, single
disc rear.
Weight: 435 lbs.
Horsepower: 105.

*(Photo courtesy of Ducati North
America.)*

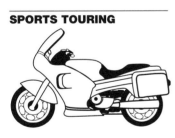

SPORTS TOURING

Sports Touring Bikes

Sports touring bikes are a cross between sports and touring bikes. That classification stems from blending the best characteristics of both into one machine. But a sports touring bike should not be confused with a motorcycle that is a collection of components from the parts bins of sports and touring machines. The sports touring motorcycle has its own unique technology blend.

Compared to touring bikes, sports touring motorcycles are lighter, handle better and offer more performance. Like a sports bike, these bikes often feature:

- Leading edge, high-performance engines
- Aerodynamic fiberglass fairings and panels
- High-tech suspension

Compared to sports bikes, the sports touring motorcycle offers some long distance features of the touring machine, such as:

BMW K1100LT

Class: sports touring.
Engine: liquid-cooled, longitudinal in-line 4-cylinder 4-stroke.
Displacement: 1093cc.
Valve Arrangement: DOHC 4 valves per cylinder.
Transmission: 5-speed.
Final Drive: shaft.
Brakes: dual disc front, single disc rear.
Weight: 551 lbs.
Torque: 77 lb.ft.
Horsepower: 100.

(Photo courtesy of BMW of North America.)

- Plush seating for two
- Low vibration, smooth shaft drive
- Removable luggage (saddlebags) often incorporated into frame
- Fairing providing good wind and rain protection
- Adjustable suspension

Custom Bikes

The variety of motorcycles found in today's showrooms did not always exist. This is a recent phenomena in motorcycle history that began in the 1970s, coming to full fruition in the 1980s. It used to be that you bought a basic motorcycle and customized it to suit your needs and taste. You chromed it, repainted it, added lights, changed the forks, did whatever you wanted to create an individualized machine. This is how the custom was born. Customs feature:

CUSTOM BIKES

- Unique exhaust systems that produce a deep, heart-thumping exhaust note
- Raked front forks, swept-back or high handlebars, and low seat position creating a laid-back James Dean "I'll let the babes come to me" look
- Usually seating for two (for when you select from one of the many women who have clustered around your custom), but often very austere second seat
- Eye-catching, high-fashion paint jobs
- Lots of chrome.

YAMAHA VIRAGO 1100

Class: custom.
Engine: air-cooled, 75° V-twin 4-stroke.
Displacement: 1063cc.
Valve Arrangement: SOHC 2 valves per cylinder.
Transmission: 5-speed.
Final Drive: shaft.
Brakes: dual disc front, drum rear.
Weight: 487 lbs.

(Photo courtesy of Yamaha Motor Corp., USA.)

Customs come in a wide variety: factory customs, made-to-order and exotics.

Factory Customs—The sales potential of custom motorcycles has not been lost on the large Japanese motorcycle companies. As a result, factory-made customs are produced, despite the fact that "factory-made custom" is an oxymoron. Although produced in large numbers, the bikes faithfully fulfill the requirements for a custom motorcycle with appropriate frame geometry and special styling cues.

MADE-TO-ORDER CMC

Class: custom.
Engine: S&S air-cooled, V-twin 4-stroke.
Displacement: 88 c.i.
Valve Arrangement: OHV 2 valves per cylinder.
Transmission: 5-speed.
Final Drive: belt.
Brakes: disc front & rear.
Weight: 630 lbs.
Torque: 77 lb.ft.
Horsepower: 75.

(Photo courtesy of California Motorcycle Company.)

Made-to-Order—If you want an American made motorcycle built to your specifications, all you need is 20 grand! There is a thriving industry of well-established motorcycle manufacturers building V-twins to order. You can specify frame dimensions to exactly fit your body, choose seating and accessories to precisely fit your riding style, and select paint and chrome to suit your disposition. Delivery takes about six weeks.

Exotics—Manufacturers sometimes produce a bike of rare quality, in low production runs, at extremely high per-unit costs. These hand-crafted bikes incorporate cutting-edge technology in both the design of the bike and the manufacturing and assembling process. Examples include Honda's 210 m.p.h., oval piston NR750 V-2; the $160,000 Italian Morbidelli 850 and the $50,000 Australian Drysdale V-8 featured here.

DRYSDALE V-8

Class: custom.
Engine: water-cooled, transverse 90° V-8 4-stroke.
Displacement: 750cc.
Valve Arrangement: DOHC 4 valves per cylinder.
Transmission: 6-speed.
Final Drive: chain.
Brakes: dual disc front, single disc rear.
Weight: 420 lbs.
Horsepower: 160.

(Photo courtesy of Drysdale Motorcycle of Australia.)

Choppers

In the 1940s, "chopper" described a bike that was made as light as possible by "chopping off" every unnecessary component. Later, the term referred to a bike that had its geometry radically changed. The

CHOPPER

Class: outlaw chopper.
Engine: Shovelhead air-cooled V-twin 4-stroke.
Displacement: +74 ci.
Valve Arrangement: OHV 2 valves per cylinder.
Transmission: 4-speed.
Final Drive: chain.
Brakes: drum front & rear.
Weight: 430 lbs.
Torque: 75 lb.ft.
Horsepower: 54.

(Photo courtesy Gypsey Jokers.)

CHOPPER

chopper was *the* way to customize a motorcycle in the 1950s, and you can see the chopper heritage in many customs. Factories do not make true choppers. There are various legal and market reasons for this. Given that the factories now produce "customs," bikes truly made unique by their owners are even more radically chopped than ever before. Features of a chopper include:

- Highly raked front forks
- Often ape-hanger handlebars
- Way, way back seating
- One-of-a-kind paint job
- Often austere human interfaces
- Often minimalist to an extreme
- Often stylistically exaggerated
- Thematic in design, perhaps embracing sex, drugs, God, satan, death, rock & roll, pig farming, etc.

By today's definition, a chopper is a handcrafted affair. There is true artistry here—a real personal statement made through the machine about the man. The medium is the message.

Standards

This category of motorcycles is difficult to define. This is partly a result of the diversity of the machines in this class; it is also a result of the size of engine displacement, which ranges from 100cc to over 1300cc. And partly, this is because a standard motorcycle was viewed as a pariah, a bike without a market, by world manufacturers. The manufacturers felt that a universal bike was simply unworthy, and no one would buy a standard. But the world motorcycle manufacturers learned from this grievous mistake, and standards are now part of all full market lineups.

A standard is a good city commuter bike, yet also capable of one or two long distance trips per year. It has enough power and performance to be competent on the highway or a river valley road. It should accommodate a load and passenger. Standards are often characterized by:

- Clean, simple designs
- "User-friendly" ergonomics
- Multipurpose road capabilities
- Limited molded plastic body work
- Upright "American" riding position
- Pullback handlebars

Standards can be divided into three displacement divisions: entry level (100cc to 500cc), multipurpose (500cc to 1000cc), and muscle bikes (1000cc up).

STANDARDS

HONDA REBEL

Class: entry level standard.
Engine: air-cooled, in-line twin, 4-stroke.
Displacement: 234cc.
Valve Arrangement: SOHC 2 valves per cylinder.
Transmission: 5-speed.
Final Drive: chain.
Brakes: disc front, drum rear.
Weight: 306 lbs.

(Photo courtesy of American Honda Motor Company.)

SUZUKI LS650PW

Class: thumper.
Engine: air-cooled, single
4-stroke.
Displacement: 652cc.
Valve Arrangement: SOHC
2 valves per cylinder.
Transmission: 5-speed.
Final Drive: belt.
Brakes: disc front, drum rear.
Weight: 352 lbs.

*(Photo courtesy of American Suzuki
Motor Corp.)*

Entry Level—Small standards are often the best "first" motorcycle. These bikes are easy to purchase, easy to master and easy to repair. To be an entry level standard, a bike must meet three conditions: (1) it must be versatile; (2) it must be practical (in a motorcycle sort of way); and (3) it must be inexpensive. To meet all these categories, small standards are often older technology bikes that use what's available in a manufacturer's parts bin for components.

Of special note in this class is the "thumper," a single cylinder, large displacement motorcycle. Simple, sound and with enough displacement that a new rider probably won't insist on replacing it after a year, this bike is often a good compromise for a beginner. Here you will find a bike with mid-range power at an entry level price.

Multipurpose—Multipurpose standards handle all road conditions competently. You can take a standard on a round trip of the Continental

TRIUMPH THUNDERBIRD

Class: standard.
Engine: liquid-cooled, in-line
triple 4-stroke.
Displacement: 885cc.
Valve Arrangement: DOHC
4 valves per cylinder.
Transmission: 5-speed.
Final Drive: chain.
Brakes: disc front & rear.
Weight: 485 lbs.
Torque: 53 lb.ft.
Horsepower: 69.

*(Photo courtesy of Triumph
Motorcycles Limited.)*

YAMAHA V-MAX

Class: muscle standard.
Engine: liquid-cooled, transverse 70° V-4 4-stroke.
Displacement: 1198cc.
Valve Arrangement: DOHC 4.
Transmission: 5-speed.
Final Drive: shaft.
Brakes: dual disc front, disc rear.
Weight: 560 lbs.
Torque: 82 lb.ft.
Horsepower: 115

(Photo courtesy of Yamaha Motor Corporation, USA)

Divide and use it everyday to commute to work. You can load two people on it and still merge into Houston beltway traffic or roll through the curves on a Black Hills ridge road. More technology is applied to this category of standards than to the entry level motorcycles, so the "relatively inexpensive" requirement gets stretched. But insurance is affordable, and repairs are not too expensive.

Muscle Bikes—Muscle bikes are standards with one very important difference: massive, unforgiving bulk power. Straight testosterone. Displacement *uber alles*. There are no secrets, no hidden agendas, no tricks of the trade. The concept is simple enough. Slam in the largest engine the cradle will hold.

Harley-Davidsons

Hogs (Harley-Davidsons) are in their own class for several reasons. No other manufacturer throughout the world produces a bike with the iconoclastic image of Harley. And that image cuts several ways. Harley is the machine of the lone wolf, the desperado, the one-against-the-world, the "I-do-it-my-way" crowd. It's the rebel without a cause. It's a lifestyle. It's an art form. Harley-Davidson survives despite its lack of super or superior technology. Harleys command premium dollars, even though the competition is higher tech, more competently executed and less expensive. Ergo, Harleys must be something different. There is something about them, and most people entertain the idea of owning one at some point in life.

HARLEY-DAVIDSONS

HARLEY-DAVIDSON DYNA WIDE GLIDE

Class: Harley-Davidson.
Engine: air-cooled, 45° V-twin 4-stroke.
Displacement: 1338cc.
Valve Arrangement: OHV 2 valves per cylinder, hydraulic lifters.
Transmission: 5-speed.
Final Drive: poly chain belt.
Brakes: front & rear disc.
Weight: 618 lbs.
Torque: 77 lb.ft.
Horsepower: 59.

(Photo courtesy Harley-Davidson Motor Company.)

The key to a Harley is the individualization of the motorcycle. Because of this, and because Harley technology leaves much to be desired, a huge third-party industry has developed to supply Harley owners with high-tech, custom replacement parts. The result is that there are now so many of these suppliers, it is possible to assemble an entire motorcycle with third-party parts. Several manufacturers are doing this, offering bikes similar to Harleys but with better technology, fancier paint and full warranties. Harley riders disparagingly refer to these bikes as "clones." By the time the hard-core Harley owner is

BIG DOG

Class: Harley clone.
Engine: air-cooled, 45° V-twin 4-stroke.
Displacement: 1442cc.
Valve Arrangement: OHV 2 valves per cylinder, hydraulic lifters.
Transmission: 5-speed.
Final Drive: belt.
Brakes: single disc front & rear.
Weight: 650 lbs.
Torque: 96 lb.ft.
Horsepower: 90.

(Photo courtesy of Big Dog Motorcycles.)

finished chroming, replacing and upgrading the parts on his new Harley, he could have bought one of these third-party bikes for a thousand or so more and only waited six weeks for delivery.

TRAIL BIKES

Trail bikes, or off-road bikes, are designed to take you wherever you want to go, accepting the terrain as it comes. These bikes are built for dirt, mud, sand, clay, colechie, brush, desert, swamp, jungle and ancient forest. Trail bikes are usually characterized by the following features:

- Engine
  - ☐ Single cylinder, often 2-stroke
  - ☐ High routed exhaust systems
  - ☐ Five- or six-speed gear box
  - ☐ Chain final drive
  - ☐ Relatively high power-to-weight ratio
  - ☐ Spark arresting muffler

- Frame, suspension, and steering
  - ☐ Minimal seating
  - ☐ Long travel suspension
  - ☐ Neutral steering geometry
  - ☐ No center or side stands (kickstands)
  - ☐ High fenders
  - ☐ Straight across handlebars
  - ☐ Smaller, weaker disc brakes

- Wheels and tires
  - ☐ Deep, biting tire tread patterns
  - ☐ Relatively strong wheels

- Controls and gauges
  - ☐ Often none
  - ☐ Sometimes a speedometer or tachometer

- Electrical system
  - ☐ Small headlights (if any)
  - ☐ Incorporated blinkers and taillights (if any)
  - ☐ Loud horn
  - ☐ Electric start (on newer bikes)
  - ☐ Relatively simple and lightweight charging and ignition systems

Off-road bikes are classified by the type of racing competition in which they are designed to compete. The American Motorcycle Association sanctions nine different types of dirt riding: hare scrambles, hare-and-hound, enduro, trials, motocross, dirt track, hill climb, ice racing and reliability enduros. Competitors' off-road bikes are customized for each type of competition. Even so, to satisfy this wide-ranging market, only four basic types of motorcycles are built: enduro, motocross, trials and cross-county.

Enduros

Enduros waste no energy conforming to street requirements. The bikes have a straightforward mission: Conquer the wilderness. Enduros are legal (under federal law) for use on designated public lands. They must meet certain noise restrictions and have a spark arresting muffler. (Some states require lights, brakes, off-highway registration and vehicle title.) Enduro competition is called "time trials" in Europe. Rules vary, but generally competitors are started one at a time, with one minute intervals between riders. Points are lost when a rider does not make it to a check point on time. The winner is the rider with the fewest penalty points. Characteristics of these bikes include:

- Lightweight
- Strong frame
- Advanced travel front and rear suspensions
- Powerful engines

ENDUROS

HONDA XR600R

Class: enduro.
Engine: air-cooled, single 4-stroke.
Displacement: 591cc.
Valve Arrangement: SOHC 4 valves per cylinder.
Transmission: 5-speed.
Final Drive: chain.
Brakes: single disc front & rear.
Weight: 271 lbs.

(Photo courtesy of American Honda Motor Company.)

- Knobby tires designed for soft or hard terrain
- Generally, two-stroke engines
- Often water-cooled
- Strong muffler/spark arrestor
- Plastic gas tank
- Skid plates and brush guards

Motocross Bikes

Motocross racing used to be called "scrambling." Motocross is simply a race to the finish line. Everyone starts at the same time in one huge swarm and hopes they aren't crushed, side-swiped or run over in the first turn. Motocross bikes are designed for "closed course" competition races. Closed course means that the route is fixed and on private land. As such, features that add weight, and would make a motocross bike legal for enduro riding, are missing. These bikes are similar to enduro bikes, and often have the following features:

- Technologically advanced suspensions
- Powerful two-stroke and four-stroke engines
- Knobby tires designed for course terrain
- Often water-cooled
- Sophisticated brake systems
- Engines tuned for low-range power

ATK 250

Class: motocross.
Engine: liquid-cooled, single 2-stroke.
Displacement: 249cc.
Valve Arrangement: n/a.
Transmission: 6-speed.
Final Drive: O-ring chain.
Brakes: disc front & rear.
Weight: 230 lbs.
Torque: 28 lb.ft.
Horsepower: 50.

(Photo courtesy of ATK America.)

TYPES AND STYLES OF MOTORCYCLES

Trials

Historically, trials bikes originated from street bikes and share ancestry with road racing bikes, although you wouldn't recognize it today. In the 1930s road courses were set up for riders to negotiate within certain time restrictions. Today, trials competition resembles sadomasochistic enduro events, and the trials bike resembles a minimalist interpretation of an enduro bike. The competition challenges a rider to negotiate a course of tortuous terrain, large boulders, fallen trees, cliffs and rock slides. Penalty points are awarded for putting a foot down, walking the bike, stopping or riding outside the course limits. Total machine control, not speed, wins trial races. Trials bikes have the following features:

- Engines tuned for maximum low-speed torque
- Wide ratio gear boxes, usually with six speeds
- Super-low first and second gears
- Often water-cooled
- Sophisticated brake systems
- Controls set for a standing rider (since most riding is done standing)
- Virtually no seat
- Long action suspension
- Extremely high ground clearance (12 inches minimum)
- Extremely austere so there is not one extra ounce of unnecessary weight

GAS GAS CONTACT-T25

Class: trials.
Engine: liquid-cooled single 2-stroke.
Displacement: 239cc.
Valve Arrangement: n/a.
Transmission: 6-speed.
Final Drive: chain.
Brakes: disc front & rear.
Weight: 160 lbs.

KAWASAKI KLR650

Class: cross-country.
Engine: liquid-cooled, single 4-stroke.
Displacement: 651cc.
Valve Arrangement: DOHC 4 valves per cylinder.
Transmission: 5-speed.
Final Drive: chain.
Brakes: disc front & rear.
Weight: 338 lbs.

(Photo courtesy of Kawasaki Motors Corporation, USA.)

Cross-Countries

A variation of the enduro and the motocross is the long-distance, arduous terrain race. The Paris-Dakar and California Baja 1000 are the two most famous of these races. Bikes designed for these races must be able to carry lots of cargo and fuel. In addition to the features found on enduro bikes, the bikes often have "desert" features for crossing large expanses of wilderness or wasteland. These features include:

CROSS-COUNTRIES

BMW R1100GS

Class: dual-purpose.
Engine: air- and oil-cooled, opposed twin 4-stroke.
Displacement: 1085cc.
Valve Arrangement: high cam, 4 valves per cylinder.
Transmission: 5-speed.
Final Drive: shaft.
Brakes: dual disc front, single disc rear.
Weight: 495 lbs.
Torque: 72 lb.ft.
Horsepower: 80.

(Photo courtesy of BMW of North America.)

- Engine torque tuned for both on- and off-road riding
- Oil-coolers or features to reduce engine temperature
- Front and rear disc brakes
- Expanded tool kits
- Extra engine guards
- Headlights (often with protection wire)
- Large capacity fuel tanks (up to 10 gallons)
- Baggage racks and storage compartments
- Modified cafe fairings

DUAL PURPOSE

DUAL-PURPOSE BIKES

Dual-purpose bikes are also called dual sport or "universal." Their history is similar to sports touring bikes. Once a manufacturer had both street and trail versions of a motorcycle, it was a small evolutionary step to get a "dual-purpose" bike. Manufacturers simply took a few parts from the street bike parts bin and a few from the trail bike parts bin to make the dual-purpose bike. However, instead of being universally good, the parts bin approach created a bike that was universally bad.

This has changed. Dual purpose bikes are now specially designed, highly advanced machines that incorporate specially tuned suspensions, tires and components to suit highway and trail use. Features of these bikes include:

BIMOTA BB-500 COLLECTIBLE

Class: collectible.
Engine: liquid-cooled, V-twin 2-stroke.
Displacement: 499cc.
Valve arrangement: n/a.
Transmission: 6-speed.
Final Drive: chain.
Brakes: dual disc front, single disc rear.
Weight: 145 kg (247 lbs.).
Torque: 9 kg.
Horsepower: 110.

(Photo courtesy of Tonkin Gran Turismo.)

- Street legal lighting
- Mirrors and gauges
- Large gas tanks
- Universal tires designed for street or trail
- Electric starters
- Engines tuned for mid-range power
- Battery-operated lighting
- Wider range transmission speeds

VINTAGE AND COLLECTIBLES

The affinity between man and machine has always led man to collect the machines he builds. Motorcycles have always been collected. But a collectible motorcycle is something more than just a machine. It is an investment. The owner's desire is not just to have and hold it. He or she desires to see the motorcycle appreciate in value over time. Therefore, to be collectible a bike must have some unique qualities, such as scarcity or outrageous technology, that make it rare in the eyes of the buyer.

The Bimota BB-500 Vdue is a prime example. Bimota is a company described by world renowned motorcycle writer Spiros Gabrilis as "always reaching for stellar goals, seldom hitting the mark but when they do, it's magic." Their most challenging goal was to rise from the ashes of financial ruin and build a direct-injected, clean-burning, compact, two-stroke engine in a racer-like chassis. The prototype received laudatory reviews in 1997 and led many to believe that the motorcycling

VINTAGE

1924 HENDERSON

Class: vintage 1924 Henderson deluxe.
Engine: air-cooled, in-line longitudinal 4-cylinder 4-stroke.
Displacement: 1301cc.
Valve Arrangement: side valve.
Transmission: 3-speed with reverse.
Final Drive: chain.
Brakes: external band on drum (rear only).
Weight: 549 lbs.

industry was on the verge of a two-stroke renaissance. But Bimota could not deliver a production bike. Ultimately, about 100 of the BB-500s were distributed around Europe. Five arrived in the United States via the gray market.

The distinction between a vintage bike and a collectible is important. While all vintage bikes are collectibles, not all collectibles are vintage bikes. Two definitions of *vintage* are in common use. One definition says that, to be considered vintage, a bike must have been manufactured before World War II. The other says that the bike must be at least half the age of the industry.

VARIATIONS: SIDECARS AND TRIKES

The affinity between man and machine also means that man constantly experiments and seeks new expressions of old themes. Some of this is the mother of invention. Some of this is a kind of research. Some of this is artistic expression. Some of this is simply trying to find out just what an acetylene torch is all about. Two such variations have become their own specialty in the motorcycle market: sidecars and trikes.

Sidecars are a natural development growing out of a need to carry more than one passenger. Riding with a sidecar is a totally different experience since the sidecar changes the riding telemetry of the bike. Riding in a sidecar is also its own experience.

Trikes combine the front end of a motorcycle with the differential of an automobile to produce a high capacity, relatively more stable at

TRIKES

URAL SIDECAR

Class: Ural sidecar
Engine: air-cooled, "Boxer" opposed twin 4-stroke.
Displacement: 649cc.
Valve Arrangement: OHV 2 valves per cylinder.
Transmission: 4-speed with reverse.
Final Drive: shaft.
Brakes: drum front & rear.
Weight: 690 lbs.
Torque: 45 lb.ft.
Horsepower: 35.

(Photo courtesy Ural America Inc.)

HONDA GOLD WING TRIKE

Class: gold wing trike.
Engine: liquid-cooled, horizontally opposed, flat four 4-stroke.
Displacement: 1182cc.
Valve Arrangement: SOHC 2 valves per cylinder, hydraulic adjust.
Transmission: 4-speed plus overdrive 5th.
Final Drive: shaft.
Brakes: twin piston caliper dual disc front, disc rear.
Weight: +789 lbs.
Torque: 75 lb.ft.
Horsepower: 86.

(Photo courtesy of Chrome Plated Hearts.)

slow speeds, open-air form of transportation. These motorcycles have become popular with riders who find they no longer want to toil with keeping a two-wheeled device upright but still cannot give up riding motorcycles.

IMITATORS

Mopeds, scooters and minibikes seem like miniature versions of motorcycles. While they do have the same basic construction, these motorcycle wanna-bes are not reasonable substitutes for most riders.

Mopeds

Mopeds are hybrid vehicles combining features of a bicycle and motorcycle. Hence the name: "mo" for motor, "ped" for pedal. A moped is powered by the rider via pedal or by the engine, or both. A clever mechanism called a centrifugal clutch smoothly transfers power to the rear wheel from either or both sources.

The machine is usually peddled only to help accelerate from a stop or up a steep hill. On flat smooth ground a moped will maintain a speed of about 35 to 40 m.p.h. Mopeds are commonly 50cc machines with very low tech design and cheap construction. (Many European countries allow youngsters to get an early driver's license that is restricted to under 50cc, one horsepower mopeds). Advantages of the moped include:

MOPEDS

- Inexpensive to purchase
- Very high gas mileage (over 100 m.p.g.)
- Easy to repair

But mopeds are not particularly reliable or safe. Disadvantages of mopeds include:

- Underpowered (underpowered machines are more dangerous than overpowered machines)
- Inadequate suspension
- Inadequate brakes
- Rudimentary controls
- Difficult for automobiles to see
- Cheap in design and materials
- Generally unsafe

These machines are generally acknowledged as the least desirable of the motorcycle kingdom. Poor performance, poor safety, shoddy construction and low status combine to make them a nonstarter for almost any rider or riding situation.

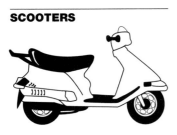

SCOOTERS

Scooters

Scooters are more sophisticated than mopeds. They do not have pedals, which is a step in the right direction (if you'll pardon the pun). Most scooters have the engine situated over the rear wheel behind a vented and bulbous cowling. Scooters have wide monocoque frames which are shaped to create a floor board for the rider's feet. Footpegs are absent. This arrangement allows for a variety of foot and riding positions. All controls other than a foot brake are at the rider's hands. To change gears, the rider must pull in the clutch lever and rotate the lever, and the housing to which it connects, to one of (usually) three gear positions.

Scooters also have high negatives. The engine placement prohibits proper weight distribution. Too much of the weight is rearward and high. The floor board arrangement fails to ensure that the rider's weight is positioned correctly on the machine, and that the rider's foot is proximate to the brake located on the right side of the floor board. Thus, scooters are inherently less stable and do not handle well. The floor board arrangement fails to ensure that the rider's weight (via the footpegs) is positioned correctly on the machine, and that the rider's foot is near the brake, which is located on the right side of the floor board.

They are also relatively heavy, generally under powered (although Japanese manufacturers are producing scooters that really scoot), and equipped with pathetic suspensions. In the front, they have a rudimentary version of what is known as leading link suspension. In this set up, the shock from the road is transferred via a lever (leading link) to a preloaded shock absorber. This means that road shock is transferred through an indirect route and feels (to use a technical term) "wobbly and strange." (In a conventional suspension, the road shock is transferred directly from the road up the front fork, which houses a preloaded shock absorber. This direct route gives much better feel, and much better road control.)

Even worse, the scooter has small 10-inch diameter wheels, a feature that has been abandoned on most other vehicles and all motorcycles. Here's why:

- A 10-inch diameter wheel will fit in a 10-inch diameter hole. Thus, the scooter wheel will "fall" in a hole that would be spanned by a larger motorcycle wheel (commonly, motorcycle wheels range from 16 to 21 inches). On a scooter, every bump is felt, and there is risk on every pothole.
- Ten-inch wheels have considerably less gyroscopic effect than, say, an 18-inch motorcycle wheel. The gyroscopic effect is key to keeping a motorcycle upright at speed.

Advantages of scooters include:

- Inexpensive to purchase
- High gas mileage (up to 100 m.p.g.)
- Easy to repair
- Carry their own spare tire
- Great humor value

Disadvantages of scooters include:

- Underpowered
- Poor and nonresponsive suspension
- Awkward controls
- Poor weight distribution
- Weak small diameter wheels

Scooters are not recommended. They are slow, poorly designed and unstable. Like the moped, scooters are particularly poor machines for the novice rider. The common belief that small, slow and simple machines are best suited for beginners is not correct. In fact, the

MINIBIKES

opposite is true. It is much wiser to learn on a machine that incorporates safe and sophisticated technology.

Minibikes

Minibikes range from the most primitive of all powered, two-wheeled transports to miniature motorcycles. At the primitive end of the spectrum, minibike engines are nothing more than lawn mower engines fitted with a centrifugal clutch. The frames are often simple; the suspension often nonexistent. Brakes . . . optional. Wheels are often small diameter, pressed steel affairs.

At the other end of the spectrum are minibikes that are fully equipped for safe trail riding, only sized for children. These minibikes are fully competent little motorcycles, although usually with inexpensive and outdated technology.

It's unfair to trash minibikes with the other half-breeds. They're fun, and not intended for more than backyard excursions. I recommend that you remain within walking distance from repair facilities at all times!

SUZUKI JR50W MINIBIKE

Class: minibike.
Engine: air-cooled, single 2-stroke.
Displacement: 49cc.
Valve Arrangement: n/a.
Transmission: single speed, centrifugal clutch.
Final Drive: chain.
Brakes: drum front & rear.
Weight: 82 lbs.

(Photo courtesy of American Suzuki Motor Corp.)

3

MECHANICS AND MECHANISMS

Today's motorcycles are very high tech. Even your common garden variety motorcycle employs technology that is found only on the most exotic and expensive cars. Super performers employ materials and technology that would be at home on an AB-2 bomber. Fact is, any Joe with several thousand dollars can purchase a 162-horsepower, 180-mile-per-hour machine off today's showroom floor that could have won the Daytona 500 just a few years ago.

Motorcycles are collections of castings, tubes, wires, hardware and materials formed and machined into "components." Components are united into "systems" that perform particular functions. Systems are united into a whole that becomes the romantic machine we know as the motorcycle. This is a classic, real world example of Plato's philosophical one and the many. The one (the system) has an identity and existence all its own. As a part of the many, it shares in a totally new identity. To understand the one, notes Plato, you must understand the many. To paraphrase: "To understand the motorcycle, you must understand the systems."

Systems give the rider the facilities to make the motorcycle go, stop and turn. The average rider must have a basic understanding at the systems level to properly select and safely ride a motorcycle.

Understanding a motorcycle at a component and materials level is important to the technophile and engineer, but generally not required of the average rider. However, some knowledge of materials is useful to maintain and detail a motorcycle properly.

A BASIC UNDERSTANDING

Once you have a basic understanding of motorcycle systems, you will be prepared to purchase, ride and maintain the motorcycle knowledgeably. Admittedly, some of these components are so simple and have purposes that are so obvious that they warrant little or no description. Footpegs, for example, serve a crystal clear purpose: They support your feet. Probably no one ever spent much time trying to figure out how they work, or what kind to have on their motorcycle.

On second thought, maybe this is not true. There are many different types of footpegs:

- Big rubber ones that diminish vibration to your feet to provide comfort on long rides
- Serrated ones that dig into your boot soles to give maximum grip when you are standing up and riding off-road
- Solidly affixed pegs as used on drag bikes
- Pegs that fold up when you take a high speed corner
- Rakishly forward-placed highway pegs for comfort and style
- Huge flat ones that offer long distance comfort but not much grip
- Running boards (not really pegs at all)

Get the point? Every part of a motorcycle has been through tremendous design research—including the lowly footpeg, simplest of component parts—yielding considerable variety.

This may have you thinking, "How can one possibly choose among the dozens of different types of engines or frames or brakes or drive trains on the market?" It is not so tough. You do not need a vast technical knowledge to purchase or to ride a motorcycle. You need a basic understanding of the systems. This lays the foundation for:

- Choosing the proper motorcycle to match your lifestyle
- Riding safely
- Making an occasional emergency roadside or shade-tree repair
- Ensuring your professional mechanic does a good, fair and safe repair job at a reasonable rate
- Being cool, fashionable or totally retro

Warning: Without a basic understanding at the systems level, you are at risk. You may discover you purchased a machine that won't do what you want. You may make a haphazard or dangerous decision about when or what to repair. Or, perhaps worst of all, you may commit an unforgivable fashion faux pas in the complex and unforgiving world of motorcycle vogue.

EIGHT BASIC SYSTEMS

All motorcycles, from the 600cc cafe racer to the 125cc standard, share eight basic systems. These systems are:

- Engine
- Carburetion
- Exhaust
- Frame and suspension
- Wheels, tires and brakes
- Drive train
- Controls and gauges
- Electrical

Each system comes in a variety of designs for, and methods of, executing its function. The design can be quite specialized and therefore correct (or incorrect) for your riding needs. This chapter describes the variety of basic systems available in motorcycle design and presents the basic understanding of motorcycle systems every motorcycle rider needs.

MOTORCYCLE ENGINES

In the old days, there were three basic types of motorcycle engines: four-stroke, two-stroke and rotary. Alas, the two-stroke is all but gone for street bikes. Stricter noise and emission regulations have made the two-stroke uneconomical or impossible to manufacture for street use. This apparently has changed manufacturers' engine choices for most of the other street/dirt bikes in their lineups as well. On a recent trip to the bike shop, two-stroke engines were found only on jet skis, snowmobiles and some motocross racing bikes.

The rotary is almost extinct as well. It never caught on. Poor marketing strategies and rider unfamiliarity caused the rotary's unpopularity. The last producer, Norton, fell victim to venture capitalist, leveraged buy-out greed. The company's last rotary came off the assembly line in 1994. It seems that only the four-stroke is able to survive decade after decade.

This section gives you a rundown of all three engine types, along with the significant differences and variations. This is done partly for nostalgia, and partly because the two-stroke may return as soon as manufacturers' efforts to conquer noise and emissions problems are successful. And there are even new rotary designs being patented, so it may return, too.

Before we begin, a bit of elementary rubbish about internal combustion engines. The name stems from the fact that the combustion happens internally. This is contrasted to, say, an old steam engine where coal was burned externally beneath a closed tank of water to produce steam power. The first internal combustion engines were built in the 1820s, but the concept of combustion under high pressure was not theorized until 1838 (by William Barnett). In 1876, the German firm of Otto and Langen began producing a "silent engine," based on Alphonse Beau de Rochas's 1862 theory of a four-stroke engine. This was the first modern four-stroke engine. Hence, the four-stroke engine is often called an Otto engine. Otto's engine, like most of the era, burned coal gas.

In 1878 Dougald Clerk developed a two-stroke engine. Clerk's design used a secondary piston and cylinder that would take in a charge of fresh fuel vapor. It would pass this charge to the working cylinder, scavenging the working cylinder of burned fuel and providing fresh fuel. It was not until 1891, when Joseph Day simplified the two-stroke engine by using the crankcase to perform the duties of the secondary cylinder, that the modern two-stroke was born. In Day's design, the fresh charge is drawn into the crankcase, rather than a secondary cylinder.

The rotary concept has been around since the 16th century when water pumps used a rotary, as opposed to a reciprocating, design. Today the rotary design is often used in compressors, but harnessing its power proved quite vexing in the past. Dr. Felix Wankel is the father of the modern rotary engine. His first operational design, in 1957, had a housing and rotor, which rotated around each other. This design was theoretically ideal, but not practical. Wankel eventually developed a successful design in which the housing was stationary. The rotor moved within the housing in a planetary motion. This engine went into production in 1963.

To round out our discussion of engine history, in 1892, Rudolf Diesel patented an engine in which very high compression (1/25 of original volume) resulted in high enough temperatures (538° Centigrade) to ignite fuel sprayed into the cylinder. This is, of course, the Diesel internal combustion engine.

Internal combustion engines are wonderfully simple in concept. An internal combustion engine requires three things to run: air, fuel and spark.

- Air—A colorless, odorless, tasteless gaseous mixture, containing 78% nitrogen, 21% oxygen, with small amounts of argon, carbon dioxide, neon, helium and other trace gases.
- Fuel—Usually gasoline or gasoline mixed with oil or alcohol. Fuel can also be more exotic. Internal combustion engines run on diesel, propane and other combustible substances as odd as fumes from decomposing chicken droppings (methane). The best economy is obtained when one part fuel is mixed with 17 parts air (notated as 1:17). For power, a richer 1:12 mixture is required. For a cold engine, an extraordinarily rich mixture is required.
- Spark—In gasoline engines, detonation is caused by a 20,000 to 30,000 volt electric spark. The spark plug provides a gap between electrodes across which the high tension voltage jumps, which is the spark. (Detonation is caused by the heat of extreme compression in diesel engines.)

These are combined via compression to produce an associative event called combustion, which produces power, as defined below:

- Compression—Usually attained by pushing a piston up a closed-ended tube (i.e., the cylinder) toward the closed end (a.k.a. combustion chamber) to squeeze the fuel and air to a density that will permit detonation via spark.
- Combustion—The rapid oxidation of fuel, or the conversion of gasoline and oxygen into carbon dioxide and water ($C_8H_{18} + 12.5$ $O_2 = 8 CO_2 + 9 H_2O$).

When all these factors are present in the proper quantities, and delivered at precisely the correct time, you have a running internal combustion engine. Of course, the engine won't run for long if you do not have other systems dealing with many residual by-products of the detonation, such as a cooling system for excess heat, a lubricating system to keep metal parts from grinding themselves into shavings, an exhaust system to control noise and fumes, etc. It is all quite clever.

Knowledge of air, fuel and spark is an important trouble shooting tool. A motorcycle mechanic will begin a dead-engine diagnosis by searching for air, fuel and spark. Finding all three operating correctly, a check for compression comes next. The absence of one of these is an immediate clue to what is ailing the engine, and directs the mechanic where to focus his or her attention.

Four-Stroke Engines

The name "four-stroke" comes from the fact that the piston makes four passes (strokes) in the cylinder to complete an entire cycle. The strokes

4-STROKE ENGINE

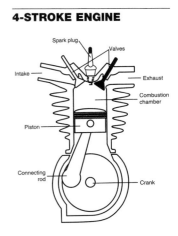

4-STROKE INTAKE

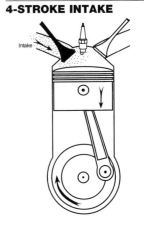

4-STROKE COMPRESSION

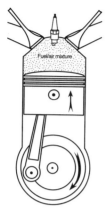

4-STROKE POWER

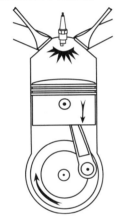

4-STROKE EXHAUST

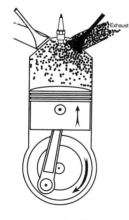

are intake, compression, power and exhaust. Two of these strokes are down (intake, power), and two are up (compression, exhaust), of course. Valves open and close to route gases or create compression. Further defined, the strokes of a four-stroke are:

- Intake—Let us begin with the piston at top dead center, or TDC. At TDC, the piston is as high (or far) into the cylinder as possible. The piston starts its way down, away from the combustion chamber, creating a low pressure area in the space vacated. The exhaust valve is closed. The intake valve is open, allowing the pressure differential (vacuum or suction, if you will) of the retreating piston to pull fuel vapor into the cylinder.

- Compression—At the bottom of the intake stroke (called bottom dead center or BDC), the intake valve closes. The piston reverses its course and heads for the combustion chamber. The fuel and air have nowhere to go since both the intake valve and exhaust valve are now closed. The mixture gets compressed between the advancing piston and the top of the cylinder. The compression ratio is the measurement of the extent to which the fuel and air are compressed within the cylinder. Most gasoline engines have somewhere around a 9:1 ratio (total BDC cylinder volume compared to total TDC volume). Diesels run from 12:1 to 25:1 ratios.

- Power—At almost exactly TDC, when the fuel and air mixture are fully compressed, the spark plug ignites, setting off the burning and expansion of the fuel mixture. With both exhaust and intake valves closed, the detonation forces the piston back down the cylinder under considerable force.

- Exhaust—When the piston again reaches BDC, the exhaust valve opens. The piston changes direction and heads upward toward the combustion chamber. The burned fuel and air that just powered the piston on its downward journey are pushed out the open exhaust valve, into the muffler and eventually the atmosphere.

Pretty neat, huh? All of this happens thousands of times a minute. It results in the crankshaft (the item to which the piston is affixed via a connecting rod) circulating to power the vehicle.

Two-Stroke Engines

Two-stroke engines manage to achieve all four functions (intake, compression, power and exhaust) in only two strokes. Examine the illustration of a two-stroke engine. Two-strokes do this by letting the crankcase handle the intake functions. Two-strokes route the incoming fuel mixture first into the crankcase, then into the cylinder (not directly into the cylinder as in a four-stroke engine) via a transfer port. This clever move allows a two-stroke to produce power on every second stroke (four-strokes produce power on every fourth stroke). Since this design prevents use of the crankcase as an oil sump, as in a four-stroke, lubricating oil is mixed with the fuel.

The Two-Stroke Intake/Compression and Two-Stroke Power/Transfer/Exhaust illustrations show the two-stroke sequence. These figures first show the intake of air, fuel and oil into the crankcase via the intake port. The vacuum required in the crankcase to draw in the fuel mixture is caused by the piston moving to TDC, increasing crankcase volume. The force necessary to push the fuel mixture from the crankcase, through the transfer port, into the cylinder, is created by the piston moving down to BDC. Fascinating! Forcing the mixture into the cylinder also has the effect of flushing the burned fuel out the exhaust port.

In general, two-stroke engines use one of three intake designs: piston-port, reed valve or rotary-valve (although there are other variations, old and new). In a piston-port engine, the piston alternately blocks the intake piston port and intake transfer port, channeling the direction of fuel mixture flow. The skirt of the piston blocks the intake port as it reaches BDC while the intake transfer port is unblocked. The pressure caused by the descending piston forces the fuel mixture from the crankcase into the cylinder via the transfer port. As the piston moves back to TDC, the transfer port is blocked and the intake port is opened, drawing fuel into the crankcase through the intake port.

Reed valves are used on engines where the carburetor throat tube opens directly into the crankcase. A thin metal flap acts as a check valve to control the direction of the fuel mixture flow, rather than a piston port. The vacuum created by the motion of the piston moving to TDC opens the flap. The pressure caused by the piston moving to BDC, and the natural spring of the reed itself, closes the flap. This pressure also forces the fuel mixture through the intake port as the port is uncovered by the piston.

In a rotary-valve engine, a cut-away disk on the crank, rather than the piston skirt, controls the intake port, leaving it open or closed as the crankshaft rotates.

A new breed of motorcycle two-stroke is on the horizon. Instead of using any port controls at all, the fuel mixture is directly forced into the intake transfer port via supercharging. This engine, when combined with modern computer and emissions technology, will burn clean enough to meet clean air standards.

In each of the three types of two-stroke engines, the fuel is initially routed into the sealed chamber that surrounds the crankshaft and flywheel, and drawn into the cylinder space (i.e., compression area) above the piston. This one/two approach to intake means that the

2-STROKE ENGINE

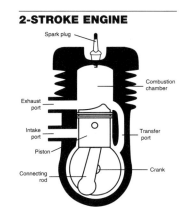

2-STROKE INTAKE/ COMPRESSION

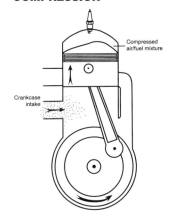

2-STROKE POWER/ TRANSFER/EXHAUST

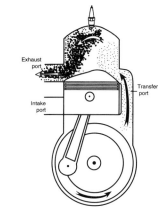

two-stroke does not have camshafts, valves, timing belts, rocker arms, pushrods, lifters, valve covers, valve guides, etc. This makes the two-stroke considerably lighter and more powerful pound-for-pound than the four-stroke.

Though a two-stroke has twice as many power strokes as a four-stroke, a two-stroke is not twice as powerful as a four-stroke engine of equal displacement. There are three reasons for this. First, there is a reduction in the effective cylinder volume of a two-stroke due to the piston movement required to cover exhaust and transfer ports. Second, there is appreciable mixing of burned exhaust gases with the fresh combustible charge, reducing the effectiveness of the next combustion. Third, some of the fresh combustible charge actually passes straight across from the transfer port and out the exhaust port during the scavenging phase of the two-stroke sequence, again reducing the effectiveness of the combustion.

The desirable attributes of the two-stroke engine, in comparison to the four-stroke engine, include lower manufacturing costs, greater reliability due to greater simplicity, superior power to weight ratio, higher power density and packaging flexibility.

The disadvantages, however, are significant. Two-strokes present a horrendous environmental problem. Here are some facts about two-stroke engines:

- According to the Environmental Protection Agency, 30% of the fuel and oil that powers a two-stroke engine is emitted unburned in the engine's exhaust, making a typical two-stroke up to 250 times dirtier than a typical four-stroke (horsepower for horsepower).

- One hour of operation of a 70 horsepower two-stroke emits the same amount of hydrocarbon pollution as driving 5,000 miles in a modern automobile.

- Two-strokes emit many more toxic, carcinogenic and mutagenic hydrocarbons, such as polycyclic aromatic hydrocarbons (PAH), than four-strokes do. (An interesting complication is that when PAHs are exposed to sunlight, they become thousands of times more toxic.)

- Off-road vehicles generally contribute more to air pollution than do cars. Off-road motorcycles and all-terrain vehicles (ATVs) using four-stroke engines produce 118 times as many smog-forming pollutants as modern automobiles on a per-mile basis. Off-road two-stroke engines emit 10 times as many smog precursors as the four-stroke engines for each mile of travel. Or, looked at another way, 90% of the 34 tons of smog precursors currently emitted each day by off-road motorcycles and ATVs comes from two-stroke engines.

- Marine two-strokes dump 1 billion (1,000,000,000!) pounds of hydrocarbons and spill as much oil, by volume, as 15 Exxon *Valdez* disasters, into American waterways every year. (An average outboard engine dumps up to four gallons of unburned fuel into the water during an afternoon of use.)

Several new breeds of motorcycle two-strokes are on the horizon. Most avoid using any port controls at all. Some use designs where the fuel mixture is directly forced into the intake transfer port via supercharging or injection. Some use different fuels, such as diesel. The hope is that these engines, when combined with modern computer and emissions technology, can burn clean enough to meet the strictest clean air standards.

Wankel Engines

Rotary engines are a motorcycle curiosity and worth mentioning. They have been around since the dawn of the piston engine, but it was not until 1954, when Dr. Felix Wankel presented his breakthrough rotary design, that the idea moved from an academic exercise to a working engine. The first engine, the NSU DKM 54, became operational in 1957. During the 1970s so-called world oil crises, great interest was paid to the Wankel rotary engine. Yamaha, BSA, Norton-Villiers-Triumph, Hercules, Van Veen and Suzuki experimented with the engine. Suzuki and Norton are the only two motorcycle manufacturers to produce the engine.

The 497cc Suzuki RE-5 Wankel, built from 1975 to 1977, produced 62 horsepower and was capable of 115 m.p.h. From 1983 to 1994, Norton produced 588cc twin-rotor engines in both air- and liquid-cooled variations. The F1 version produced 95 horses. A Norton Wankel set the British land speed record at +191 m.p.h.

Rotary engines achieve compression by rotating a convex triangle concentrically in a figure eight-shaped oblong chamber. At various points along its path the triangle creates compression between itself and the chamber. This design has several advantages:

- It is inherently smooth and quiet, producing very little vibration and offering an extremely sweet power curve.
- A two-rotor engine is naturally counterbalanced.
- Mechanical simplicity. Rotaries have fewer parts.
- It is capable of extremely high r.p.m. because of the lack of reciprocating parts (it has only two moving parts—the crankshaft and the rotor).

WANKEL

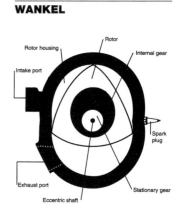

- Lighter and more compact than reciprocating engines of equivalent power.

Despite its advantages the Wankel has not enjoyed the success of the piston engine because the piston is more abundant and more widely understood. Much more money has been spent on four-stroke research than on Wankel research.

Engine Variations: Number of Cylinders

The majority of motorcycle engines have one to four cylinders, although six- and eight-cylinder models are not unknown. Multicylinder engine design offers the great advantage of allowing for large displacement with relatively smaller mass parts. For example, a 500cc single-cylinder four-stroke engine must have one very large piston, a strong and heavy connecting rod and great big valves. This kind of engine is known as a thumper, for obvious reasons. This design produces gobs of torque, vibrates like a washing machine on an out-of-balance spin cycle and is unable to attain very high r.p.m.s (although some smaller versions really crank!).

Alternately, a multicylinder 500cc four-stroke engine can have either two, three or four smaller pistons, each serviced by commensurately smaller parts. This design will vibrate less, rev higher and produce more high-end power (as opposed to torque). In a multicylinder engine, the mass of reciprocating (back and forth) parts is smaller per cylinder. Overall, the total reciprocating mass of a multicylinder engine is higher. More cylinders equal: more parts, more power, more weight and more possible points of failure.

Engine Variations: Layout of Cylinders

There are several different multicylinder layouts. The three most common designs are:

- In-line—In an in-line layout, the cylinders and crankshaft are usually "transverse"; that is, the engine is set into the frame perpendicular to the longitudinal axis of the bike (sideways to the front and back of the machine). The more cylinders, the longer the crankshaft, the wider and smoother the engine. At one time or another, nearly all motorcycle manufacturers have embraced this design. Motorcycles with in-line engines tend to be the most top heavy.
- Horizontal—Horizontal engine layout (also called flat, opposed or pancake) is fundamentally different in that the crankshaft runs along the longitudinal axis of the bike. That is, the crank runs along

IN-LINE ENGINE

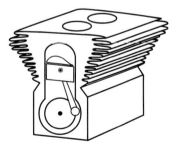

the line of the front and back wheels. Its pistons are set 180° apart. Honda, Ural and BMW are the most notable of the horizontal engine manufacturers. The horizontal engine is ideal for machines having shaft drive because the front-to-back crankshaft revolves in the proper direction for mechanical attachment to a driveshaft. This design tends to have the lowest center of gravity. But steep turning angles are obstructed by the cylinders sticking way out on the sides.

- "V"—The name describes the cylinder arrangement well. The cylinders are set at 90°, 45° or other variation of degrees apart. Taken to its logical extreme, "V" engine design will result in a radial engine like the ones found on larger aircraft powerplants. Harley-Davidson, Moto Guzzi, Hesketh, Moto Morini and Ducati are famous for their V-twin layouts. In fact, they have produced virtually nothing else for many years. Over the last two decades, all of the Japanese manufacturers have been producing "V" designs. The "V" is a favorite because the design has a natural tendency to vibrate less than an in-line design while being more compact than a horizontal design.

Engine Variations: Valve Layout

Four-stroke engines generally employ one of three basic valve and camshaft layouts: side valve flathead, pushrod overhead valve (OHV) and overhead camshaft (OHC).

- Side Valve—The side valve layout is almost a thing of the past. One will find it on older machines and on intentionally simple machines like minibikes. Side valve layout is almost synonymous with flathead design, where a flat piece of metal serves to "cap" the top of the cylinder. It generally houses no moving parts, although there are combinations of overhead and side valves. In a side valve layout, the valves run along the outside of the cylinder. The business end of the valves point "up" and the stems point down. The valves are actuated by a camshaft driven through meshed gears or chain off the crankshaft. This design is simple to manufacture, but does not produce high compression ratios or let the engine breathe easy.
- OHV—Overhead valve layout, though more advanced compared to flathead design, is found on few motorcycle engines today (but it is still common in many modern automobile engine designs). This design allows the valves to be housed in the head, "above" the pistons, so that they enter the combustion chamber from the top. Pushrods activate rocker arms that open the valves. An OHV layout allows for more efficient routing of fuel and air into the combustion

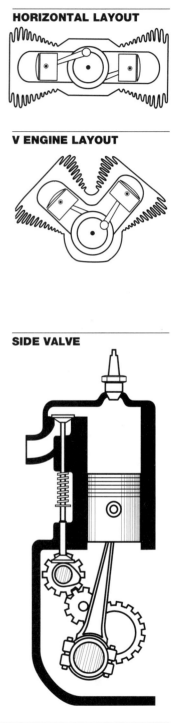

HORIZONTAL LAYOUT

V ENGINE LAYOUT

SIDE VALVE

OHC

DESMODRONIC

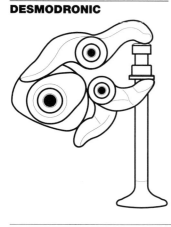

chamber, but has the disadvantage of considerable reciprocating mass in pushrods, rocker arms, and sometimes lifters.

- OHC—Overhead camshaft is the most advanced of valve design layouts. It is found on most modern motorcycles. The valves and the camshaft are situated above the combustion chamber. See the OHC diagram. With valves and camshaft in close proximity (i.e., no more pushrod, and often no lifters) the camshaft actuates the valves. This layout greatly reduces reciprocating mass, and allows the engine to rev higher before valve float occurs. This layout can employ either a single cam (SOHC) or dual cams (DOHC). With SOHC, one camshaft actuates both the intake and exhaust valves. With DOHC, intake and exhaust valves are actuated by independent camshafts.

Overhead camshaft designs often have three, four or even five valves per cylinder. Additional valves and valve actuating mechanisms seem at first glance only to create extra reciprocating mass, reducing the effectiveness of the design. This is not always the situation. The value of multivalves lies in the fact that single exhaust and intake valves cross a design line between mass and the size of the opening they can regulate. Stated differently, two small valves can control a larger total port opening than one large valve, while having a combined mass less than one large valve. Multivalve design also permits the fuel mixture to be routed into the combustion chamber via a more efficient path.

BMW offers a hybrid design on their R series motorcycles. They refer to this design as either "high cam" or "cam-in head." In this design, the cam is not right on top of the cylinder, but on the side. It utilizes short, half-inch pushrods. This design has two advantages. First, engine width can be reduced. Second, the problems with mass in the OHV design are significantly reduced.

There is a fourth valve mechanism: Desmodronic. The closing action on a traditional valve system uses a spring to retract the valve. The OHC Desmodronic valve control system, unique to Ducati, uses no springs. Under this arrangement, one cam is used to open the valve and another to close the valve. The Desmodronic system was developed because springs become unpredictable at very high r.p.m. With the Desmo system, valve closing is more precise at high r.p.m.

Engine Variations: Method of Cooling

Motorcycles are cooled by air, water, oil or some combination of the three. Air-cooling is simple, light and requires no moving parts. Water and oil-cooling are more effective, but are heavier, require a radiator, some moving parts and are more expensive.

Air-cooling works very well on motorcycles, although the present trend is for water-cooling. In fact, Soichiro Honda was adamant that engines should be air-cooled. (Pollution control laws ended that!) With an air-cooled engine, the motion of the bike causes air to pass over cooling fins located on the cylinder and heads, the hottest part of the engine, to draw heat from the engine. The fins work as heat sinks. They are added to the engine to increase the amount of surface area that is available to contact flowing air. More fins or fin surface area means more cooling. This method works extremely well unless: the motorcycle is stopped while the engine is running for a long period of time and no air is flowing over the fins; or the fins are clogged with mud or other material (as happens when riding off-road).

Water-cooling requires passages in the cylinder block and head through which coolant can circulate. The coolant collects the excess heat from the engine and transports it to a radiator. Cool air is pulled though the radiator via a fan or forced air, dissipating the heat. Like fins, the radiator is a heat sink with a large surface area to contact flowing air.

Oil-cooling is similar in concept to water-cooling. Oil naturally picks up heat as it is pumped through the engine. Passing this oil through a radiator dissipates the heat.

There are three main advantages to liquid-cooling. First, it continues to work when the bike is stopped with the engine running. Second, it is easier to keep the engine within defined temperature limits, giving the design engineer greater control over the engine. The greater control an engineer has over an engine, the more efficient, clean and powerful it can be designed. Third, addition of a water jacket reduces engine noise.

CARBURETION

The carburetion system supplies a controlled mixture of fuel and air to the engine, taking into consideration engine temperature, load and speed, to optimize engine performance and fuel economy, while keeping emissions low. This is not a simple task. Carburetion is achieved in one of two basic methods: fuel injector or carburetor. These methods can be assisted through engineering designs, computer control and turbocharging to make the engine more efficient.

Fuel injection is the current rage, although it has been around for years. This system delivers fuel to the fuel injectors via a pressurized fuel line. The injector is an electromechanical device that sprays and atomizes the fuel into the intake air. In other words, the injector is nothing more than a solenoid through which fuel is delivered to the air stream.

Modern fuel injection systems are computer controlled. Older systems were mechanically controlled. Using a series of sensors, the engine, exhaust and environmental conditions are monitored. This information, accompanied with throttle position information, is used by the computer to determine the optimal fuel mixture. When determined, the computer instructs the injector system to provide a certain quantity of atomized fuel.

A carburetor is a mechanical fuel atomizing device. Carbureted systems can also be computer controlled, using the same types of sensors for controlling the fuel mixture as noted above. The major difference is, instead of electronic devices controlling the amount of fuel delivered to the air stream, mechanical devices are used. Inside a carburetor, fuel is pulled into the air stream by creating lower pressure (i.e., high vacuum) areas around a venturi cluster supplied with higher pressure fuel. The higher pressure fuel will flow to the lower pressure air stream. This concept, known as Bernoulli's principle, is the basis for all mechanical atomizing devices.

Added complexity comes from the fact that the engine does not draw a smooth steady air flow. Instead, the air flow is a series of high-demand/no-demand draughts compounded with reverse valve shock waves and exhaust suction. Coupled with the need to change the fuel mixture based on engine speed, engine temperature, air pressure, etc., the role of the carburetor is very complex.

The advantages of fuel injection are obvious. A mechanical device cannot control the countervailing forces and demands as well as an electromechanical device. Fuel injection is a more precise method of measuring fuel. Fuel injection can increase horsepower, increase torque, improve fuel economy, improve cold starting and reduce emissions. The disadvantage has been cost, although computer-controlled carbureted systems can be as expensive as computer-controlled fuel injection systems.

How the carburetion system channels air to the intake valve is extremely important. The engineering of the air intake path plays a significant role in engine power. Designs that provide a lower resistance path for the air to flow will be much more powerful than designs that do not. The reason is simple. An engine is an air pump. For any given engine, if you reduce the energy it must expend pumping air, you increase the energy available for other uses. The ideal path for air flow would be a straight line from the air filter through to the piston.

Engines with well-designed intake systems are said to be "free breathing." This can be achieved through good design or through turbocharging or supercharging. Superchargers and turbochargers help overcome the friction losses of the intake system by blowing air into the cylinder. They use a turbine or impeller to compress the intake air.

Superchargers derive their power from the engine using belts or gears to power the impeller. Turbochargers use a turbine in the exhaust system to power the compressor. The effects are an impeller spinning at 200,000 r.p.m. and an increase in power of up to 40% over a normally aspirated engine.

Neither system has found acceptance in the mass-produced motorcycle market, although a significant effort to build turbos was made by the Japanese motorcycle makers in the early 1980s. Factory turbos were shipped by Honda (the 82-horsepower CX500T V-twin), Yamaha (the 85-horsepower XJ650T transverse-four), Suzuki (the 85-horsepower XN85, using a GS650 transverse-four) and Kawasaki (the 110-horsepower ZX750 transverse-four). At the top end, they were fantastic speed machines, but only once you got into fifth and opened the throttle. Too many compromises were made to get that fat juicy top end. Retarded ignition timing; extra weight due to the turbo and beefed-up crank, rods, bearings, etc.; exotic carburetion; extra cooling devices and turbo lag all hurt the bottom-end performance. (Turbo lag is the time it takes for the boost from the turbocharger to kick-in.) Almost anything over 100cc could beat these hot-looking bikes off the line. And mechanically, with computer controls, sensors, surge tanks, pressure regulators, wastegates, etc., the turbos were extremely complex. Riders did not buy them.

EXHAUST

Exhaust systems perform four basic functions: direct burned gases away from the engine and passengers, dampen noise, enhance performance and control emissions. On trail bikes, a fifth function is performed: spark arresting. Moving from the engine to the back of the motorcycle, the major parts of the exhaust system are: exhaust cooling flange (handles exhaust immediately from the exhaust valves); exhaust pipe, catalytic converter (on more and more bikes to reduce emissions); the muffler (reduces broad band noise); and spark arrestor (incorporated into the muffler design).

The exhaust system is designed according to use. Trail, motocross and dual-purpose motorcycles route the exhaust high on the frame to keep the system from being damaged in the brush or submerged in water. Cruisers, and bikes designed for riding two people, will route the exhaust low on the frame to allow for a passenger on the back and to create a lower center of gravity. Sport bikes and racers route the exhaust so to reduce back pressure and maximize engine performance, which may be high, low or somewhere in between.

In the past, mass-produced bikes came with dismal exhaust systems. The exhaust was one of the first components to be modified. A simple change of the exhaust system delivered whopping increases in power. This is no longer the case. Modern motorcycles right off the showroom floor come with advanced exhaust systems. It is an old wives' tale that modifying the exhaust system will improve performance on a contemporary motorcycle. Even a straight pipe does not help performance of modern emission-controlled bikes. Check with an expert before modifying the exhaust system. Your plans may actually decrease performance or require rejetting of the carburetor. Be particularly conscientious when replacing a two-stroke exhaust system. Two-stroke exhaust systems are designed to assist in the scavenge and intake of the cylinder through the control of secondary reverse exhaust gas pulses.

FRAME AND SUSPENSION

Frame and suspension have evolved slowly, but steadily. As far as the frame is concerned, evolution was slow in part because the first designs were sufficiently suited for the stresses and demands of other motorcycle components. The diamond steel tube frame did the job well, and no new frame technology was needed for decades. As far as the suspension is concerned, evolution was slow because the problems that needed to be resolved were significantly beyond the available technology. In the 1890s motorcycles had no suspensions. It was not until 1906 when Alfred Drew invented the parallel-slider front fork that a good front suspension became available. A good rear suspension would not arrive until the swing-arm was invented in the 1940s.

PRESSED STEEL FRAME

Frame

The frame provides the supporting skeleton to which the components are attached. A frame must be light, strong and rigid. Although often hidden from view, made of simple materials and manufactured using simple techniques, the frame contributes as much to the "personality" of the motorcycle as any other component. To a large extent, frame geometry determines the motorcycle's handling characteristics.

Modern frames on standard production motorcycles can be grouped into three basic types: tube, pressed steel and monocoque. Tube frames are historically the oldest and now the most common. Tube frames are inexpensive to manufacture yet are lightweight and offer good strength and high stability at highway cruising speed. Like bicycle frames, tubed frames come in welded and "tube and lug" varieties. The welded frame is self-explanatory. The tube and lug variety fits the tubes into manufactured joints, much like a tinker toy.

Frames may be either "cradle" or "spine" designs. In the cradle design, single or double downtubes support the engine in the classic bicycle "diamond" design. In a spine design, the engine literally hangs down from the frame.

Pressed steel or fabricated sheet metal has been used to create "backbone" frames. These frames consist of stamped sheet metal that is welded together, as shown in the accompanying figure. It is economical, but heavier and less rigid than tube designs. This makes the pressed steel frame ideal for small, inexpensive motorcycles. Although through extensive engineering and use of modern materials, pressed steel frames are also well suited for larger applications.

Monocoque frames are an extension of the pressed steel frame. Monocoque frames incorporate many motorcycle components (e.g., fuel tank, rear fender, seat pedestal, engine mount) into cast sections that comprise the frame structure. Scooters are the classic example.

Variations of these frames exist, and it is not uncommon for manufacturers to combine technologies. One common variation is the engine-based frame. Instead of using a down tube, this frame incorporates the engine as a stressed member of the support skeleton. The Yamaha Virago and BMW R1100 are good examples.

Frames are traditionally made of steel, aluminum alloy or chrome alloy. Each has its appropriate use. Aluminum alloy is one-third the weight of steel, but also one-third the strength. There is no inherent weight-to-strength advantage for aluminum or steel. Steel is used in traditional triangle frames, where the tubes can be connected in a series of triangles. Steel has properties that make it great for this purpose because it is strong and resistant to fatigue. But the tubed design does not withstand super-bike racing stresses. Aluminum can be designed in boxed tube sections that have greater stiffness for a given weight compared to steel.

Front Suspension

Historically, with motorcycles borrowing so heavily from bicycle technology, the first front suspensions were nothing more than bicycle forks reinforced with various forms of link girders. The link girders provided limited vertical movement of the front wheel. Slowly, better systems were developed.

Front suspension systems come in three basic varieties: leading link, telescopic fork and swingarm. Leading link forks began appearing as optional add-ons to rigid forks. Leading links are characterized by a fork pivot positioned behind the wheel spindle. Vertical wheel movement is allowed by the action of the link. Damping is then possible through some form of spring or hydraulic device. (You may have heard about an Earles suspension, which is a variation of leading link.) Although not common, this design is still in production and found on low-end motorcycles and scooters, and the upper-end retro-classic Harley FXSTS Springer.

Originally found on production motorcycles as early as 1908, the telescopic front fork did not become the standard until right after World War II. Most modern bikes use a double-acting internal spring telescopic fork. This type of fork uses a progressively wound coil spring fitted inside the fork tube to provide most of the suspension action. Components inside the fork are activated anytime load is placed on the front fork or whenever the front wheel receives a shock. Shock absorption is accomplished through spring action, air compression in an inner tube and resistance to the flow of oil forced into a cylinder by outer tube movement. There is a compression stroke action and an extension stroke action to provide constant shock absorption and rebound control. If both directions of fork travel were not regulated, the bike would buck uncontrollably.

Front wheel swingarm design has only recently been introduced into mass-produced motorcycles. Bimota and Yamaha lead the pack. In this design, the steering and shock absorption functions are separated into two totally independent mechanical systems. This separation provides engineers the luxury of tuning each system to perform at maximum effectiveness.

Rear Suspension

Historically, rear suspensions have been one of three designs: hardtail, plunger and swingarm. Hardtails still exist in name through the Harley line, but this is a marketing and fashion statement rather than a technological need. Real hardtails have no shock absorbing features other than the cushioning provided by the tire, seat springs and rider's butt and spinal column. (You can get a custom-built hardtail, but why?) Modern hardtails have a shock mechanism keenly hidden from view to provide the "hardtail" look.

The plunger suspension separated the rear wheel from the rigid frame via a small spring device permitting limited vertical rear wheel travel.

After World War II, the swingarm became the standard rear suspension. The swingarm is a pivoting fork (or cantilever) generally attached to the lower section of the frame. Shock absorbers can be placed on both sides of the swingarm, which is the conventional layout. But there is no inherent reason for this design. On trail bikes a single shock (a.k.a. monoshock) is attached to the frame and swingarm near the fulcrum, allowing for greater suspension travel.

WHEELS, TIRES AND BRAKES

No matter how sophisticated the rest of the motorcycle, the wheel and tire (literally just the tire) are the motorcycle's only contact with the earth (or, at least, should be the only contact). Together, they are critically important to motorcycle performance and safety. Wheels are simple to understand. Tires are a bit more complex.

Wheels

Motorcycle wheels come in three basic varieties: pressed steel, spoke and "mag" casting. Pressed steel wheels are found almost exclusively on cheaper, lower performance machines such as entry level standards and scooters. Everybody knows about spoke wheels—they're found on bicycles. The spoked wheels designed for motorcycles are larger, stronger and more expensive. There is some variety in design of spoke wheels. The major design variables are the shape and material of the rim and the pattern of the spokes that hold the rim to the hub.

- Rim design—Commonly, rims are made of steel, and usually this works fine. If one has some real performance considerations, one may want rims made of alloys such as aluminum, titanium or another stronger and lighter material. Alloy rims are found on off-road bikes and high-performance machines on which the wheels are going to take a real beating. Rim maintenance involves a periodic check to determine that they are true and round, and firmly affixed to the hub by the spokes.
- Spokes—Spokes come in a number of sizes or gauges, and are laced between the hub and the rim in a variety of patterns. The engineers who designed your machine know more about spokes and rims than you do, and settled on a spoke gauge and lacing pattern to match the motorcycle's intended purpose. Size or lacing pattern knowledge is not required unless you are planning serious racing.

Increasingly, the trend in motorcycle wheels is to mag wheels. Mag wheels are generally lighter, stronger and more likely to stay "true" (i.e., round and straight) than spoke wheels. Mags require less maintenance and inspection.

Wheels size plays a significant role in bike performance. Larger diameter wheels are more stable, but they require more effort to turn. Smaller wheels are more responsive, but are not as stable. This is why cruisers have large diameter wheels and sport bikes have small diameter wheels.

Tires

Tire designs fall into six basic categories: high performance/sport, touring/sport touring, original equipment manufacturer (OEM), classic replacement, motocross/enduro and dual purpose. Within each of these categories are various subdivisions such that you can buy a tire that matches exactly the surface conditions you expect to encounter. Tire variations include: speed rated, radial, bias, belted, rain tread, touring tread, slick, knobby, raised white letter, load rated and multicompound.

High-performance tires maximize grip. They provide excellent traction and confident cornering capabilities, usually at the expense of carcass life. Touring tires are designed for carrying heavy loads and for high mileage, although offering less high-performance traction and cornering capabilities. Sport tires, and sport touring tires, are hybrids of performance tires and touring tires.

OEM tires are the same quality or design as those that come with a new motorcycle. In theory, the OEM tire is designed and tested for maximum compatibility with the capabilities and characteristics of the motorcycle. This is not always true. Some bikes come with great OEM tires. But too often, manufacturers save a buck and put crummy squared off tires on their new bikes. These tires barely meet the minimum requirements for the motorcycle. Junk these. The difference between a great tire and a mediocre tire is almost immeasurable.

Classic replacement tires offer the proper style and design to fit older motorcycles, and often come in uncommon sizes or offer unique features, such as wide white side walls, to complete the classic look. These tires incorporate new technology and are better tires than those they replace.

Motocross/enduro tires are designed for chewing the earth. These tires come in subgroups specifically designed for hard (baked adobe), medium (clay or grass) or soft (loose, loam, sand, mud) ground conditions. You can also get "paddle" tires, which are tires that turn your motorcycle into a virtual stern wheeler. The paddles are for riding in dunes or swamps.

Dual-purpose tires are hybrids between enduro and street tires. You can buy these tires designed for mostly street use, 50/50 street/trail use or mostly trail use. Dual-purpose tires are sometimes mistakenly called universal tires. There is no true universal tire; no tire can be great for all purposes. See Chapter 10 for more information about tires.

Brakes

Motorcycle brakes come in two basic varieties: drum and disc. On all but the smallest and slowest of machines, or the biggest and fastest machines, the rear brakes are engaged by a foot lever on the right side of the machine. (Several race bikes are now using hand-operated rear brakes.) The front brakes are activated by a hand lever near the throttle or right handle grip.

Brakes work through friction. Most apply force against a rotating disc or drum affixed to a wheel. Some apply force to the engine countershafts. The force causes the wheel to turn less freely, causing the motorcycle to slow. In theory, this is no more sophisticated than is dragging your feet to slow a moving tricycle. Motorcycle brakes are critically important to safety and you should know a bit about them.

- Drum brakes—Drum brakes are named for the drum-shaped hub, affixed to the wheel, to which force is applied to slow rotation of the wheel. Force is applied by two semicircular "shoes" that reside inside the drum, positioned to press against its inside surface. When disengaged, the shoes are retracted just enough to not touch the inside surface of the drum. When engaged by a cam, the shoes are forced outward, pushing against the inside surface of the drum. Sufficient friction is created to slow the wheel and, consequently, the entire motorcycle. Drum brakes may be either mechanically or hydraulically activated.
- Disc brakes—Disc brakes are named for the disc-shaped hub to which force is applied. This design has the disc affixed to the wheel with its outer edge passing through a U-shaped part (called the caliper) which is affixed to a non-rotating portion of the motorcycle. To slow the rotation of the disc, pads are forced in by hydraulic activated pistons from the inside arms of the caliper, "squeezing" the disc.

Both disc and drum brakes work well, though disc brakes are lighter, have more stopping power, are easier to maintain and work more consistently when wet or muddy.

MOTORCYCLE DRIVE TRAINS

The drive train consists of the transmission, primary drive and final drive. All components are perfectly mated to the intended use of the motorcycle by the manufacturer. Riders are confronted with few choices of transmission and drives once more important choices have been made. A brief description of each component here is sufficient.

Transmission

Transmissions range from one-speeds to clutchless two-speeds to six-speeds to automatics. Whatever the number of speeds, the duty of the transmission is the same: to transfer usable power from the engine to the final drive. The emphasis here is on usable power. One engine cycle (intake, compression, power, exhaust) produces a small amount of power. Usable power is created only when many of these cycles are combined. Combining them, however, is not sufficient. Engines produce good power only within a narrow range of r.p.m.s. Too few r.p.m.s, no power. Way too many r.p.m.s and the engine self-destructs.

The transmission allows the engine to operate within a selected r.p.m. range to produce usable power.

The most common motorcycle transmission is the constant-mesh design, which has two shafts: the primary shaft and the countershaft. The primary shaft is driven via gears or a chain by the crankshaft. The countershaft is driven by the primary shaft, and is also connected to the drive chain, drive belt, or shaft drive, which powers the rear wheel. Power comes from the crankshaft, is transmitted to the primary shaft, meshed to the countershaft, driving the rear wheel.

The primary shaft and countershaft each have one straight-cut or cross-cut gear for each of the "speeds" of the transmission. A five-speed engine will have 10 transmission gears, five on the primary shaft and five on the countershaft. In this design, all gears on the primary and countershafts are in constant contact with their mate on the other shaft (hence the name constant mesh). All gear pairs except the selected pair (i.e., the selected speed) freewheel on their shafts. Instead of engaging and disengaging gear pairs to select a speed, this design locks and unlocks specific pairs to the shafts.

Final Drives

One of three methods is commonly employed to transfer power to the rear wheel: belt, chain or shaft. Each has different performance characteristics. Each has inherent advantages and disadvantages.

Belt drive is the oldest final drive method. The first belts were made of leather. Belts fell out of favor when chain technology advanced to a sufficient level to be used as the final drive. Belts have always been used on some smaller bikes, and are becoming popular again on larger bikes. Modern belts are constructed out of special synthetic rubber with elastic reinforcement. Belts are lighter and simpler than shaft drives and rob less power. Belts are smoother than chain; there is no lash when you roll off the accelerator. Belts are low maintenance, experience almost no stretch, require no lubrication, and last three to four times longer than a chain.

Chain drive is the most common of the three final drive types. Leonardo da Vinci produced a series of sketches illustrating the basic roller chain concept in the 15th century. But it was not until the 19th century when roller chains were adapted to bicycles that chains were mass-produced. When the first motorcycles were produced, however, roller chains were not sufficiently strong, so belt technology was used.

Chain offers several important advantages compared to belt or shaft drive. First, chain is inexpensive, making it ideal for standard and introductory motorcycles. Second, chain is extremely durable in degrading conditions such as a mud pit or swamp, making it ideal for motocross, off-road and dual-purpose motorcycles. Third, chain is lightweight. Fourth, chain does not produce additional forces that impact handling and control (as does shaft), making it ideal for high-performance sports bikes. Finally, if properly adjusted, a chain consumes only about 1% of the transferred power, which is extremely efficient.

Chains have a few disadvantages. First, they are not as smooth as the other drive mechanisms, which is why touring motorcycles do not favor chain. Second, chains need constant maintenance: An improperly maintained chain can consume 20 times the energy of a properly maintained chain. Third, chains are noisy.

Shaft drive is similar to a driveshaft of a car, only totally enclosed. Shaft has several advantages. It is smooth, durable and low maintenance. Shaft is ideal for cruisers. However, shaft is heavy, which is not desirable for trail riding. And shaft produces a good deal of gyroscopic torque, pushing a bike up or down in a turn, which is not desirable for high-performance bikes.

CONTROLS AND GAUGES

Controls and gauges handle the man/machine interface. An inexhaustive list of controls and gauges includes: seat, handlebars, footpegs, speedometer, tachometer, neutral light, gear indicator, rearview mirror, throttle, brake pedal, gear selector, horn button, turn signal switch, kill switch, high beam indicator, light switch, oil pressure indicator, oil level indicator, temperature gauge, starter button and turn signal indicator. These all do one of two things:

- Let the bike tell you something
- Let you tell the bike something

It is beyond the scope of this text to devote detail to every possible control and gauge combination. A few axioms of ownership should suffice. A motorcycle should have the necessary controls and gauges to:

- Be legal where you want to ride—street or trail
- Provide the information you need to ride
- Suit your riding style
- Enhance your pride of ownership

ELECTRICAL SYSTEM

The electrical system can be viewed as three basic systems: charging, ignition and accessory. These systems can work independently or in concert with each other.

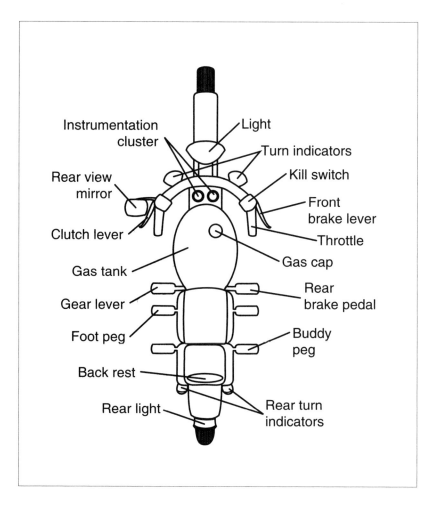

Instrumentation cluster

Light

Turn indicators

Rear view mirror

Kill switch

Front brake lever

Clutch lever

Throttle

Gas tank

Gas cap

Gear lever

Rear brake pedal

Foot peg

Buddy peg

Back rest

Rear light

Rear turn indicators

Charging System

The charging system consists of an alternator, rectifier, battery and regulator. The alternator generates alternating current (AC) electricity. The rectifier transforms the AC into direct current (DC). The battery accepts the charge and stores the charge until it is required.

The alternator does not produce a constant quantity of electricity. The quantity increases with engine r.p.m. At low r.p.m., the battery must be called on to supply extra power. At high r.p.m., extra power must be channeled to the battery until charged. Once fully charged, electricity must not be sent to the battery at all.

These systems go about their business all under the control of the regulator. The regulator controls the charging system so that the voltage and current output will not exceed predetermined specifications. The

Tail light
Turn indicator
Stepped seat
Mirror
Turn indicator
Light
Shock
Disk
Fender
Shock
Side stand
Horn
Reflector
Disc brake callper
Mufflers

regulator senses the amount of alternator voltage present, determines whether the battery needs to supply a charge or receive a charge, and directs and controls the alternator output accordingly.

Ignition System

The two most common ignition systems are battery/coil and magneto. Battery/coil ignition systems are standard on most cars and many motorcycles. Battery/coil ignition systems are logically divided into primary and secondary sides. The primary side consists of the components that carry battery level voltage. The secondary side consists of those components that are part of the circuit once the electrical voltage is boosted to 30,000 volts. For our purposes, we will discuss the ignition system in terms of functionality and parts, ignoring the primary and secondary classifications.

A basic battery ignition system consists of a battery, coil, spark timing mechanism (either distributor or electronic ignition) and a spark plug. The battery provides the initial current to the coil when the engine is started. This current is directed to the primary windings of the ignition coil by the electronic ignition, or by the distributor when the points are closed. At the direction of the electronic ignition (or when the points open), the electricity stops flowing.

What happens next is one of those incredible, hard to understand electrical events. The coil transforms the six (or 12) volts into 400 volts and then into 30,000 volts which rip out of the coil to the spark plug. Viola, spark. This process happens once for each cylinder during every power stroke, and takes only a fraction of a second to complete.

The major types of battery ignition systems are either electronic or mechanical. Mechanical systems use some form of distributor (consisting of points, capacitor and cam) to direct electricity to the coil. Electronic systems use an electronically controlled switch to perform the same function. Electronic ignition is higher tech, providing more dependable timing control and better spark. The disadvantage of electronic ignition is that when the system fails, it fails completely.

The magneto, invented in 1903 by German engineer Robert Bosch, combines most of the features of a battery/coil ignition system into a single unit. It performs the same functions as the coil and distributor of a battery/coil system. The magneto ignition has the advantage of generating its own power, eliminating the need for a battery. A magneto is used on motorcycles where reducing weight is important, such as trail bikes.

Magnetos operate on a very simple principle. An armature wound with a primary and secondary coil rotates between poles of a stationary magnet. As the armature rotates, current is "induced" in the primary winding when the contact breaker points are closed. When the breakers open, the magnetic field associated with the current collapses, and very high voltage is induced in the secondary winding. This voltage is discharged through the spark plug.

The ignition system is critical to the operation of the motorcycle. Every motorcycle must have some version of the ignition system, although some have highly abbreviated versions. Motorcycles of any size and complexity have some version of a charging system, unless the bike is highly specialized and the charging system has been stripped away to save weight. Everything else hanging off the electrical harness but not part of the charging or ignition systems is lumped together in this final category: accessories.

Accessory System

Although variations do exist in accessory systems, buyers are not given a choice of basic wiring harness and electrical system design options. You certainly get a choice of options to string onto the system. Here is where caution is advisable. Motorcycle electrical systems are incredibly fragile. Some systems don't produce one extra volt of power. New accessories or reverse grounding can overload and destroy part or all of an electrical system. One small anomaly may lead to several vexing symptoms. Two anomalies, independent yet happening simultaneously, may create a situation that is virtually impossible to troubleshoot. Do not mess haphazardly with a motorcycle electrical system! As with all motorcyclye repairs and modifications (but even more so), if you are not sure, seek the help of a professional mechanic.

SELECTING THE RIGHT BIKE—AVOIDING THE $7,000 MISTAKE

4

The most fundamental question to ask is, "Should I ride?" I addressed that in Chapter 1. If the answer is yes, you need to know what to ride—which will be carefully examined in this chapter.

Be forewarned: Motorcycles are designed to appeal to the heart, not the brain. It is extremely easy to make a $7,000 mistake purchasing a motorcycle. Conversely, it is just as easy, and a good deal of fun, to make a great purchase. If you avoid the most common mistakes and follow a dedicated methodology for selecting a motorcycle, you will select a fine machine that fits your needs well.

THE TWO MOST COMMON MISTAKES

The worst purchase scenario goes something like this: You pass the storefront window of a local motorcycle dealer on a beautiful 82°F day. Sunlight flashes off the chrome fuel tank of a Tricati 1500cc Cow

Charger, catching your eye. You stop to admire the well-groomed lines and swept back four-into-one exhaust. You've toyed with the idea of getting some sort of two-wheeled transportation since you were four years old. Those passions are rekindled. There is no reason you can't take your hard earned money and buy that bike. Ten minutes later, you sign the papers and drive home a bike you know nothing about. Congratulations, you made the most common mistakes of motorcycle purchasing. You did not control your passions or use a little common sense.

Control Your Passions

Buying a motorcycle is made difficult by the simple fact that motorcycles are part utility, part toy and part personal statement. The motorcycles that strike you, those that cripple the unprejudiced left side of your brain, are the ones that totally seduce the bestial right. These are the ones that have all the sizzle designed into them by the marketing department. Don't let the carnal and erotic override the cool, calm and collected. If you do, you will waste your money, and possibly your life. Some motorcycles sell sizzle, some sell steak. Given today's slick capabilities in one-piece injection molding plastic technology, there is at least a 50/50 chance that the bike that is best for you is not the one that strikes your fancy when you walk into the showroom.

Consider, for example, one of the most popular of today's motorcycle styles, the cafe racer. These are sleek, low and potent-looking machines. Usually they have a small "cafe" fairing, a "rider forward" seating position and are adorned by prominent decals proclaiming their manufacturer and heritage. You crave one of these. The author longs for one too, for the same reasons as you. These machines are stylish and often tremendous performers: nine-second quarter miles, zero to 60 in 5.5, face melting 170 m.p.h. top-end speed! A bike like this will make you an instant bad boy hero and broadcast to the world in no uncertain terms your sexual prowess.

Your primitive, instinctual self wants a bike that is fast and looks fierce. But, assume you are purchasing the bike primarily for your "Rodger Flannel" life consisting of short trips around the suburbs and a daily commute to work. These are not high speed trips. Your instinctual feelings are not leading you toward a smart purchase.

Why is this bike not for Rodger Flannel? First, the seating position causes you to lean forward. Much of your weight is supported by your wrists. Only during relatively high speed highway riding can you settle comfortably when the force of wind against your body helps hold you up. On a trip when you support more of your weight with your wrists, the eventual aching of your wrists from supporting your body weight will detract considerably from the pleasure of your ride. The rider forward position also makes it difficult to maneuver at slow speeds. But second, and more important, other bikes will better suit your needs (short trips and commuting) and your wants (performance and style). Off hand, a good recommendation would be either a sport touring or dual-purpose bike.

Consider, for example, the first time or inexperienced buyer, who is easily seduced by the clean lines, jaunty stance and overstated prowess of the latest high-tech enduro-style bike. But he may find himself riding alone on a Sunday afternoon when all the other guys have hopped on their street bikes for a run to the local beach party hangout.

There he sits, with his leathers, gas can, gloves, tools and other expensive (and equally seductive) paraphernalia. Meanwhile, all his buddies take off for a high speed, got-your-honey-and-picnic-basket-on-the-back run to the ocean. Not that this novice won't enjoy plunking around in the woods by himself, but wouldn't it have been nice to have a street bike, too?

Conversely, Dad, (this kind of talk was big when I was learning to ride) consider that the race bike guys have their bad days, too. They can't bushwhack around in the woods on a sunny day, nimbly scoot through congested traffic on the way to work, zip past the gas pump or smile as they sign the check for their insurance premium. In any of these scenarios was a bad bike purchased? No. Great bikes were purchased. These bikes were just the wrong bikes.

Try to be realistic about your needs. A bad purchase is made when someone buys a motorcycle that:

- Does not serve the purpose it was intended to fulfill
- Does not deliver the economy the purchaser had in mind
- Is not reliable
- Is not easily maintainable
- Will not carry a passenger comfortably (if needed)
- Will not carry enough cargo (if needed)
- Does not possess the style or elan the purchaser desired
- Is too darn slow
- Is too darn fast (the most common purchase mistake made)

Well built as they may be, some bikes are not powerful enough to take on the highway. Others are fast enough to keep up with a Tomahawk cruise missile, but are extremely uncomfortable for some riding (albeit quite stylish). Others simply aren't economical. Others are maintenance nightmares. Others are not reliable. Others are grossly under- or overpowered.

Also, some are just stupid looking or unfashionable. Yes, motorcyclists are style conscious. Very style conscious. So is the viewing public. If you show up at the Burger Princess Drive-In on your new mauve 450cc Kowadaka Trend Bender, no one will talk to you. You may hear a few snickers, or, if you parked at the wrong place, even receive an invitation to get beat up. Showing up at a Harley-Davidson convention without a Harley can get you the same invitation. Control your passions and take the time to make an informed decision.

Use Common Sense as a Guide

If it looks like a rocket ship, it probably performs like one. Do you want/need this kind of power—and the danger, expenses and maintenance costs that will accompany it? If it looks like a tinker toy, it is probably as light, nimble and under-powered as one. Do you want/need this kind of agility . . . and the fragility and lack of power that accompany it? A common sense look-over will also tell you how well the machine is built. Finish, fit and attention to detail are all good indicators of the overall quality of the machine. Do not confuse these surface indicators with marketing techniques or gimmicks such as good television advertisements, really cool paint jobs or sleek molded plastic side panels.

A PURCHASING METHODOLOGY

What should you buy, then? You should buy a motorcycle that is made to do what you intend to do, given the skill level you bring to it, at a price you can afford. Profound, no? But it is a simple fact that is often overlooked in the passionate heat of a motorcycle purchase.

Determining what you should buy is a simple five-step process. First, become educated. Second, decide what it is you are going to do with the bike. Third, make an appraisal of your riding and mechanical skill levels. Fourth, determine what you can afford. Finally, combine the information from the four previous steps. There will only be a few motorcycles that meet all of your criteria.

Become Educated

Most of today's motorcycles are marvels of technology. The technology available to the average buyer today is comparable to what was only found on the big-time race circuit just a few years ago. Almost every model built today is well engineered and superbly crafted, although lemons are not extinct. Choices in style and technology abound. There are literally hundreds of different motorcycles on the market. They range from 50cc mopeds, suitable only for short slow trips to the corner store, to 1600cc behemoths capable of eyeball-flattening 160 m.p.h.

acceleration. Obviously, no one would be in the market for a single motorcycle with all of the positive characteristics of a moped and a behemoth. The person shopping for a 50cc Yamokozi Turtle Chaser is not usually the person who would also want a 1600cc Motodevarnaski Canyon Raptor. The purchaser must deal with a wide spectrum of choices in which every conceivable niche or specialty purpose has been filled (and usually filled quite well).

A savvy purchaser will become familiar with all of the makes, models, types, styles and features offered by all the manufacturers before buying. A purchaser should understand the trade-offs made in relationship to safety and performance with respect to price, style, frame geometry, suspension, engine type and maintenance schedules. A smart purchaser will understand what it takes to safely operate and maintain a machine, and know how his own experience and capabilities rate. These are very important considerations that should be totally detached from the heart because these aspects determine which new or used motorcycle is best for you.

What is significant is this: You must know the nuances as well as the outright functions of a type of motorcycle to make the most of the hard earned cash you plunk down on a purchase. Few people want a motorcycle solely for the economy and simplicity it offers. A greater majority of riders have some additional passionate attachment for their machine. At a minimum, most riders have a strong appreciation of the craftwork and beauty of their machine, and some sense of pride in its ownership. At the extreme end of the scale are people who immerse themselves in motorcycle culture and motorcycling to the point that their identity is inseparable from the machine.

So how does one educate oneself? The motorcycle press is the first place to look. There are dozens of magazines dedicated to motorcycles. Many are specialized and cover only trail bikes, street bikes, touring bikes, classic bikes, race bikes, European bikes, British bikes, Harleys, etc. The next place to look is the library or bookstore for books on the sport. Finally, check out as many dealerships as you can. But do not expect much help from the sales folks. There are many dedicated motorcyclists selling motorcycles, but there are just as many salespeople who know nothing about bikes but pretend to know it all. You've got to know, if only so that you can protect yourself.

What Are You Going to Do with the Bike?

This should be simple enough. Look at an average week of your life. How would a motorcycle fit into that week? If you are only going to trail ride, you will be best off with a motorcycle dedicated to trail use, such as an off-road, motocross, or trials motorcycle. Of course, the type of trail riding you will do will determine which of these bikes you get.

If you are only going to do street riding, you need a bike designed for paved surfaces. You also need to decide how comfortable you want to be on long trips compared to how fast you want to go. Touring bikes are on the expensive, "comfortable" left end of the scale, and sports bikes are on the expensive, "fast" right end of the scale. In the middle of this scale (because the bikes are becoming somewhat less expensive) are sports touring, standards, customs (expense, speed and long-range discomfort start going up here) and choppers.

If you might do both street and trail, you need a dual-purpose motorcycle.

What Is Your Skill Level?

Make an honest appraisal of your skill level. If you are a beginner, buy a low-end, inexpensive motorcycle to learn on. This most often means a used motorcycle. Most beginners overestimate their skill level and buy way too much motorcycle. Your first bike will be dumped once or twice (at least), sustaining some cosmetic damage (at a minimum). This is not the sort of treatment you want to give to a $12,000 motorcycle.

If you have over one year of safe riding experience, almost any motorcycle will work for you. But remember that experienced riders on unfamiliar motorcycles have a higher rate of accidents than experienced riders on familiar bikes. Even experienced riders must be careful on an unfamiliar bike, and it takes about a year to become accustomed to any new purchase. Also remember that few riders are prepared for their first true sports bike.

If you are a seasoned rider looking to compete, you need to consider the top-of-the-line motorcycles in the area in which you wish to compete.

What Can You Afford?

This question needs to be asked two ways. First is, "What can you afford?" Second is, "What do you want to spend?" It is, of course, the lower of these two numbers that restricts your motorcycle purchase.

A motorcycle purchase involves many more expenses than just the cost of the bike. The purchase also involves buying those things that make it possible to use and enjoy the bike, such as: insurance, gas/oil, repairs, safe riding classes, equipment (tools, manuals, locks, covers, waxes, etc.), clothing (leathers, helmet, etc.), license/registration and user fees (parking, park entrance fees, etc.). Even if you pay cash for the motorcycle, these are significant additional costs that you must budget for. The Equipment Costs table illustrates the costs of owning a used bike for one year.

These numbers are conservative. It is not uncommon for the total cash outlay during the first year of motorcycle ownership to exceed

EQUIPMENT COSTS			
Purchase	One Time Cost ($)	Monthly Cost ($)	Total Annual Cost ($)
Motorcycle (1991 750cc)	2,800		2,800
Insurance		61	732
Gas/Oil (@ 5,000 miles)		20	240
Repairs		40	480
Safe Riding Course	50		50
Equipment	200		200
Clothing	350		350
License/Registration	200		200
Fees		20	240
Total			5,292

$5,000. Expect the costs to be much greater if you are buying a new bike, a fast bike or a bike coveted by motorcycle thieves.

Given such high initial costs of motorcycle ownership, many purchasers rely on credit to acquire the bike. Some folks think a motorcycle is like a car since both are forms of transportation. One might think that if you can afford a $5,000 car, you can afford a $5,000 motorcycle. Not true. A motorcycle is a luxury purchase, pure and simple. You can afford a lot less motorcycle than car. This is how the banks and finance companies look at it, and this is how you should, too. Also keep in mind that during bad weather most people will need another mode of transportation in addition to a motorcycle.

It is not difficult to figure out how much motorcycle you can buy on credit. Make a budget of your current debt and expenses. If you are a home owner, or are thinking about becoming one, you know that lenders operate under the 28/36 rule. This rule says that a home buyer's payments for housing should be no more than 28% of gross income. It also says that house payment plus total long-term debt (i.e., installment or revolving debt having one or more years remaining contractual payments) should be no more than 36% of gross income. This means that a mere 8% of your gross income is available for covering debts such as car, furniture, credit card and motorcycle purchases.

If home buying is not part of your economic profile, you need to use different budget metrics. Most people find that they have over extended their capabilities to pay off debt if their debt to net income ratio is above 15%. Thrill seekers may let this ratio go to 20%.

What Is Going to Fit Your Body?

In general, motorcycle manufacturers design bikes for average male *Homo sapiens* with ordinary dimensions. If you are far from average in size or shape, getting a motorcycle that is compatible with your body dimensions can be a chore. Almost any bike should fit you if you are of typical size. Naturally, everyone is different. Average height does not mean average reach or inseam. Fitting a bike properly is not just an issue of comfort, it is an issue of safety. Be sure that your hands, arms, feet, legs and head fit the bike you are buying.

Neck, Back & Butt—I start with the neck, back and butt because alignment of the spine is fundamental. The more the motorcycle design allows you to obey the rules of good posture, the more you will enjoy life in general. Not only will you be able to stay in the saddle with less discomfort, but your back won't be a wreck when you get to where you are going. Here are the rules of good posture while seated on the motorcycle:

- Natural curves of the spine remain naturally curved
- Pelvis tilted forward (Slouch in a chair. That is pelvis tilted backward)
- Head squarely above the neck with chin in
- Lower back supported (Either through lumbar support [touring] or with your arms bearing the load [sports])
- Ears, shoulders and hips in line
- Hips and shoulders parallel (No twisting!)
- Knees level with hips and directly over ankles

Unfortunately, motorcycle design can create a riding position that cranes your neck back, collapses the small of your back, and rotates your pelvis backward. It is the price you pay for speed. As you check other remaining "fittings," always be aware of what is happening to your neck, back and butt alignment.

Arms & Hands—A motorcycle that fits allows you to perform various tasks without extra effort. For example, you should be able to do the following:

- Cover the hand brake—This is a safety requirement. You need to have your right hand covering the brake at all times. This means fingers over the brake lever and thumb firmly wrapped around the handlebar grip.
- Rest with weight on the palm or heel of the hand—This is the favored position of most riders. It distributes your weight better, reduces strain on the back and keeps fingers from suffering fatigue. The best measure of this is how well your arm and wrist are in alignment. While in the riding position, your arm should make a straight line to the center of the handlebar grip as viewed from the side. If the wrist is bent, it is carrying the load and will fatigue.

- Reach the clutch lever without moving arms—In an emergency, from your standard riding position, you need to have instant access to the clutch. If you cannot reach out with your fingers and have full control, the lever needs to be moved and perhaps the handlebars need to be adjusted or replaced.
- Ride one-handed—There will be many situations when this is necessary. Examples include shading your eyes from the sun, adjusting a rearview mirror, putting a tape into the stereo or shooing a hornet.
- Turn the fuel petcock—You must be able to reach the fuel petcock while underway. There will be times when you run out of fuel riding the highways and have nowhere to exit to switch to reserve.

Legs & Feet—For short-legged riders the most limiting factors are seat height and width. For those with long legs it's footpeg placement. Every rider should be able to do the following:

- Maneuver the bike in tight parking lot situations—For short riders, this is a critical test. You must be able to turn the handlebars into a sharp turn and push the bike backward while retaining your grip on the handlebars and keeping the ball of your foot on the ground. Although this riding position is awkward, you will encounter it.
- Pay at a toll booth—You must be able to roll to a stop, put the bike in neutral, put a foot down, release the handlebars and search your pockets. This scenario happens elsewhere: you might be searching for change, sunglasses or a map.
- Leg grip the tank—This is an issue for tall riders. The location of the pegs must not cause you to spread eagle. If your legs do not firmly grip the tank, you do not have full control over the motorcycle.
- Shift and brake—The brake and shift levers on most motorcycles are adjustable. For the brake, your foot needs the ability to activate the full power of the rear brake, locking the rear wheel. You must be able to lock the rear wheel. For the shift lever, you need to have instant access to both lower and higher gears. The lever should not be so high that downshifting is a problem, or so low that upshifting is difficult. Shifting should be a simple toe flick action.

Head—Your head has a unique relationship to the fairing, although this might not be obvious at first. Fairings offer two very detracting features: turbulence and optical distortion. The severity of these problems depends on the positioning of your head relative to the fairing.

The wind pocket behind the fairing (basically where the rider is located) can experience a great deal of turbulence. This turbulence can be deafening, quite literally, if your head is buffeted by it.

Fairings are supposed to improve the field of vision. But they can obstruct vision just as much as they can help it. First, few fairings are optically perfect. Most have some distortion in the plastic, right in your line of vision. Second, some fairings are meant to be looked over, some are meant to look through, some offer a rider the choice. If the top of the fairing is set such that you cannot fully look through it or fully look over it, it will obstruct your view of the road.

The ergonomics of any motorcycle can be adjusted or modified. Handlebar levers can be moved and foot levers raised or lowered. Fairings can be adjusted. Some bikes even come with adjustable handlebars. But these are minor adjustments. If a minor adjustment cannot solve the problem, consider a different motorcycle. Replacing a handlebar, seat or suspension system can cost hundreds of dollars.

What You Should Buy

Once you have determined what you will do with the bike, what skill level you bring to the situation, what you can afford, what you want to spend and what fits your body, your choices will be narrowed to only a few motorcycles. By identifying these few motorcycles, you can use your time becoming fully literate in all their features and capabilities. This is time well spent. An obvious choice will emerge.

PURCHASING A NEW MOTORCYCLE

Selecting a motorcycle is fun. Putting together the deal and purchasing the bike is work. Previous chapters have discussed selecting the motorcycle that is right for your particular needs, temperament, style and ego. However, the motorcycle purchase involves more than just walking into a showroom and riding out with a dream machine. It involves, in order of priority: selecting a good dealer, contracting the best financing, getting insurance, striking an honest deal and taking delivery. Note that striking a deal with a salesperson is the next-to-last thing you do, although it is often the first and only thing some buyers do.

Doing the groundwork is very important. Once you put the first quarter mile on that bike, it is yours. Its value is significantly less than when the sales manager rolled it into the parking lot just minutes ago. The last thing you want is to get a bike home only to discover you cannot insure it, park it or get warranty/repair work performed on it. Worse, you could wake up one morning to discover that the repo man performed a midnight collection. Be smart: Do the groundwork.

SELECTING A GOOD DEALER

How significant is the dealer? Let us say that you have picked out the bike, a Hawker Blackburne 350. There is only one place to get it, the local Hawker dealership. Your second motorcycle choice, a Miller-Bolsame Jupiter 250, is a somewhat distant second. But you can tell that the Hawker dealership is not as well run as the Miller-Bolsame. My advice is to buy the second bike at the quality dealer. That is how important the dealer is! The dealer makes all the difference. A knowledgeable, well-run dealership will provide you with the right motorcycle, service and parts. A poorly run dealership will provide you with the opposite.

Selecting a motorcycle based on the quality of the dealer may seem inconsequential, too difficult to figure out and not worth passing up the motorcycle that gives you Technicolor dreams. It is not. I cannot explain the agony caused by a poorly run dealership (clamping the meat of your thumb in the jaws of needle nose pliers comes close). Non-skilled mechanics, uninformed parts counter personnel and fly-by-night sales staff can make life hell. Imagine a service department that makes you come back time and time again for warranty work. Imagine a parts department where the staff does not know the subtle differences between virtually identical parts in virtually identical parts bins, and sells you the wrong part. Imagine an accessories department where the staff will only sell you what they have on the floor, rather than work with you to get the accessory you really need. A poorly run dealership can make your motorcycle experience a nightmare and can result in many wasted Saturdays.

Why? Basically, a poorly run dealership is one that is probably fighting for its economic life. It is a dealership that has been cutting corners over the years, slowly reducing its customer base. As the customers leave, more corners get cut. And then more customers leave. When you see a dealer who cuts corners, it goes hand-in-hand that the dealer puts short-term profit ahead of other priorities. And you can bet the dealer is going to cut corners with you.

It is not difficult to check if a dealership is well run. Dealerships are generally divided into five departments: management, new bikes, used bikes, service and parts. Visit each department and look for signs of a well-run business.

Management

Management attitude is the single most important aspect to a good dealership. Are managers on the floor scrutinizing the operation? Do they treat customers well? Do they expect their staff to treat customers well? Do they treat their staff well? Do they invest in their business by purchasing new equipment, keeping the facility clean and modern and supporting the training of their staff? Does the dealership participate in the community (e.g., helping with poker runs, trail cleanups, charity fund-raising)? Does the dealer work to create a positive public image for the sport? A dealer who does all this is clearly in it for the long haul and will work to keep your business.

Management attitude is of special importance when it comes to warranty repairs, a fact discussed later in this chapter.

New and Used Bikes

A good dealership will have sales personnel on the floor who know about their manufacturer's full lineup of motorcycles and about the competition's bikes as well. You may find sales personnel who know more about sales than about the sport. You may also find sales personnel who know more about the lawn mower or ski jet lines than the motorcycle line. If you find no one who knows about the sport and the motorcycle lineup for that manufacturer, be cautious. A dealership that is more interested in closing deals or selling generators may not be so interested in dealing with you after the sale.

A dealership can also provide you a full set of services such as registering your bike with your state's motor vehicles department, installing options and setting you up with financing and insurance. The fact that the dealer does or does not provide these should not be an indictment of the dealer. But if you need these services, it is a consideration.

One important sign to look for is whether the dealer assembles the new bikes or has an assembly company do the work. Motorcycles come from the factory in crates and partially assembled. The dealership must complete the assembly. It is a positive sign when the dealership does its own assembly. It means it has total control over the quality of the motorcycle you buy.

Another important sign of a good dealership is one that does customer satisfaction follow-up on sales. This is the process of surveying customers on what they liked and did not like about the dealership. Ask the dealer if this is done and what the satisfaction percentage is.

Do not let a small inventory or shop persuade you that the dealership is poorly run. A good dealer may or may not have a large inventory of motorcycles or work out of a huge building. "Mom-and-pop" operations are often the best when it comes to service and satisfaction.

Service Department

The motorcycle industry is an industry that lives off technological innovation and change. Many great engine advances were first seen on motorcycles. You should be sure that the dealer is able to make repairs to the new breed of motorcycle. In other words, the dealer has the trained mechanics and modern repair facilities to do the job.

One good sign is when the dealership keeps statistics on its mechanics. Ask the service manager. If the dealer keeps stats, you know that they monitor the performance of their mechanics and really care about the quality of work. You should also ask how long the mechanics have been there. A long work history suggests that the dealership tries to keep their mechanics (and other employees) happy. This is a critical detail when that employee is working on your motorcycle. The last thing you want is some disjointed mechanic taking out management enkindled aggression on the head bolts of your Moto Morini.

Another good sign is a well-organized work area. Look at the service department and see how they do business. The area should be clean and organized, with good working areas and space. You should not see bikes on makeshift apparatus, greasy floors or mechanics yakking to their girlfriends (or boyfriends) while working on a motorcycle.

Another sign is up-to-date mechanic certifications from the manufacturer and motorcycle training institutes, often proudly displayed on shop walls. It takes great skill to diagnose and repair super modern, computer-regulated, pollution-controlled motorcycles. Manufacturer and institute certifications tell you that the mechanics are receiving continuing education on modern diagnosis techniques, system designs and high-tech repairs. It also tells you that the dealership is willing to invest time and money into developing a strong staff.

Parts

If you plan to do any of your own work, the counter help in the parts department is an invaluable resource if they know their stuff. If they are unknowledgeable or uncaring, you will experience many exasperating weekends at their hands. Like the service department mechanics, parts personnel should be well trained and have long tenures in the job. The parts department should be well organized and clean. If the dealership does not care about these employees, the dealership also does not care about you. You want counter help that will recognize the part you need (and if the part they gave you even comes close to looking like that part), know the parts they have in stock and can offer some advice (just a bit, they are not in the business of training).

As a kid, I once had a Harley AMF Sprint. It needed a head gasket. One parts staffer leveled with me and said that getting a gasket was going to take a very long time. The staffer also said that a Sprint was probably not a good thing for a novice to be into right then. I could have ordered the part and waited several months while warehouse workers in Wisconsin and Italy searched for the gasket. I could have dumped hundreds of dollars into the beast over the next few months and still not had a running motorcycle. Instead, I took the clue, sold the bike and bought a Honda CB 175 twin. Today, that Sprint is worth good money as a collectible, but 20 years ago it would have just been a pile of junk. The parts staffer saved me from myself.

CONTRACTING THE BEST FINANCING

New motorcycles routinely cost several thousand dollars. Almost everyone needs some financing to buy a new bike. There are three basic sources for this money and two basic types of loans. The sources include manufacturer sponsored financing, financial institution financing and repo artist financing. The loan types are motorcycle loans (where the bike is the collateral) and personal loans (where you are the collateral).

Since the financial market changes rapidly, the best that can be said here is to shop around. The manufacturer may offer some financing help, but not all dealers offer their manufacturer's financing. Banks and credit unions may offer either a motorcycle loan or a personal loan, depending on the motorcycle and your credit history. If these sources do not want to lend you money, you can get financing from "organizations" that specialize in high risk loans. However, if you need to go to one of these "organizations," seriously question your need for a motorcycle. These companies make their money through repossession. They expect you to miss a payment and in fact *want* you to miss a payment. And the day you do is the day you wake up to find your motorcycle missing.

Lenders view motorcycles as luxury purchases. This means that, in a pinch, a borrower will make car, rent and other debt payments before the motorcycle payment. Ergo, compared to other things in your life, a motorcycle is expendable (i.e., a luxury). Lenders also recognize that motorcycles depreciate fast, and are subject to theft, abuse and destruction. They do not like to make loans where the motorcycle is the collateral. So, they loan only a fraction of the motorcycle's value, meaning you need to come up with a large down payment. Or you must offer some other form of collateral. Or you must take out a personal loan with no collateral and pay a tremendous interest rate. Or you need a cosigner.

Note: Many finance companies insist that you have comprehensive insurance on your bike. Some also insist that you have life and/or health insurance. It is not that they care so much about you. It is just that they want their money back if you T-bone a Freightliner with your Lambretta 200 Super Scooter. These additional costs can be significant, so shop around for your loan before you shop your motorcycle. The dealership may also have a finance department. Shop them, too. They will have a variety of lenders they do business with, and they may just have the best rate around.

GETTING INSURANCE

Given the rider, the location and the bike, some motorcycles simply cannot be insured. Some can only be insured at extortionary rates. Won't you be surprised if you buy one of these bikes before finding out you can't insure the beast? Are you a first time buyer, male, under 26, not married, buying a bat out of hell? Do you have a few traffic transgressions on your driving record? Are you buying a Harley and living in a low income neighborhood? Lots o' luck finding insurance! As with financing, the savvy motorcyclist shops around for insurance before purchasing a bike.

There are eight basic flavors of motorcycle insurance. These are: liability, passenger, uninsured motorist, comprehensive, collision, personal injury protection, no-fault and road service.

- Liability coverage includes bodily injury and property damage for damages you cause to other people or property. A motorcycle can do just as much damage to human flesh as a car. You should carry enough liability insurance to fully rehabilitate a victim. This means several hundred thousand dollars of coverage. Anyone who has been hit by a punk knows that no amount of money fully restores the body, mends the spirit, recovers lost time or compensates for pain. At the very least you must carry enough liability insurance to restore the body of someone you annihilate. (It is too common for motorcyclists to carry very little liability insurance. It is too common for some stupid little jerks to ride with no insurance at all!)
- Passenger insurance covers claims by your passenger when you are at fault. In some states this is included in bodily injury liability, but it may be an option (or you may increase the limits separately).
- Uninsured motorist coverage pays you and your passenger for injuries caused by other drivers. [Note: Most collisions between motorcycle and car are the fault of the car driver.]
- Comprehensive covers your bike from damage due to such things as fire, theft, vandalism, acts of God, etc.
- Collision coverage will cover damages to your bike caused by an accident regardless of fault. It generally covers driver and passenger.

- No-fault insurance is offered in some areas. It covers the property damage and medical bills of a motorcycle rider involved in an accident despite fault.
- Road service protection covers the cost of on-site repairs and towing when your motorcycle is disabled.

Most states require drivers to have some minimum level of liability insurance. Others also require uninsured motorist insurance. Lenders will insist on comprehensive insurance for bikes they finance if the bike represents collateral. Be realistic about motorcycle insurance. The deductibles are often quite high for comprehensive coverage. The market value of your bike is often much lower than you would imagine, so you won't get a lot if your V-twin Russian 1200cc Ish is totaled. However, even the smallest parking lot incident can result in over a thousand dollars in damage. The same insurance company that provides your auto or home insurance may also provide motorcycle insurance, but often at very high rates. Look at companies that specialize in motorcycles. You can find these listed in the Yellow Pages or in advertisements in motorcycle magazines. The dealership may also have an insurance department. Shop them, too. They will have a variety of underwriters they do business with, and they may have the best rate around. Mix and match the various insurance types as you will, but you must have enough insurance to cover the damage you do to others. It is the fair thing and the right thing.

If you have not yet read enough reasons to take a Motorcycle Safety Foundation novice or experienced rider course, how about this: Many insurance companies offer discounts to riders who take these courses.

STRIKING A GOOD DEAL

Motorcycles are "mixes" of technology. Trade-offs are made for comfort, speed, handling, performance and cost. The idea that one bike is "better" than another only applies to a specific riding situation. No one motorcycle can do it all. If you have an open mind and are willing to select from one of several motorcycles, you can generally negotiate a good price. If, however, there is only one bike that will do, you may be forced to pay a premium price for a premium bike.

The first and best advice is to have an open mind. Select two or three motorcycles that will fit your needs from two or three different dealers. Some riders get carried away with the "machismo" of one particular motorcycle. It really strokes the ego to have the most recent motorcycle edition to a particular market niche: to have the highest horsepower, latest innovations, fastest track times. It is also deeply satisfying to do some serious ball-busting, talking trash about someone's bike because it can't do sub-eleven quarter miles, or won't do 0 to 60 in less than three seconds, or tops out at less than 173 m.p.h. In reality, many motorcycles are overbuilt for how the average Joe will use them. The fact that one bike has higher performance specifications over another is interesting, but hardly applicable to any riding other than on the Autobahn. If you won't be riding this bike in Deutschland, consider a "slower" bike that only tops out at 157 m.p.h. It can save you thousands of dollars. If you must have 120 horses at the rear wheel and 92 foot pounds of torque (Lord knows why), your choices are limited. And you will pay dearly.

The second piece of advice is to have some backbone. Getting the best deal requires some panache and guts. Haggling over prices is not a great 20th-century Western tradition. Most of us are conditioned to pay the price bar-coded onto the product label. On some motorcycles, you will be forced to pay full price simply because that is what the market will bear. On showroom dogs, you can negotiate several thousand dollars off the price.

The only way to do such negotiating is to show up at the showroom. What you want to know is the "out the door price." The ODP equals the cost of the purchase plus tax, license, freight, setup and finance differences. You can't call up dealers and just ask what the purchase price is. They may give you some low ball number knowing that they will make the low price up by beefing up the freight, setup or finance margins.

Here are some tips on negotiating. First, ask the salesperson what the manufacturer's suggested retail price is for the bike. Have him or her prove it. This is the figure from which to start negotiating. Bikes on the showroom floor may have a sticker price higher than this amount. Dealers have around a 20% profit margin and "dealer pack" (the minimum compensation a dealer gets from the manufacturer even if you only pay invoice) to negotiate with from the manufacturer's suggested retail price. Second, ask if there are any rebates on the bikes. Manufacturers often move slow-selling bikes by giving dealers rebates, which the dealer may or may not want to pass on to you. Third, look a those additional fees, such as setup. Here is where going to other dealerships really pays off. Every dealer should match the lowest fees you find.

Keep in mind that the motorcycle dealer deserves a profit. If you are working with a dealership where sales volumes are small, part of the price you are paying is for the convenience of having that dealer near you. It is a real, tangible element that many buyers overlook in their zest to get the best price.

The best way to acquire information for negotiating with a dealer is to talk to the competition and read the motorcycle press. Other dealers will offer reasons why the competition's bike is not as good as their motorcycle. They may also know what is and is not selling. A little showroom reconnaissance talking to sales personnel will yield good results and is fun.

In general, you can get a better price at the end of the season. Dealers do not want to hold stock over winter if they do not have to. Conversely, do not expect a dealer to take an end of season trade-in willingly. (Of course, you will always do better selling your motorcycle yourself. A dealer sees every flaw, many that an average buyer does not see. A dealer must also make a profit on the transaction that cuts into the trade-in value.)

Unless you are a mail-order mechanic, or experiencing poverty, buy the bike fully equipped from the dealer. You can negotiate a discount on options that you are adding (e.g., case guards, back rests, fairings). This is a good deal for both you and the dealer since the dealer still makes a profit on the entire package, but you save off the full retail. Many dealers throw in free labor on these options.

One note on "sticker" prices. If the bike is in high demand, you will probably pay sticker or more. Otherwise, have some respect for yourself and for your own self-interest, dicker with the man.

TAKING DELIVERY

Too many buyers take delivery on a new motorcycle with defects. Inspect your new motorcycle before you drive it off the lot. Check it out just as you would a motorcycle with 50,000 miles on it. Have the dealer fix any defect, no matter how minor, before you drive away. Once you are off that lot, your odds for getting a quick and satisfactory warranty repair diminish. Check for the following:

- No nicks, cracks or cuts in the paint, plastic or vinyl
- All options and accessories are installed and working properly
- With the bike on the center stand, check that the tires are aligned and that the chain is aligned
- Check all lighting and electrical options
- Have the dealer start the machine. Be sure it warms up well and idles down to its normal idle r.p.m.
- Check for the tool kit and any other included options (e.g., wheel chain lock, vent covers)

If there is anything wrong or missing, the dealer will probably try to correct it on the spot. Otherwise it will be only a day or two. But leave the bike on the lot! That few days wait will be much shorter than the amount of time it would take if you drive off the lot first. Remember that you do not formally take delivery of the bike until you ride it out onto the street. And then, all things change.

The salesperson should provide you with an orientation to the bike. He or she should go over all of the controls and features, show you where all the technical information is located and serial numbers are stamped and demonstrate how to remove the quarter panels that you will often remove. Be sure you understand all of this before you hit the road.

If the bike checks out, enjoy. But take your time on the way home. These first few miles are the most dangerous miles you will ever ride. Studies show that motorcycle riders on unfamiliar motorcycles are at extremely high risk of accident.

WARRANTIES AND WARRANTY REPAIRS

This is a big issue in the motorcycle industry. Franchise dealers have a contractual requirement with the motorcycle manufacturer to perform warranty repairs on any bike brought to them of that manufacturer. In reality, some dealers refuse to perform warranty work on a bike bought from the local competition. Some dealers take this too far, refusing to do any warranty work on any motorcycle not bought at that dealership.

I have sympathy for the dealer who refuses to perform warranty work on a bike bought from a competitor. Warranty work does not pay the bills. Most manufacturers pay a reduced rate or attach caveats to what warranty work they will and will not pay for. If you did not give a dealer the fat, juicy business opportunity to sell you a bike, why should this dealer take your dregs warranty work? If it is not too far to go to buy the bike, it should not be too far to go to have the warranty work performed.

But there are situations where a dealer should perform warranty work on a bike not bought at the dealership. I have heard plenty of stories of military personnel and other folks being moved across the country only to find that some local goofball dealer will not make good on the manufacturer's warranty. This is not only unpatriotic, it is an insipid business practice that alienates potential customers. If you find yourself in this situation you have tough choices. You can force the dealer to perform the work through legal wrangling and much letter writing. This wastes a good deal of energy and takes time. Then again, do you really want that dealer touching your bike? Take your business elsewhere and spread the word about the jerks at the intransigent shop.

Some dealers will do warranty work on bikes bought at other dealerships. These dealers are saints and should be rewarded with your loyal business.

To be reasonably sure that the dealer is *willing* to make repairs, check the dealer's reputation with motorcycle groups, local consumer groups and the Better Business Bureau. The time to do this is *before* you buy.

Know What the Warranty Says

Know what the warranty says before buying a motorcycle. The typical warranty on motorcycles is 12 months with unlimited miles. This changes from time to time, with the big cruisers generally covered with warranties more like those found in the automobile industry. Some manufacturers offer warranty transfers for a small fee.

Know the Break-in Requirements

Break-in is the process of deliberate riding so that the anomalies and irregularities of machined parts can be worked out (i.e., rings to seat, gears to mesh, etc.). Read your owner's manual. Know what the required break-in period is. Know the technical requirements and limitations during this time. Learn the maintenance requirements. In most cases you must maintain your motorcycle according to the manufacturer's maintenance schedule to collect on warranties. It is for this reason that I recommend having all service during the first year performed by the shop where you bought the motorcycle. This may cost a few more dollars, but it is well worth the "insurance" should a component fail.

Remember that a good break-in covers a variety of riding conditions and situations. During the break-in you want to expose your motorcycle to a variety of loads, speeds and engine temperatures. That means doing some city driving, some freeway driving, some hills, some country roads, some touring and perhaps some two-up riding. Do not hit the turnpike with the intention of doing all couple-of-hundred miles of break-in during one day.

Document all maintenance. Save the repair orders and sales receipts. These prove you maintained the motorcycle according to the maintenance schedule. You will have fewer (or no) courses of action in a warranty or "lemon" dispute without this documentation.

A cautionary note for all of you oil additive nuts. The value of these additives is questionable at any time, but certainly do not use them during break-in! Their additional properties may prevent a full and proper break-in of the engine and transmission.

When You Need a Warranty Repair

When a component fails, or your motorcycle is not performing as it should, take the bike back to the dealer as soon as possible. Do not let a small problem turn into a big problem. Provide the dealer with a full description of the problem, preferably in writing. Your description might include observations that answer questions such as:

- What does the problem sound/feel/smell like?
- Where does the sound/feel/smell come from?
- Under what weather and road conditions does the problem happen?
- Under what speed/engine temp/r.p.m./gear does the problem occur?
- Under what load conditions does the problem occur?
- How does it affect your driving? How do you respond?
- Do your gauges provide any helpful information?

Be as specific as possible. Vague descriptions such as "it makes a ping sound" will not help the mechanic. And no matter how much you know about motorcycles, be descriptive, not prescriptive. Provide the symptoms and let the professionals diagnose the cure. If you tell them the cure, such as "I need a new alternator," and they do the cure you recommend and it is not the cure at all, congratulations, you bought a new alternator needlessly.

Date the written description and include the current odometer reading. Keep a copy for your records. If you do not put these observations in writing, make sure the service technician writes down a full description.

Your Rights

A warranty gives you certain rights. During the warranty period, any failed covered part, which has been properly maintained, must be fixed by a franchise dealer. In addition, there are special circumstances that may qualify a repair as warranty work. First, if you find yourself in the unfortunate situation where a component under warranty fails and you cannot get to a factory authorized repair shop, you may qualify for financial reimbursement from the manufacturer. To qualify, save the failed parts, fully document the repair and contact your manufacturer service representative.

Second, if a problem with your motorcycle exists during the warranty period, you have the right to have the problem resolved even when the warranty expires. To qualify, you must be able to prove that the problem existed during the warranty period. Without full documentation the dealer may claim that what you think is an old problem covered under warranty is really a new problem not covered under warranty.

Finally, it may be that you get a motorcycle that legally falls into the definition of "lemon." A typical legal definition of a "lemon" would be:

> A passenger car, pickup, van, motorcycle, RV or moped, except off-road vehicles, that requires four or more repairs for the same problem, or is out of service for 30 days for multiple problems, during either (1) the first 12 months or (2) 12,000 miles of ownership or (3) the warranty period.

Each state defines vehicle types, the number of repairs and the time and mileage periods differently. Some "lemon" laws describe the costs to include and deductions to be made when determining a settlement value. Your Attorney General's Office can provide your state's definition.

Most motorcycle buyers would refer to their new motorcycle as a "lemon" long before it met the legal definition requirements. To be exact, if the dealer you bought your motorcycle from is unable or unwilling to make warranty repairs, you have a "lemon" on your hands, and a real problem. The dealer's ability and willingness to make a good faith effort performing warranty repairs is the single most important difference between owning a motorcycle you enjoy or owning a "lemon." As noted above, check out the dealership before buying.

WHEN YOU GET THE PURCHASE HOME

Get to Know the Motorcycle
The very first thing you do is park that puppy and read the owner's manual cover to cover. This is sure to save you hours of grief and several hundred dollars in repairs. Memorize that maintenance chart. Memorize those tire pressures, shock settings, etc. If you can't remember them, write them down and stick them in a storage compartment or under the seat. Also buy a service manual, such as the manufacturer's, or a Haynes or Chilton manual.

Document the Daylights Outta This Thing
You will also want to start a file on this motorcycle. I recommend an expanding file folder, called a wallet, available at your local stationery store. Stuff every receipt, instruction booklet, warranty card, repair order and document related to your motorcycle into the wallet. You might also collect all those articles you've read over the last 12 months about your bike here. Keep all sales brochures.

While you are at the stationery store, get an automobile log that lets you enter all kinds of repair information about the vehicle. (Those pages in the back of the owner's manual will not be sufficient.) Be diligent and enter every repair and interesting piece of motorcycle information you can.

Why do all this work? First, it will increase the odds that you will keep the bike properly maintained over the years. Second, it means a higher resale value at trade-in time. (Used bike purchasers look for the conscientious owner.) Third, it holds the information you may need in the event of a "lemon" dispute.

Detail and Lubricate the Bike

Start the bike out right by coating all plastic parts with a good protectant, all polished metal with a good wax, all chrome with a quality chrome polish and all rubber with a rubber preservative. Don't use the cheap stuff. You will work just as hard only to have it last half as long.

There is some contention in the industry about changing the oil. Some say to change the oil immediately after delivery because some dealers fill their bikes with cheap oil. Others say to change the oil and filter once before the recommended first break-in oil change. Others say to simply follow the owner's manual. My recommendation is to follow the owner's manual to the letter. This is not only because of warranty concerns (although these concerns are significant). It is also because oil is becoming so good, some bikes do not totally break-in during the break-in period. An extra oil change might exacerbate this problem.

Get an Extra Key and Extra Lock

You only get two keys, so immediately get a third. Triple redundancy is the standard for the space shuttle, and it should be for you. Also, write down the number on the key in your owner's manual. Even without the key a locksmith can make a new one with just this number.

Get a good security lock. It is easy for some punk to smash an ignition lock with a screwdriver and ride away on your Norman Villier 197.

Supplement the Repair Kit

The tool kit that comes with your bike will probably be filled with real cheesy, knuckle-buster gadgets. There will also be some common sockets, drivers, Allen and box wrenches, etc., that you will want and that are not in there. Take the time to find out what you need, what is cheesy and what is missing. Then go buy some good American-made tools. There is nothing like being in the boondocks with nothing but cheap tools and a few stripped nuts on your Motosacoche MAG 850 to make you wish you'd spent the extra cash upfront. Be sure your tool kit includes the following:

- Spark plug socket (5/8 or 13/16)
- Sliding T handle with extension
- Wrenches: Allen wrenches for all hex socket bolts; combination wrenches to fit all regular bolts (especially ones for removing tire axles and adjusting chain or belt); one adjustable
- Pliers: one slip joint or locking, one with wire cutting jaws
- Valve stem puller
- Tire irons and spare tube if running tubed tires
- Spark plug and gapper
- Flat repair kit
- Chain breaker and master link
- Duct or electric tape
- Magnetic screwdriver with interchangeable bits in storage handle
- Electrical wire (3 feet)
- Bailing wire (3 feet)
- Two extra fuses and a 3x5 inch strip of aluminum foil
- Cable ties
- Pencil and paper
- Light stick (yes, it can provide enough light to work by in a pinch)

6

PURCHASING A USED MOTORCYCLE

The cost of a new motorcycle has become prohibitive for many would-be motorcycle owners. It used to be that spending five grand on a bike was a lot. Now, with all of the specialized high-tech bikes, five grand barely gets you in the market. When you add the cost of financing and insurance, total cash outlay can approach $10,000 (even $20,000).

This does not take into consideration depreciation. After you drive off the lot, your bike has depreciated considerably. The wholesale value of an average motorcycle is about 40% to 50% less than the new full retail price after the first year of ownership. This, of course, varies widely. Some bikes hold almost all of their retail value, like BMWs and Harleys. Some bikes hold none at all, such as dirt race bikes. This is why used bikes are how most riders "get into" motorcycles. And there are plenty of great used bike values out there.

THE PRELIMINARY STRATEGY

It may seem like there are millions of motorcycles to choose from. To some degree this is more true of used bikes than of new bikes. After you analyze your needs, skill level, budget and determine what fits you, there will only be a few motorcycles that will work for you. In the used market, there may be 20 or more examples of those models in the Sunday paper that meet your needs. Each is unique, individual and must be inspected as such.

You should know the following before looking for a used bike:

- The style or type of motorcycle you want
- Your price range
- How you will get financing
- Where you will get insurance
- How you will get cash to the seller
- How will you get the bike home

If you know these things, you also know that many other issues are wrapped up in them. If you do not understand that now, read on and you will.

There is one major postulate of used bike purchasing: Keep it simple. Simplicity is the quintessence of a good used motorcycle. Bourgeois exotic bikes, rare bikes and bikes with super high technology and lots of slick options are cool and exciting. But exotic bikes are difficult and expensive to repair and maintain. Rare bikes are often too valuable to ride, and finding parts for them is difficult. Super high technology bikes fail more often than time-proven "old" technology bikes. For these reasons, low-tech bikes make the best used bikes for the proletariat. This is especially true for buyers who are learning to ride, and may be laying the bike down a lot, or for those who are short of cash.

WHERE TO LOOK FOR A GOOD USED BIKE

Bikes can be bought from a private seller, from a manufacturer's franchise dealer, from a secondhand dealer or at auction. Each method has its particular points.

Manufacturer dealers need to turn over trade-ins because their profit is often locked up in the trade-in. These dealers generally keep the cream puff trade-ins and sell the less desirable used bikes to secondhand dealers. The advantages of buying from a dealer are:

- Wide selection in one location
- The selection is of higher quality bikes
- Financing is often available
- Knowledgeable sales staff

- Warranties are sometimes available (although most bikes are sold "as is")

The disadvantage is that you will pay more for a used motorcycle at a manufacturer dealership than if you bought the bike from the original owner directly.

Secondhand dealers offer the same wide selection, but of older bikes that need closer scrutiny. Secondhand dealers offer lower prices, often on very good bikes. However, do not expect all of the services you find at a manufacturer dealer. Dealers of both ilks may not let you check out a bike as well as this book suggests.

Auctions are the only places to get some bikes (such as police specials and collectibles). Auctions are also interesting places to get a standard machine. A word of warning: The uninitiated should be cautious and do a great deal of research about the bike(s) they are interested in and the rules of the auction. For example, bidders often pay a registration fee. Bikes are sold as is, usually for cash only. You arrive early to review the offerings and make detailed inspections of the bikes you will bid on. The owners may or may not start the bike for you. Auctions are a high risk way to buy a bike. The advantage is that you might get a great bike at an outrageously low price. Check with the police and local wrecking yards for upcoming auctions.

Private sellers are the preferred source for used bikes. Advantages of buying from a private seller are:

- No middlemen, which makes the price more attractive to both seller and buyer
- You have a better chance to fully inspect the bike
- You can inspect the owner's records
- You meet the person who cared for the bike

But private sellers are not without disadvantages, which include:

- It can take a substantial amount of time to go from seller to seller
- He or she may be selling "hot" goods
- The bike may be a lemon
- The bike may be assembled from several junked motorcycles.

INSPECTING A USED MOTORCYCLE

No rider wants a "lemon." No rider wants a used bike that will cost them a small ransom to keep on the road. Therefore, the inspection of a used bike should be a methodical practice based on modern mechanical techniques.

Fortunately, you do not need to be a mechanic to properly inspect a used motorcycle. Good bikes are easier to spot than one might think. The following inspection process will give you a high degree of confidence that the bike you are looking at is sound. Followed in order, the inspection process will also help you quickly eliminate a dog.

Over the Phone Inspection—Twelve Questions

Surprisingly, you can learn a lot about a bike during the first phone call with the seller. Take notes while you ask the seller the following questions:

- What is the general condition of the bike?
- What is the history of the bike?
- How has the bike been used?
- How has the bike been stored?
- Does the seller have documentation, such as title, tags, repair orders, etc.?
- What repairs and maintenance have been performed?
- What enhancements and modifications have been made?
- What repair does the bike need right now?
- What "extras" come with the bike?
- How many miles on the bike?
- What is the selling price?
- Why is the bike being sold?

Although you have not seen the bike, you will know a great deal about the bike, and the person who rides it, after this first phone call. Perhaps knowing about the person who rides it is more important than knowing about the mechanical condition of the bike. No matter how favorably a motorcycle guide rates a particular model, who maintained the bike and how well it was maintained are more important factors than who manufactured it.

For example, most folks who keep documentation are very conscientious owners, which is a good sign. On the other hand, someone who keeps no records, or whose answers are vague, maybe seems a bit shifty, is probably someone with whom you do not want to do business.

Do not try to negotiate the price over the phone. It is ridiculous for you to set a price without seeing the bike. If the price is within or a bit above your price range, and you like what you have heard, go look. Be cautious of the seller who drops the price over the phone or is trying to push a sale.

Preliminary Once Over—Four Steps

The preliminary check is a simple "at-a-glance" check. It is your first face-to-face meeting with the motorcycle. Like a first date, this will be somewhat superficial. No reason to get your hands dirty if the bike cannot pass the simplest of requirements. Follow these four steps:

- Engage the seller in conversation. You want to accomplish two things. First, you want to repeat the questions you asked over the phone. Be cautious if you get dramatically different answers. Second, you want to develop some sort of simpatico rapport with the seller. The better the seller feels about you, the better the bargaining will go.

- Check the documentation. Match the license plate number with the number on the registration. Sometimes plates are switched! Match the odometer reading and the frame and engine identification numbers to the numbers on the title. If they don't match, you may be looking at stolen goods. Look for sales receipts and repair orders. You want to know about major repairs and see a constant attention to scheduled maintenance.

- Check general wear and tear. If the bike has 15,000 miles on it, the bike should show signs of being used that long. Areas that wear with use (e.g., tires, footpegs, seat, grips, knobs, buttons, handles, hinges) should match the odometer. Areas that age with time (e.g., rubber boots, plastic parts, the finish) should match the age of the bike. If these do not match, find out the reason.

- Everything should be clean and straight. Clean not only means free from leaks and stains, it also means that the seller does some detailing on the bike to keep it polished and bright, or at least respectable. If the bike has lots of road grit on it, be wary. A head leak, cracked case or leaking shock may be hidden by the dirt accumulation. Note anything brand new. Brand new parts may suggest a recent fix of crash damage. Ask about it.

Clean means clean everywhere, not just in the easy-to-reach places. Ask the seller to remove all easily removable plastic covers and to pop the seat. Have a look. Look under metal fenders for rust.

Straight means, quite simply, straight. Forks should run parallel when examined from different angles. Handlebars should align with the front wheel. The front wheel should align with the back wheel. The back wheel should align with the frame. If things are not straight, and on many good used bikes some things will not be straight, know the reason.

If the bike passes these four inspections, there is an honest chance you have a good used bike on your hands, and you'll want to examine it further. If the bike fails, pleasantly say your good-byes and go on to the next motorcycle.

Full Inspection—Thirds and Inspection Points

A systematic check of the motorcycle is the most efficient and effective way to ensure that you do not miss critical details. Divide the bike into thirds. The front third is everything from the steering head and handlebars forward. The middle third is the engine cradle. The back third is everything behind the engine. Examine each third. Start at the stem. Work to the stern.

A motorcycle has only 12 major inspection points:

- Wheels, tires and brakes
- Suspension and steering
- Instrumentation and controls
- Engine
- Fuel system
- Exhaust
- Power train
- Cooling
- Lubrication
- Frame
- Electrical system
- Options

By dividing the motorcycle into thirds and then checking the inspection points that reside in that third, you will perform a quality check of all systems of the motorcycle.

Wheels, Tires and Brakes

Wheels—Wheels should be free from defects. Defects include major impact damage, and bent, missing or twisted spokes.

Tires—Tires are visually inspected for wear, abrasion and damage. Look at the entire tire. Sidewalls should not have cracks from aging. (Tires must be at the recommended pressure or you may not see these cracks.) Use the Lincoln head penny test to ensure that tread depth is not less than 3/32 for a front tire, and 2/32 for the rear. Insert the penny into the main tread groove, Lincoln's head first. If the tire tread is not deep enough to cover the top of Abe's head, the tires need replacing. Remember that tires are organic. They decompose. They rot. From the inside out. Tires that are more than four years old should probably be replaced, even if their tread is deep and the carcass looks good.

Brakes—Drum brake wear can be noticed in two areas. First is at the indicator on the cam arm. Second is at the slack adjustment on the brake cable or rod. These can give you a good indication of remaining shoe life. Disc brakes have windows for pad inspection. The disc itself should not be deeply grooved or scored. Brake lever and pedal action should be smooth. If the brakes are activated by a hydraulic system, check the reservoir window for fluid level and fluid condition. Inspect all hoses for cracks and fluid leaks. Pumping hydraulic brakes should not significantly help build up additional brake pressure after one or two pumps. This would suggest the need for brake servicing.

Suspension and Steering

Suspension—The suspension is checked while sitting on the motorcycle. Pump the front forks. Then do the same on the back shock(s). The forks and shocks should take no more than two and a half strokes to absorb the push. The movement down should be resistant but smooth. This is the first stroke. The bike should not bottom out. The movement up should be just as smooth. This is the second stroke. The bike should settle in. This is the half stroke.

On monoshocks, check bushing areas for excess wear. Check for oil leaks around seals. On coil spring shocks, check the springs for breaks.

Steering—Uncertain or wobbly movement of the handlebar suggests worn bearings in the steering head. With the bike on the center stand, move the handlebars from full left to full right. No roughness should be felt. To check for bearing wear, push and pull the handlebars.

Instrumentation and Controls

Instrumentation—All gauges, indicators and switches should be in working order. Some components cannot be checked without the engine running or without a test ride. Others can. With the engine off, turn the ignition on. Look for the warning lights (euphemistically called "idiot" lights) and neutral lights to come on. These lights come on when the ignition is on (but engine off) to show that the bulbs are not blown. If the bulb does not light, this may mean only that the bulb is out. But it may also mean that the seller has disconnected the light to prevent you from knowing there is a problem.

Controls—While in the saddle, check all controls, such as the brake lever, clutch lever, choke, kill switch, gas reserve petcocks, etc. Everything should work smoothly. Inspect the clutch and brake lever clamps for cracks around the mounting bolts. Check that the cable adjustment screws are not stripped.

Engine

Note if the motorcycle is hot, warm or cold. Ask for the owner to start the bike. A hot or warm bike should start right up and idle reliably near 1,000 r.p.m. A cold bike may be tough to start. You must use your judgment if this is normal or a sign of problems. A hard-starting cold engine is a sign of wear.

As the bike is started, listen for noise and notice the exhaust. Unusual warm-up noise may be due to piston slap. Unusual noise after the engine is warm (and the oil has thinned) may be due to worn main bearings. These noises can be very hard to distinguish by the uninitiated. But after you hear several motorcycles, you will have an idea of what a smooth engine sounds like.

Look around the head gasket. Small areas of burned gas may be an indication of a defective head gasket. Crystallization around the head gasket is a possible sign of a water leak.

Visually check the shift lever rod for damage. Oil leaks often develop here.

Fuel System

Check the fuel tank for rust. Look inside with a flashlight. Feel around the edge of the fuel cap. Check the petcocks for smooth operation. You don't want to be fighting to get your bike on reserve while going 65 m.p.h. in bumper-to-bumper rush hour traffic.

Exhaust System

Exhaust on a cold engine may be white from steam, but not after it has warmed. Notice the exhaust as you lightly blip the throttle. Black smoke is a moderately bad sign of a rich fuel mix, which may be cheap or expensive to fix. Four-stroke exhaust should never be blue. Blue exhaust smoke is a bad sign of burning oil for a four-stroke engine. This may suggest worn valves, guides or rings. Blue smoke from a two-stroke is expected. The exhaust system itself should be free from pinhole leaks and heavy rust.

Power Train

The power train consists of the transmission, clutch and final drive. The transmission and clutch should work smoothly and never slip. But checking the tranny and clutch without a test ride is difficult.

Final drives come in chain, belt and shaft. There is not much to say about shaft drive. All you can look for is fluid leaks. Shaft drives are generally smooth and quiet. If the bike has a center stand, raise the bike and push on the rear wheel side to side to check for bearing wear.

If the final drive is toothed belt, look at the condition of the belt and the sprockets. It is possible for the sprockets to become chipped from flying road debris. This may reduce the life of the belt. But belts rarely show signs of failure. They simply haul off and fail one day. Although belts have a service life that is often longer than the expected life of many motorcycles, it is important that the belt be on a rigorous replacement schedule just so you do not get stranded.

If the final drive is chain, there is quite a bit to inspect. For this inspection you are looking for proper alignment and kinking links. Alignment is checked several ways. First, sight down the chain from above and behind the motorcycle. The chain should be straight between the countershaft sprocket and rear sprocket. Most chains are not properly aligned. So the next question is, how poorly aligned is it? Look at the chain and sprockets for unusual wear, signified by bright shiny spots on either.

Kinked links can be seen on the rear sprocket. Put the bike on a center stand so the rear wheel turns freely. Rotate the wheel and notice if any of the links do not follow the sprocket smoothly.

Check for worn sprocket teeth by rotating the rear wheel. Worn chains and worn teeth go hand-in-hand. Sprocket teeth should not be hooked, bent, broken or filed on one side or another. If the chain is out of alignment or the sprockets worn, have the owner pitch in toward a new chain and sprocket set.

You can visually inspect the chain, but visual inspection will only uncover the most abused cases. The only way to know if a chain has been stretched beyond safe limits is to take the chain off the bike and measure. This is far beyond the scope of this inspection. Checks such as trying to pull the chain off the rear sprocket tell you nothing. The chain may come off for a variety of reasons, one of which is that the chain is worn beyond the manufacturer's specification. Then again, the chain may not come off even if stretched beyond specification.

Cooling

Motorcycle engines come air-cooled, oil-cooled and water-cooled. Some offer a combination of the three.

Air-cooled engines must be inspected for fin damage and for options improperly added by the owner that may inhibit cooling. V-twins are of special concern. With the rear cylinder receiving so much hot air off the front cylinder, V-twins often run very high head temperatures.

Oil-cooled engines must be inspected for damage to the radiator and oil leaks along the oil lines to and from the radiator.

Water-cooled engines should be checked for proper coolant level and condition. You don't want to find oil or corrosion in the coolant. You want to see fresh, clean coolant at the proper level in the radiator. Check the radiator and radiator hose for cracks, damage and leaks. Also check for a properly functioning fan.

Lubrication

Inspect the oil. It should be up to a proper level. Look at the oil. It should look clean and translucent. Feel the oil. There should be little or no grit and no sludge. Smell the oil. It should have the dull, soft, sweet smell of clean, fresh oil. There should be no burned odor. Oil with a gray color is an indication of water contamination. It is critical that the owner show proof of regular oil changes.

Scheduled oil changes are the single most important element of motorcycle maintenance. It is critical for the life of the engine. Although a conscientious owner may not be able to demonstrate that the bike received timely oil changes, it is a great bonus to find an owner who can. It means that you are not only looking at an engine that is probably in good shape, but also that the bike was owned by someone who cared.

Frame

The frame is inspected for damage and repair. Look for scrapes and impact damage. This may be covered by new paint and welds. Damage does not automatically disqualify a bike as a good purchase. But you do need to ask the seller about it. Inspect all frame member welds, such as the steering crown welds, for cracks. Try to get a good look at the underside of the bike. Check that all motor mount bolts are in place. Visually check the alignment of the rear wheel and rear fender with the frame. (If this alignment is incorrect, the bike has landed on its rear fender hard!)

Electrical System

The electrical systems of many motorcycles are quite fragile and complex. If anything seems wrong with the electrical system, walk away from the bike. Electrical problems can be the most vexing to diagnose, impossible to fix and can leave you stranded at any time.

Be sure all electrical parts work. Check all lights, horns, instruments and turn signals. Check accessories such as radios, CBs, air horns, etc. Check the wiring harness for reworked, supplanted or bypassed circuits.

Check the battery for proper maintenance. The acid level should be correct, the battery posts free from corrosion and the battery top should be free of dirt. The cradle holding the battery should also be free of dirt and corrosion. The battery case should be free of cracks and small holes. If the battery has been neglected, be concerned that the rest of the electrical system has been put under additional strain. One or two other electrical parts may be ready to fail, especially with electronic ignition. Also worry that the owner really has not given a damn about the bike. The battery is the most critical component of the electrical system and deserves proper care. If the seller misses doing battery maintenance, he's probably missed other important maintenance.

When the engine is running, check that the headlight gets brighter when the engine is revved. This is normal and suggests a properly working charging system.

Options

There are too many options to discuss an inspection of every type. But do try each option to make sure it works. Be realistic about options that do not work. Some options are important to your riding needs. Others are not. Do not be gun shy of buying a used bike with one or two broken options if you would not use them anyway. It is more important that the powerplant, drive line and safety features check out well.

Test Ride

Test riding is a big issue in the motorcycle trade. On one hand, you cannot thoroughly test a bike without a test ride. But on the other, plenty of sellers have been ripped off by giving test rides. Motorcycle culture is filled with stories of sellers who had an uninsured rider crash the bike on a test ride. And, there are many stories of sellers who let some guy test ride their bike, only to see the rider disappear over the horizon, never seen again. Do not expect to test ride a motorcycle.

If a test ride is important, there are several solutions to this situation, none of which are really good. The first is to offer the seller enough ID and perhaps something of value (such as your car) to settle his mind that you won't steal the bike. Another is to get, in writing from the seller, the contingency agreement that he offers you a 15-minute full refund warranty if you buy the bike. If, within the first 15 minutes of owning the bike, you are unhappy with how it fits you, you can bring it back for a full refund. A third is to have along a legal document saying that you will take full responsibility for all damage done on a test ride. A fourth solution is to have the seller take you for a ride on the back of the bike. Some dealers resolve this problem by putting homing devices in the frames of their demo bikes.

Further Mechanical Inspection

If you really want to be certain about the health of a particular bike, you can have it inspected by a mechanic. There are several good tests that only a trained mechanic can perform on a motorcycle, including a spark plug inspection, compression test, leak down test and several electrical system tests.

GUIDE TO A FAIR PRICE

Checking the classifieds, web sites and publications specializing in motorcycles and dealers will give you some idea of what certain bikes are worth. But, if you are going to spend several thousand dollars on a bike, it is well worth it to get a subscription to *Motorcycle Consumer News* or the *AMA Official Motorcycle Value Guide*. *MCN* is a monthly motorcycle magazine. Seasonally, *MCN* publishes the retail values of all the major street-legal motorcycles sold in the United States. The list covers about 15 years worth of motorcycles. The *AMA Guide* is more comprehensive. It includes retail, trade-in and wholesale values for street and dirt bikes.

Determining a fair price with the seller is a matter of dickering. After inspecting the motorcycle you will have a list of repairs that need to be made or potential problem components that increase the risk of buying the bike. Every bike will have a few marks against it. Figure out what you are comfortable paying, offer the seller something lower than that price, leaving yourself room to dicker up.

OWNERSHIP OF A NEW USED MOTORCYCLE

At some point you will buy a used motorcycle. Once you give the seller the cash you have little or no recourse should you have made a mistake. But you have gone through the steps in this chapter; you are confident.

Once you do forge that gulf, you are the owner of a new used motorcycle. It is yours. Congratulations! Whether you did it right or cut some corners, know that everyone who purchases a motorcycle, new or used, has some lingering doubt. And that causes stress. Many people do not sleep well the first few nights of motorcycle ownership. Your motorcycle has meant a significant allocation of scarce monetary resources put into a depreciated (and depreciating) asset. That is stressful. The motorcycle may have mechanical problems (unlikely for anyone who has read this book). That is stressful. And the motorcycle might not live up to the job it must do. That is stressful.

To reduce this stress, follow a basic strategy of business: Always have a secondary plan of action. In this case, the primary plan is that you love this motorcycle and keep it for 150,000 miles. The secondary plan is that the motorcycle is a lemon and you will want to unload it. No matter which scenario, during the first few days of ownership you follow the same procedure. These processes will help you discover if this is a bike you can love, or if this bike is a lemon.

Buy the Book

Now that you own a new used motorcycle, it is imperative that you maintain the bike properly. Buy a manual covering basic repairs of the motorcycle. Become familiar with the basic maintenance repairs for your motorcycle. If you do decide to sell the motorcycle, the book will go with it and the buyer will feel like he got a little extra premium free.

Get to Know Your Motorcycle

If an owner's manual came with the bike, it is required reading. Although these manuals are often superficial in their coverage of the bike, they contain the most important information about the bike. Be sure you know how to operate the cruise control, set the radio/clock, operate the power controls, fill the tank without pouring fuel down the side of the bike, adjust the chain, check and increase tire pressure, etc.

Detail the Motorcycle

Wash that bike. Buy some good motorcycle detergent. Mild soap is best. Don't be cheap and use that bargain basement white dishwashing detergent. It doesn't work worth a darn, and some newer paints can be damaged by these basic detergents. Get yourself a good sturdy sponge, several plastic wire brushes and a window sponge covered with nylon mesh—maybe a chamois cloth if you are really into it. As your sponge passes each washed surface, look for signs of corrosion or damage that you may have missed.

Be careful when pressure washing a motorcycle. A forceful spray from even a garden hose can force water into electrical parts and intakes where water does not belong. The chain is the only component that should be pressure washed. This removes all road and trail grime. If you oil the chain immediately, this will help the chain last much longer.

Wax that bike. Waxing protects the custom paint jobs of street bikes and makes cleaning a trail bike easy. A good paste wax is worth the price. A good wash and wax takes an hour or two. Given that kind of effort, you want the wax to shine for a couple of months. Cheaper waxes do not last. It is not worth anyone's time to save a few cents on the materials only to have to repeat the process every few weeks. If you don't have five or six old soft shirts or diapers, buy some cheese cloth and rags for waxing the motorcycle.

Wax it right. Don't do it in direct sunlight or on tremendously hot days. Don't splay on huge gobs of wax. Apply an even coating. Avoid covering all the decals, brand insignias, locks, handles and side molding with wax. Gently wax around and over these items. Nothing looks worse in the nooks and crannies of a motorcycle than crusting sun-baked wax. If you do get wax in unwanted areas, use a semi-stiff paint brush to "dust" away the wax.

Buy the necessary leather, vinyl, plastic, aluminum and chrome cleaners. Products designed for motorcycles or top quality products sold in auto parts shops are best. Avoid "one-product-does-all" and generic products. If you have some particularly gruesome cleaning to do, and want to buy a specialty product, be careful. Alloy and plastic surfaces can be destroyed by using the wrong chemical cleaner.

Clean the "inside" of the motorcycle. That is, clean every area you can get to, such as under the seat, under the gas tank, behind removable accessories, etc.

The idea is to become intimately acquainted with the motorcycle. Going over it in detail will give you a better understanding of its needs, parts and repairs. You may uncover some great flaw missed in previous inspections. If so, you want the bike polished to showroom condition, in the event that you discover something fatal and must sell it. Donald Trump, in his book *The Art of the Deal*, explains it this way about cars (which applies):

> . . . if you want to sell a car and you spend five dollars to wash and polish it and then apply a little extra elbow grease, suddenly you find you can charge an extra four hundred dollars—and get it. I can always tell a loser when I see someone with a car for sale that is filthy. It's so easy to make it look better.

Buy the Right Tools

Purchase a few good American-made wrenches and tools to use on the motorcycle. Don't buy inexpensive foreign sockets or universal implements. They fail at the worst moments. Buy the right tool and treat it with respect. Buy a quality tool, something that will work hard for many years. It will become your friend and ally. (Avoid making repairs with an adjustable wrench. You will strip the heads of bolts and bust your knuckles once or twice.)

Check the tool kit that comes with the motorcycle. If it is lost (something you should have picked up on the initial inspection), replace it. At a minimum you want all the tools necessary to change a fuse, replace a cable, adjust a shock, take off a wheel, remove a spark plug, adjust a mirror, remove the oil plug (some bikes require special sockets), adjust a chain and change a light bulb. You also want the requisite Allen wrenches, Phillips screwdrivers, and regular screw drivers. Also throw in a spare fuse and master link (very important!).

The right tools also include:

- The right cover, if you will be storing the bike outdoors
- The right antitheft device, such as chains, cables, steering crown locks, alarms, etc.
- Straps and bungee cords for carrying loads

Change the Oil

No matter what the owner told you about the motorcycle, christen the motorcycle by putting it on a regular maintenance schedule. This means changing the oil. Of course, you don't want to do this as a basic practice since we are all business people and hate to waste money. And we are all environmentalists wishing to make the world better for our children and therefore do not want to waste precious resources such as oil. But, in this one case, we will rationalize. An oil change only costs a few bucks and keeping a used motorcycle on the road is far more environmentally sound than junking it and expending resources building a new motorcycle.

If the previous owner did the oil changes personally, you may want to take your motorcycle to your local dealer for an oil change and lube. Most backyard mechanics change the oil but neglect to lube the chassis. If you do the work yourself, be sure to lube the chassis.

Inspect the oil plug when it is removed. Some plugs are magnetized to collect metal flakes.

Retain the sealable containers the fresh oil comes in to hold the old oil for recycling. Or buy a five-gallon jeep can designed to hold the oil. Consider doing your neighbors a favor and collect their used oil, too. This ensures that more oil gets recycled, and helps improve relations with those in the community. It also keeps your neighbors from dumping the oil in their backyards and contaminating the water flowing into your backyard, killing your roses.

Federal law says that anyone who does oil changes for a business must take your oil for recycling. This is a good law, but rarely enforced. Gas stations and repair shops do not like to take your old oil for two basic reasons: cost and contamination. Cost: When raw crude sells on the open market cheap, service stations must pay to have someone come pump their holding tanks. Contamination: Many backyard mechanics contaminate the oil with other products. The major problem is anti-freeze contamination. Put a little antifreeze in your oil and you have changed it from a recyclable resource into hazardous toxic waste. A little antifreeze in the oil tank at a gas station can turn the entire lot into toxic waste. This is far more expensive to dispose.

Perform All Basic Maintenance

Bring the motorcycle up to standard. All fluids should be at proper levels. Check the brake fluid, clutch fluid, battery acid, radiator coolant and tire air pressure levels. If headlights need aiming or bulbs need replacing, do it. Lubricate all control cables and hinges (including the kickstand and luggage lids) with a good all-purpose, water-displacing lubricating spray. You want this motorcycle road ready. See the chapter on maintenance for more detailed information.

Adjust the Bike

The controls and suspension will need to be adjusted to match your physical dimensions and riding style. Forks and shocks should be set at the air pressure and damping settings that suit your taste. Handlebars, mirrors, levers and footpegs should be adjusted so that you are comfortable in the saddle.

Why Are You Doing All of This?

If you are going to keep this motorcycle for a lifetime, you want to do all these things so that the lifetime is a long time. A motorcycle is a tool like any other. You want to know how to safely use that tool to its fullest potential. You want to take care of that tool so it will last and never fail you in a crunch. In the process you will also get some good exercise and maybe induce a little pride of ownership.

What is more important, you'll get to really know your motorcycle. You will see things you missed. If you find something surprising, something that means you made a mistake buying the motorcycle, you now have a fresh and clean vehicle to put on the market. A clean, fresh motorcycle will be easier to sell than a motorcycle that is not in such fine shape.

Special Notes to Beginners

Buying a used motorcycle for a beginner is a great idea, but there are many things to take into consideration. Here are some pointers.

Although it is smart to get an inexpensive bike, don't get a junker. Your first experience should be enjoyable. You also need a bike that will allow you to learn about riding, not about roadside repairs or emergency handling techniques. I owned a bike that sometimes cut out. For an experienced rider this is not much of a problem. It could be catastrophic for a novice. So get a bike that is reliable, fun and lets you concentrate on developing riding skills.

Beginning trail riders should consider going four-stroke and air-cooled. Two-stroke and liquid-cooled trail bikes are high maintenance machines, especially if put into competition. Two-stoke pistons need replacing after 30 hours of use; cranks need replacing once a year. Cooling systems will corrode over a season if not properly maintained. The suspension simply gets punished. It is more difficult to find a good used liquid-cooled two-stroke than a good used air-cooled four-stroke.

Whether street or trail, buy a bike that is not too small and not too large. For a trail bikes, that means something in the 250cc or 350cc range. Why? Smaller trail bikes are fast, often capable of faster times than larger bikes. To be ridden correctly, they must be run at high r.p.m.s and ridden hard. Larger trail bikes offer tons of power that must be judiciously controlled. It takes experience to properly handle these bikes.

For street bikes, buying a bike that is not too small or too large means something in the 250cc to 650cc range (and staying away from the cafe racers altogether), weighing in at no more than around 400 pounds. Why? You want enough horsepower to handle all street situations, so you do not want anything with too small a displacement. But like trail bikes, larger street bikes offer tons of power that must be judiciously controlled. Larger street bikes can also be very heavy. You want to consider a lighter weight street bike. These bikes are easier to maneuver and manhandle. Either situation, large or small, requires skills that a novice is not going to possess.

7

BEST USED BIKE PURCHASES

New bikes are frightfully expensive, drop precipitously in value once driven off the dealer's lot and cost a fortune to insure. In comparison, a used bike can be a great buy. Granted, good two-, three- and four-year-old bikes are more and more difficult to come by. (The trend is for people to nurse their favorite steeds longer and longer.) Many excellent values can be found in bikes 10 or even 20 years old. They can be found for less than $1,000, making entry into the sport afford-able for beginners, and keeping the sport affordable for everyone else.

You don't have to compromise. Many older bikes perform just as well as the current modern motorcycles. Some older bikes outperform the newer competition. Try putting anything off the showroom floor against a 1981 Kawasaki GPz 550 in the quarter mile.

A good used bike shares some of the following qualities: long production run, bulletproof drive train, proven engine, plenty of trained mechanics available, easy repair for the backyard mechanic, good supply of parts, good road/trail characteristics, technological compe-tence and excellent resale value. It probably strikes you immediately that some of these characteristics directly contradict others. For exam-ple, a bike that holds its resale value may not be inexpensive. Or a bike with great road characteristics may be somewhat high tech and therefore expensive to repair. Or a very simple motorcycle might not be technologically competent compared to bikes on the showroom floor. True. What is important is that you understand that the contradictions represent trade-offs. Evaluate these trade-offs and find a used bike that best fits your needs.

Note that really old bikes, bikes produced 25 years ago or longer, can be good used bike purchases. Although these bikes may need some repair, and parts may not be instantly available, they have the advantage of being simple and rugged. Newer bikes are often computer-controlled, rare alloy affairs that are simply impossible for the backyard mechanic to work on. Older bikes are made of iron and steel, rather than composite and plastic.

Classic and collectible motorcycles (i.e., anything you would not want to ride on a daily basis for fear of pillaging its value) are a different story. There have been a number of great motorcycles produced. The 998cc Vincent Black Lightning. The 1956 DOHC 500cc Moto Guzzi V8. Triumph Bonnevilles. 105 horsepower Honda CBXs. Harley knuckleheads. Indian 45s. Benelli 750-Sei's. These bikes are truly fine, and rare, which makes them interesting to collectors, but bad purchases for the average rider. You want a bike you can get cheap, ride cheap and enjoy for years.

Be that as it may, the following motorcycles are good values for most of the reasons noted above. The reader must be cautious, however. Despite these recommendations, no abused bike is a good value. And even though a particular motorcycle is not listed here, most motorcycles that have been given appropriate care are worth a look.

BMW

In Germany at the dawning of World War I, Bavarian Motor Works was a builder of airplane engines, agricultural machines and castings, marine engines and truck engines. The infamous Baron von Richthofen (a.k.a. the "Red Baron") attributed some of the success of his biplane squadron to the superiority of the BMW engines.

BMW has always been at the forefront of design and technology, with many firsts, such as being the first to use supercharging in road racing, hydraulic damping telescopic forks and a fully floating axle. BMW produced the first moped, called the Flink, in the 1920s. In 1923 BMW produced its first flat twin. This bike came with shaft drive. World War II ended BMW motorcycle production until 1948 when the company boomed, producing over 100,000 machines by 1953. The late 1950s market slump that put many motorcycle makers out of business almost took BMW, too. But a revival in demand for the Beemer brought production back to over 20,000 units a year in 1971.

BMW 1981 R65LS

Class: sports touring/commuter.
Engine: air-cooled opposed
twin 4-stroke.
Displacement: 649cc.
Valve Arrangement: pushrod
OHV 2.
Transmission: 5-speed.
Final Drive: shaft.
Brakes: front disc, rear drum.
Weight: 407 lbs.
Horsepower: 50.
Variations: 1981 to 1985. Also
look at 980cc, 798cc, 750cc R
series.

(Photo courtesy of BMW of North America.)

BMW has earned its reputation for longevity and dependability. The used bike shopper will find that, by and large, BMW owners maintain their vehicles well. They also tend to put more miles on a bike than average. This should not deter you. Mileage alone does not indicate value. There are many BMWs with over 100,000 miles that are reliable, marketable units. Look for one that has been ridden steadily rather one that has sat idle for long periods. Also, some BMWs have a no charge, transferable three year warranty.

1981 R65LS: The BMW R series horizontally opposed flat twin design has been around since 1923. All R series are worth looking at. The basic engine style has not changed, although the engine and motorcycle have gone through constant upgrades. The R65 is an excellent introductory BMW. It is simple, lightweight and nimble around town. This is due to a shorter wheel base and lower center of gravity on 1979 to 1984 models. Despite its displacement, when properly equipped with bags and shield the R65 is perfectly suited to cross-country touring. Nineteen eighty-five and later 65s are monoshock equipped.

If you need more speed and power, take a look at the R100s. These bikes produce 55 pounds of torque at 3,500 r.p.m. and 60 horsepower at 6,500 r.p.m. Top speed is around 125 m.p.h.; the bike will cover the standing quarter mile in just over 13 seconds.

BMW often sets the pace for technological advancements, and many state-of-the-art advancements have debuted on the R series. One note of caution: Due to the constantly changing technology, one year's model

BMW 1985 (AND LATER) K100 SERIES

Class: touring, sports touring, sports.
Engine: liquid-cooled horizontal four-cylinder fuel-injected 4-stroke.
Displacement: 987cc.
Valve Arrangement: DOHC 2.
Transmission: 5-speed.
Final Drive: shaft.
Brakes: front dual disc, rear disc.
Weight: 569 lbs.
Horsepower: 90.
Torque: 63 lb.ft.
Variations: single and multi-valve, 1092cc, 740cc three cylinder.

(Photo courtesy of BMW of North America.)

may be substantially improved over the previous year's. The most significant drawback is that BMWs tend to be very pricey used bikes.

For any high mileage bike, including BMW, check the rubber parts for cracking, the service record for maintenance, and see when the battery was last replaced.

1985 AND LATER: The K series was introduced in 1985 as BMW's bold step into the latter 20th century. The power plant is an in-line four-cylinder engine mounted on its side. The K100 and K75 models share the same frame except for engine mounting members. The K75 (as opposed to the K75S and K75RT) has a 2-inch lower seat height. The K75 is an excellent bike for smaller riders.

Owners tend to really nurse these babies, so you may not find many, and those you find will be at a high cost. Be sure to test any full dresser on a hot day. There is almost no air moving behind the fairing on some, other than heat rising from the engine.

By comparison, the 987cc K1 (introduced in 1988) produces 100 horses, 73 pounds of torque, and does 100 m.p.h. The 1100cc version of the K (introduced in 1993) produces 100 horsepower and 77 pounds of torque. The K75 produces 75 horses and 50 pounds of torque.

HARLEY-DAVIDSON

Many motorcycle companies got their start during World War I. World War I battlefield strategies incorporated thousands of motorcycles with sidecars. But long before World War I, the single motorcycle that defined United States' motorcycles began production: Harley-Davidson. Their first motorcycle, produced in 1903, was a single-cylinder, air-cooled job. The trademark 45° V-twin was first produced in 1909. At 61 cubic inch displacement (cid), the engine produced seven horsepower and raced at 60 m.p.h.

In the 1960s, Japanese motorcycle makers launched an impressive market development campaign in the United States. To broaden its lineup and fend off the Japanese challenge, Harley-Davidson joined forces with Aermacchi (a.k.a. Aeronautica Macchi S.p.A), an Italian manufacturer of aircraft and motorcycles. The merger led to the production of light- and medium-displacement motorcycles for touring, racing and trail use. In 1969, Harley-Davidson merged with AMF. By 1976 the Harley lineup included the Electric Glide (1200cc), two Super Glides (1200cc), two Sportsters (1000cc) and six lightweights ranging from 125cc to 250cc. But Harley lacked the ability to compete against the Japanese in the lightweight markets, and by 1979 the only sub-liter class bike in the lineup was the XR750 OHV aluminum engine racer.

As a general rule, the modern OHV V^2 Evolution engines (introduced in 1984) are preferable to the older shovelheads (1966), panheads (1948) and knuckleheads (1936). If you don't plan on making your motorcycle a weekend hobby, or you don't want to engage in a bidding war with motorcycle collectors, go with the modern engines. Another good rule is that used Harleys can be substantially cheaper ($1,000 cheaper!) in the winter. People who are more into fashion than motorcycles get into them in the spring, and discover they either cannot or do not want to pay for the bike when winter sets in.

Harley-Davidson has one unique feature that few modern motorcycles have: part interchangeability and availability. Engines are not radically redesigned every three or four years, as is common with Japanese bikes. New parts often fit older engines. If the factory no longer supplies a part, there is almost always a third party accessory firm that does. If an accessory firm does not make it, you can probably find the part used somewhere off of a bike 10 years older or newer.

Today, Harley-Davidson manufacturers over 20 motorcycle variations that surround three power plants. With custom detailing and after-market add-ons, the Harley owner, like no other, can express his or her own unique personality—Harley is a lifestyle!

FLSTC HERITAGE CLASSIC: The Harley Classics recreated older designs using modern equipment. The Heritage is a current production model of the old full dress "Hydraglide" touring bikes of the 1940s and 1950s. These bikes are designed to look like their predecessors with styling such as tin covered front forks, wide-wide tires and studded leather seats and saddle-

HARLEY FLSTC HERITAGE CLASSIC

Class: cruiser.
Engine: air-cooled 45 degree V-twin 4-stroke.
Displacement: 1340cc/80cid.
Valve Arrangement: OHV 2.
Transmission: 5-speed.
Final Drive: poly chain belt.
Brakes: single disc front & rear.
Weight: 650 lbs.
Horsepower: 69.
Torque: 82 lb.ft.
Variations: many. Production years 1987 and up.

(Photo courtesy Harley-Davidson.)

bags. Fat Bob fuel tanks are a signature of this Harley. You could go buy one of those 1950 monsters and be happy you did. Or you can have all the styling with all the reliability and efficiency of the newer versions.

XLH 883 SPORTSTER: The first Harley Sportster came with a 2.2 gallon "peanut" gas tank. This is still the trademark of the bike today, and can be found on the 883. Other signature design features of the Sportster include austere instrumentation and few features. Even the passenger seat is an option. Independent staggered dual exhaust on the bike's right side emits the unmistakable Harley exhaust note

HARLEY XLH SERIES 883 SPORTSTER

Class: sports.
Engine: air-cooled 45 degree V-twin 4-stroke.
Displacement: 883cc.
Valve Arrangement: OHV 2.
Transmission: 4-speed.
Final Drive: chain.
Brakes: single disc front & rear.
Weight: 478 lbs.
Horsepower: 52.
Torque: 54 lb.ft.
Variations: Sportster, Hugger, Deluxe, 900cc, 1000cc, 1200cc, etc. Production years 1957 and up.

(Photo courtesy Harley-Davidson.)

(i.e., rumble thunder). The aluminum Evolution 883 Sportster captured the essence of the new design philosophy at Harley: low maintenance, new technology, extended service intervals (5,000 miles).

All years are potential classics and highly sought after, new and used. The wise choice for the average buyer is the 1986 or later Sportster with the evolution 883cc or 1200cc engine. (The 1200 offers 71 lb. ft. of torque.) The 883s are good entry level Harleys, often with seats that ride as low as 26 inches off the ground. Good for stubby legs and stubby people. Range can be a problem, though, given the small capacity "peanut" gas tank.

If you are interested in more speed, try to find a 1984 Sportster XR1000. Nineteen eighty-four was the first year of the Evolution engine, and also the first year for belt drive, five-speed transmissions and rubber isolated engines. The "Buckaroo Banzai" XR1000 featured twin carbs, dual front discs, solo seat and protruding air filters stuck on the end of each carb. Or buy an 883 and spend two or three thousand boring it out and souping it up.

HONDA

Honda Motor Company, Ltd. is the archetypal Japanese business success story. Soichiro Honda, founder of Honda, is the quintessential Japanese entrepreneur. Before World War II, Honda owned a factory producing engine rings for Toyota. In his typical bold fashion, Soichiro started his engine ring company knowing nothing about the product. Immediately after the war Honda looked for ways to meet the transportation needs of Japan's people given that the country's economy and manufacturing capabilities were destroyed. His solution was to fit surplus military gasoline engines (originally designed to power electric generators) to bicycle frames. This solved a transportation problem, but it did not solve the fuel shortage problem. So, Honda bought a pine tree forest to manufacture turpentine (allegedly mixed with black market gasoline) to power his motorbikes. With the supply of surplus engines running out, and the need to build a sturdier form of transportation, Honda designed his first motorcycle. This bike went into production in late 1949. Today, Honda is number one in world motorcycle sales.

The Honda Motor Company is credited with creating the modern U.S. motorcycle market. In 1962, Honda hired Gray Advertising of Los Angeles to improve U.S. sales. Gray founded their Honda program on the belief that the primary resistance was the American public's lack of social acceptance of motorcycles. From this notion came the "You meet the nicest people on a Honda" campaign, one of the most successful advertising campaigns in the history of U.S. promotion.

Honda now holds 29% of the U.S. motorcycle market. Honda was the first Japanese motorcycle company to open a production plant in the United States with Gold Wing production in Marysville, Ohio beginning in 1979.

1984 GL1200 GOLD WING INTERSTATE: The Gold Wing first appeared as a 70 horsepower 1000 that you could custom into a long-distance full dresser. In 1980, Honda introduced the 84 horsepower 1085cc GL1100 Interstate. The Interstate defined the modern touring cruiser class. Honda has owned the market ever since. In 1984, Honda upped the engine displacement to 1200cc. In 1988, the massive six-cylinder GL1500 was introduced.

The horizontally opposed engine provides a low center of gravity and has demonstrated unbelievable reliability. It is not uncommon for Gold Wings to go 100,000 miles. Several have been documented at over 200,000 miles. Great values can be found in those bikes with between 40,000 and 50,000 miles.

The Aspencade is the top of the line Gold Wing. It comes with every high technology gadget a cruiser can offer. The Interstate is a bit less plush. Although the Aspencade is a great used bike in its own right, complexity in a used bike is not so desirable, and therefore the recommendation is for the Interstate. Early used models provide all of the essential touring necessities at good prices. The GL1100 offers most of what the GL1200 offers, at a lesser price, but with an engine that shows some negligible reduction in low-end power.

HONDA 1984 GL1200 GOLD WING INTERSTATE

Class: touring.
Engine: liquid-cooled horizontally opposed flat four 4-stroke.
Displacement: 1182cc.
Valve Arrangement: hydraulic adjust SOHC 2.
Transmission: 4-speed plus overdrive 5th.
Final Drive: shaft.
Brakes: dual disc front, disc rear.
Weight: 702 lbs.
Horsepower: 86.
Torque: 75 lb.ft.
Variations: all years, Aspencade, GL1100.

(Photo courtesy of American Honda Motor Company.)

HONDA 1982 CB900C

Class: cruiser.
Engine: in-line air-/oil-cooled
four 4-stroke.
Displacement: 902cc.
Valve Arrangement: DOHC 4.
Transmission: 5-speed
constant mesh with dual-range
sub-trans.
Final Drive: shaft.
Brakes: dual disc front, disc
rear.
Weight: 571 lbs.
Variations: all years.

*(Photo courtesy of American Honda
Motor Company.)*

Test ride several manufacturers' cruisers before buying a touring bike. Each handles very differently. A newer Gold Wing might not be a great city commuter, given its size and ride.

1982 CB900C: The CB series of four cylinder engines dates back to the early 1970s and the classic CB500 and CB750. The lineage includes 350s, 400s and 1100s. All have well-balanced, reliable engines. The CBs are easy home mechanic projects with good parts availability. The smaller versions are great introductory bikes for learning to ride, repair or restore. But you'll want more power, like that of the 900, after a season with a smaller bike.

Honda included key features such as rubber mounted engine designs borrowed from the CBX and RCB endurance racing engines. Special combustion chamber design, four 32mm carburetor, and four-valve cylinders give the 900 high combustion efficiency. An oil-cooler and air adjustable shocks round out this well-thought-out motorcycle.

1971 CL350: Honda has produced a lot of successful motorcycles from only one pattern. The step-through 90s are a good example of one pattern that keeps coming back every decade in a new version. The CL/CB/SL twins are like this. The CL has raised pipes with street fenders for dual-purpose use. The CB has street pipes. The SL has a spark arresting muffler and high fenders for trail use. The CB twins offer simple engines without a lot of high tech. There are many plastic parts that are metal on other bikes, but this is one of the reasons the small bikes "weather" better than others. The power plants have been around

HONDA 1971 CL350

Class: dual purpose.
Engine: vertical twin 4-stroke.
Displacement: 325cc.
Valve Arrangement: SOHC 2.
Transmission: 5-speed.
Final Drive: chain.
Brakes: drum front & rear.
Weight: 360 lbs.
Horsepower: 36.
Torque: 19 lb.ft.

(Photo courtesy of American Honda Motor Company.)

for ages, including runs as Hawk 400s. Look for years starting 1968. The 1974–77 models were punched up to 356cc.

The small displacement CL/CB line makes for great starter bikes as long as the price is good and the electronics are not shot. The bikes are light, handle well for the beginner, and provide respectable power for the street or modest touring. These are very easy home mechanic projects. Everything is right out where you can get to it. There are 200cc and 175cc versions that have similar characteristics.

HONDA 1984 CB700SC NIGHT HAWK S

Class: sports touring.
Engine: air-/oil-cooled in-line four 4-stroke.
Displacement: 696cc.
Valve Arrangement: hydraulic adjusted DOHC 4.
Transmission: 5-speed with overdrive 6th.
Final Drive: shaft.
Brakes: dual disc front, drum rear.
Weight: 474 lbs.
Horsepower: 80.
Variations: 1984 to 1986.

(Photo courtesy of American Honda Motor Company.)

1984 CB700SC NIGHT HAWK S: Hawks make periodic debuts in the Honda lineup. These are great bikes. Honda introduced the CB700SC as an attempt to make the near perfect universal machine. Do not be fooled. This is a bike designed for a chicane (a series of turns). Features of the CB700 include a high-concept engine layout tuned for top end performance and an easy to adjust suspension. Low maintenance shaft drive, hydraulic valves and oil-cooling reduce maintenance requirements. For a small bike it is quite comfortable on long trips. The high 11,000 r.p.m. redline gives you a lot of top end.

Features of the 700 include hydraulic clutch, automatic cam chain tensioner, hydraulic valve adjust, oil-cooler, spin-on oil filter and rubber mounted engine. Honda dedicated a good deal of research into reducing the total dimensions of the engine. Oil is stored in the frame to minimize the height of the engine. The generator is located behind the cylinders to reduce engine width.

Although the 650 Night Hawk that the CB700SC replaced is a totally different bike, it too has many of the same merits, and two additional. Honda flooded the market with these 650 babies in the early 1980s. There are lots of them around, lots of parts available, and, unlike the 700, the average Joe can work on the 650. Of course, the average Joe probably never needs to go into the 700.

HONDA 1991 CBR600F2

Class: sports.
Engine: liquid-cooled in-line four 4-stroke.
Displacement: 599cc.
Valve Arrangement: DOHC 4.
Transmission: 6-speed.
Final Drive: chain.
Brakes: dual disc front, disc rear.
Weight: 429 lbs.
Horsepower: 86.
Torque: 43 lb.ft.

(Photo courtesy of Cycle World *magazine.)*

1991 CBR600F2: Anyone looking for a recent sports bike that offers race track performance and agile handling right off the showroom floor will be looking at the 600 class motorcycles. Legendary names have been built in this class: Suzuki Katana, Honda Hurricane, Kawasaki Ninja. There is a constant technological leapfrogging of one manufacturer over another in this class. No one is king of the 600 hill for long. Of this class, late model CBR600F2s are what to look for. The CBR takes its lineage from the Hurricane introduced in 1987, but is altogether a different motorcycle. Others 600s may be faster, more nimble or less expensive, but the CBR offers a great blend of cost, handling and speed. If you want to cut cost, look at a Hurricane or Katana.

One note about the 600 class: You gotta know what you are doing. These bikes are fast, very fast, 143 m.p.h. fast in this particular case. The average guy can ride out on one of these puppies and think he has mastered all of its capabilities in a few miles. Forget it. The capabilities of a 600 class bike require training and experience to master. Take it easy. Check insurance before buying.

KAWASAKI

Kawasaki Heavy Industries is one of the world's largest industrial, multinational corporations. It was founded in 1878 when Shozo Kawasaki built a shipyard at Tsukiji, Tokyo. Kawasaki had long been in the business of making steel, locomotives, railcars, automobiles and aircraft before becoming concerned with motorcycles.

Immediately after World War II, Kawasaki put its engineering skill to work producing engines and gearboxes for motorcycle companies. During the 1950s there were at least 40 motorcycle manufacturers serving the Japanese domestic market. Honda, Yamaha and Suzuki were already well established both domestically and internationally. To enter the crowded field, Kawasaki Aircraft set up a research and development center in 1959. In 1960 the aircraft division bought its way into the market with the purchase of Meguro, a motorcycle company. It is doubly interesting that the aircraft side of the company decided to enter the motorcycle market, and that they would decide to build extremely potent motorcycles.

Kawasaki made its reputation racing. The first time the name Kawasaki was seen at international race events was in 1963. Their first grand prix entries were in 1965. By the early 1970s Kawasaki was racing and winning with production-line motorcycles instead of purpose-built racers.

Kawasaki's in-line fours have made a great impression on many people. Their early 80's models are great all-purpose machines, espe-

cially if you like speed. Kawasakis seem to hold their value better compared to other Japanese bikes. Super-K (a.k.a. Kawasaki, Big Green) also made some notable two-strokes beginning in 1969. These bikes, coming in 250cc, 350cc, 400cc, 500cc and 750cc varieties, have extremely high power-to-weight ratios. They offer more off-the-line punch and stunt/wheelie popping power than virtually any other bikes. For example, the 1972 350 S2 weighed 335 pounds, produced 44 horsepower, and had a maximum speed of 106 m.p.h.

1985 ZL900 ELIMINATOR: In the years that have passed since the first ZL900 came out, the market has gone full circle from loving these bikes to hating these bikes to loving them again. Kawasaki also produced the ZR1100 (earlier known as Zephyr), a direct descendant of the Eliminator. The 900 was produced for two years before it was punched up to a 1000. The ZL900 has proven itself to be a maintenance-free, rock-solid machine. All of the bikes in this lineage are good, but the 1985 is becoming a collectible, worth more now than new.

KZ1000P POLICE BIKE: Bulletproof is more than just a cliché for some bikes. The KZ1000P is a special edition made for police work. The frame and drive train are heavy duty for added loads. The suspension

KAWASAKI 1985 ZL900 ELIMINATOR

Class: cruiser.
Engine: liquid-cooled horizontal four 4-stroke.
Displacement: 908cc.
Valve Arrangement: DOHC 4.
Transmission: 6-speed.
Final Drive: shaft.
Brakes: front dual disc, rear disc.
Weight: 550 lbs.
Horsepower: 77.
Torque: 63 lb.ft.
Variations: 900cc & 1000cc, production years 1985 and up.

(Photo courtesy of Kawasaki Motor Company, USA.)

KAWASAKI 1982
KZ1000P POLICE BIKE

Class: sports.
Engine: air-cooled horizontal four 4-stroke.
Displacement: 1015cc.
Valve Arrangement: DOHC 2.
Transmission: 5-speed.
Final Drive: chain.
Brakes: front dual disc, rear disc.
Weight: 562 lbs.
Horsepower: 93.
Variations: production years 1978 and up.

(Photo courtesy of Kawasaki Motor Company, USA.)

is upgraded. The electrics are extra heavy duty for the lights and equipment used in daily police work. Safety tires come as original equipment. This is a highly stable bike that will stay together for 100,000 miles easy. It also is great off the line, although it does not offer a lot of top end (relatively). The bike, in its current form, has been in production since 1982.

The average citizen cannot buy one of these new, but you can find them around used or at police auction. One word of warning if you buy at a police auction. Some police departments take great care of their motorcycles. Others, engaged in lease arrangements and service contracts, do not. Any motorcycle officer will tell you how well his department takes care of its bikes, and how well other departments keep their bikes.

1986 VOYAGER: In the touring category, the Voyager offers one of the best values for the dollar. The Voyager has traditionally competed on price in the new bike market.

The first Voyagers were produced in 1983. These were very heavy motorcycles (900 pounds!). In 1986 the Voyager XII was introduced showing Kawasaki's new philosophy: lighter, narrower, less expensive, quicker. Voyager is the lightest of cruisers by as much as 100 pounds. This reduced weight allows the Voyager a whopping 440-pound load capacity.

Not surprisingly, Voyager offers the best handling characteristics in slow speed city driving of all of the full dressers. It is also faster off the line than the competition. This is an important consideration for commuters and multiuse riders. Voyager's power plant is strong and the package comes with many modern features such as stereo, radio, tape, cruise, clock, saddlebags, top case, etc. But other features like an on-board air compressor or reverse gear will only be found on the competition. No big deal. In the used bike market extra complexity cuts two ways, good and bad. Complexity is only great if it works and is inexpensive to maintain. The Voyager may not have all the features, but it has a great price/performance ratio.

KAWASAKI 1986 VOYAGER

Class: touring.
Engine: liquid-cooled in-line four 4-stroke.
Displacement: 1196cc.
Valve Arrangement: DOHC 4.
Transmission: 5-speed wet clutch.
Final Drive: shaft.
Brakes: front dual disc, rear single disc.
Weight: 735 lbs.

(Photo courtesy of Kawasaki Motor Company, USA.)

1973 Z1 KZ900: This bike, nicknamed "Zapper," dethroned Honda in the super-bike category. The Z1 has had a long production run with minor changes. It has been one of the best selling Kawasakis ever. There are a lot of them out there and lots of parts available. It is flat out one great piece of engineering; these bikes do not break. The first year's production is becoming a collectible.

Also to be considered is the younger brother of the 900. Near the end of this bike's production, Kawasaki produced 750cc and 700cc KZs. The smaller air-cooled, eight-valve, in-line four presents the buyer with a great multipurpose motorcycle. These engines take abuse and never whimper. Look for the LTD editions.

By the way, if speed and turns are what you are into, look at Super-K's H2 750 of the same year. All of the two-stroke three cylinders from Kawasaki produced at this time had awesome power. This one was the leader: 74 horses, 57 pounds torque. Very reliable, parts are still available and many are still on the road.

1990's ZX11: Sleek, smooth and fast. The ZX1100 covers all the bases for street use. It makes an excellent commuter bike (when was the last time you looked forward to the ride to work?), makes quick work of winding back roads (unless you turn around and run them again!) and is comfortable enough to knock down big mileage at whatever speed you choose. By 1990, Big Green had proven the technologically impres-

KAWASAKI 1973 Z1 KZ900

Class: cruiser.
Engine: horizontal four 4-stroke.
Displacement: 903cc.
Valve Arrangement: DOHC 2.
Transmission: 5 speed.
Final Drive: chain.
Brakes: front disc, rear drum.
Weight: 540 lbs.
Horsepower: 82.
Torque: 54 lb.ft.
Variations: production years 1973 to 1982.

(Photo courtesy of Kawasaki Motor Company, USA.)

KAWASAKI 1990's ZX11

Class: sports touring.
Engine: liquid-cooled in-line four 4-stroke.
Displacement: 1052cc.
Valve Arrangement: DOHC 4.
Transmission: 6-speed.
Final Drive: chain.
Brakes: dual disc front, disc rear.
Weight: 549 lbs.
Horsepower: 145.
Torque: 80 lb.ft.
Variations: 1990 to present.

(Photo courtesy of Kawasaki Motor Company, USA.)

sive 1052cc power plant. With the ZX-11, they went farther by adding forced air induction, digitally controlled main jets, and light concave pistons. The suspension is every match for the engine.

Look for the smaller ZX editions, the 997cc and 748cc, too.

SUZUKI

Suzuki succeeded as much through ingenuity as luck in the early part of the 20th century. A series of wars and natural disasters favored the company in its beginning years. The company that bears the name Suzuki was manufacturing treadle type cotton looms in 1908. Looms were to remain the backbone of Suzuki for at least the next 30 years. The outbreak of World War I offered an unexpected bonanza for Asian companies like Suzuki, and the company flourished while its European rivals floundered. In 1920 the rice, cotton yarn and silk yarn markets collapsed suddenly, forcing many of Suzuki's competitors into bankruptcy, but not Suzuki. In 1923 an earthquake destroyed many factories in Japan, but not Suzuki's. In 1937 Suzuki began research into the automotive and motorcycle arenas. But World War II ended all plans. Suzuki's manufacturing plants were converted to making war munitions.

In 1944 the company experienced its first setback. An earthquake did severe damage to several Suzuki plants. In 1945 even more damage was sustained during air raids. After the war, Suzuki suffered cash flow problems and union unrest. Silk was difficult to obtain. The loom market was in a highly volatile state. Suzuki decided to diversify rather than lay off workers. Suzuki manufactured whatever was in short

SUZUKI 1978 GS1000

Class: cruiser/muscle bike.
Engine: air-cooled horizontal four 4-stroke.
Displacement: 997cc.
Valve Arrangement: DOHC 2.
Transmission: 5-speed.
Final Drive: chain.
Brakes: single disc front & rear.
Weight: 542 lbs.
Variations: years 1978 to 1980.

(Photo courtesy of Cycle World magazine).

supply, which meant electric heaters and farm implements, to note two product lines.

In 1951, ideas of entering the automotive market again began to stir at Suzuki. Just as for the other giant Japanese motorcycle companies, the destruction of Japan's economy in World War II presented an opportunity and challenge. At that time, scooters were quite popular since supplies of everything from fuel to production capacity were limited. Suzuki decided to enter the cycle engine market with one caveat, that the company would make all components in-house.

Suzuki produced its first prototype engine in 1952. The engine was a .7 hp 36cc two-stroke to be "clipped on" to bicycles as a power assist. This engine was named, interestingly enough, the Atom. The engine was sold under the name "Power Free." The success of the Power Free and its 60cc cousin, the Diamond Free, led Suzuki toward full-scale motorcycle production.

In 1954 the one-cylinder four-stroke 90cc Colleda was launched. A year later a two-stroke racing version was produced. By 1958 Suzuki was producing 50cc, 125cc, and 250cc motorcycles.

Suzuki made its name worldwide in the 1960s with some truly mean 250cc and 500cc two- and three-cylinder two-strokes. Suzuki also manufactured the rare 1974 RE5 497cc Wankel, one of the few rotary motorcycles. It produced 62 horsepower at 6,500 r.p.m. and could top 115 m.p.h.

1978 GS1000: The GS1000 was voted the machine of the year by *Motor Cycle News* readers. It competes well against the muscle bikes of its era. A strong engine and general-purpose design make the GS1000 appealing on the open road as well as on the drag strip. User-accessible components for backyard mechanics are a plus. Later models have zoopier features, like an extra disc brake, shaft and a sports design. Performance features found on the smaller GS's are rarely found on the competition.

The GS came in ST, SZ (Katana), EN, LN and SN versions. The ST came in white and offered a cafe fairing, chrome pipes, seating for two, oil temperature gauge and quartz clock. The Katana came in silver and offered a lower riding position, sport fairing, seating for one, antidive suspension, black exhaust pipe and clip-on type handlebars. The EN came in black, was minus any fairing, but did have chrome mufflers and air boxes. The LN had a two-tone blue and maroon paint job. It offered leading axle forks, pullback handlebars, chrome front and rear fenders, chrome exhaust and mag-type wheels. The SN came in a blue and white paint job and offered low racer handlebars, mag-type wheels and a sport fairing.

Also take a look at the GS750 and 850 of that era. Both are capable of +124 m.p.h.

1982 GS850: The GS850G is noted above as a variation of the GS series. First produced in 1980, the 1982 and 1983 model years have proven themselves to be particularly strong. The bike is easy to maintain and easy to accessorize. Features found on the GS850G that are attractive to the used motorcycle buyer include long-lasting engine, large comfortable seat and low-maintenance shaft drive.

SUZUKI 1982 GS850G

Class: sports touring.
Engine: air-cooled in-line four 4-stroke.
Displacement: 843cc.
Valve Arrangement: DOHC 2.
Transmission: 5-speed.
Final Drive: shaft.
Brakes: dual disc front, single disc rear.
Weight: 558 lbs.
Variations: 1982 and 1983.

(Photo courtesy of Cycle World magazine.)

The GS850 offered CV carbs, transistorized ignition, automatic cam chain tensioner, air-assisted front forks, oil-damped rear swingarm with five load settings and four damping adjustments, mag style wheels and quartz-halogen headlight. The bike comes in GT, GX, GZ, GD, GLT, GLX and GLZ variations.

If you want a good lightweight cycle to fashion into a touring machine, this is a great model to build around. Do not overlook the 850's smaller brothers, the GS650E and GS650G (with shaft drive).

1988 (AND LATER) GSX600 KATANA: The GSX600 has great looks and lively performance supplied by a 16-valve, four-cylinder engine. There is strong usable power throughout the power curve. Roomy seating position provides full-size comfort. Special performance features include an advanced cooling system, high 11.3:1 compression ratio, steep 52° lean angle, large valves, cool air induction system, "full floater" rear suspension and decapiston brake system with metallic pads. Center or service stand were optional.

The Katana is advertised as a balance of performance, comfort and convenience—it lives up to its billing. It is a best value in the sports bike market, selling for around half of what a new bike costs. Like all bikes of this class, this bike is better than most riders, so be careful. Take your

SUZUKI 1988 (AND LATER) GSX600 KATANA

Class: sports touring.
Engine: air-cooled in-line four 4-stroke.
Displacement: 600cc.
Valve Arrangement: DOHC 4.
Transmission: 6-speed.
Final Drive: chain.
Brakes: dual disc front, single disc rear.
Weight: 429 lbs.
Horsepower: 70.
Torque: 38 lb.ft.
Variations: 1988 to present.

(Photo courtesy of American Suzuki Motor Co.)

**SUZUKI 1985 GV700GLF
MADURA**

Class: cruiser.
Engine: liquid-cooled 82 degree
V-four 4-stroke.
Displacement: 698cc.
Valve Arrangement: DOHC 4.
Transmission: 6-speed over-
drive.
Final Drive: shaft.
Brakes: dual disc front, drum
rear.
Weight: 503 lbs.
Variations: 1200cc.

(Photo courtesy Cycle World
magazine.)

time to get to know the motorcycle. Within the 600 series, this bike often leads the way.

Also look at the GSX1100E. The four-cylinder DOHC 1075cc engine delivers 110 horsepower at 8,500 r.p.m., producing a 140 m.p.h. top speed and 11.6 second quarter miles.

Check insurance first.

1985 GV700GLF MADURA: The GV700 offers a smooth, comfortable V-4 engine coupled with shaft and powerful 6-speed transmission. The bike is a combination of ultramodern power plant and customized cruiser frame. The very comfortable riding position is enhanced with forward mounted pegs and pull back handlebars. Well laid out speedo, tach, fuel gauge and gear indicator make the GV700 an easy cycle to ride. Features on the Madura include maintenance-free hydraulic valve adjusters, hydraulic clutch, overdrive, rubber-mounted engine, "full floater" rear suspension and custom flat spoke chrome wire wheels. Unfortunately, they did not make a lot of these guys.

Also take a look at the GV1200GLF Madura. The 1166cc engine offers more of the gut level furor found in the GV700.

1986 GS450L: Suzuki made four variations of the GS450 starting in 1980—the E, L, S and T. These were smooth, comfortable, standard machines. The different designations were for different styling features. All had the excellent 450 engine.

SUZUKI 1986 GS450L

Class: standard/cruiser.
Engine: air-cooled in-line twin counterbalanced 4-stroke.
Displacement: 448cc.
Valve Arrangement: DOHC 2.
Transmission: 6-speed.
Final Drive: chain.
Brakes: single disc front, drum rear.
Weight: 379 lbs.
Variations: 1986 and 1988.

(Photo courtesy of Cycle World magazine.)

Features of the GS450 included longer extended air forks, large 3.2 gallon fuel tank, counterbalanced engine, "custom look," fuel gauge and a fat 16-inch rear tire. The bike was marketed as a "middle weight custom cruiser" with "big bike features, styling and performance packed into a nimble, low cost middleweight . . . performance on a budget." These claims are not puffery or overstated. This is a good, solid motorcycle.

The GS450L is a great beginner's motorcycle. It is easy to learn on and easy to maintain. The long-lasting engine simply runs forever, providing a stingy 69 m.p.g. on the way. The low, comfortable seat has only a 29.1 inch height. The bike is only 84 inches long, 34 inches wide, 46 inches tall and has a wheelbase of 56 inches. It's great for smaller riders.

The 1983 GS450GLD is a curiosity. It came with unique two-speed semi-automatic transmission and shaft drive.

YAMAHA

Torakusa Yamaha, a clock smith and self-employed general engineer, founded Nippon Gakki in the 1880s. By the time Torakusa died, in 1916, Nippon Gakki was firmly established as a musical instruments company. In 1940, the military government of Japan took control of Nippon Gakki's factories to produce war materiels.

Nippon Gakki produced metal aircraft propellers and musical instruments during World War II. After the war, Nippon Gakki had excess metalwork machinery that was put to work at motorcycle production. Based on a German DWK, the two-stroke YA-1 125cc "Red Dragonfly" rolled off the assembly line in 1955. Yamaha Motor Company, Ltd. was founded shortly after the YA-1 went into production, when the Motorcycle Manufacturing Division was separated from Nippon Gakki.

Although the Japanese domestic motorcycle market was crowded with over 40 different manufacturers, the YA-1 attained acceptance by winning the prestigious "Mt. Fuji Ascent" and "Asama Heights" races. It was a pattern to be repeated. Yamaha's philosophy has always been that to move motorcycles out of the showroom, win on the racetrack. That is how they gained acceptance in Europe and North America.

Yamaha made its name in two-stroke production. By 1969, Yamaha was producing a full line-up of bikes from 50cc to 350cc. Of special note was the Enduro class of dual-purpose bikes. Eyeing the small number of riders who were enjoying off-road riding in unsettled areas of the American West, Yamaha developed the 250DT1, the first "true trail bike," according to Yamaha.

But Yamaha was facing a dilemma with its two-stroke dependent line-up. Two-strokes suffer from natural disadvantages when applied to large capacity engines: poor fuel efficiency and high exhaust emissions. In response to changing times, Yamaha produced its first four-stroke in 1970, the 5-speed OHC 650cc XS1 twin. Yamaha introduced an impressive number of four-stroke bikes between 1970 and 1974.

By 1982 Yamaha had grown into a huge multinational corporation. Today, Yamaha is producing motorcycles, snowmobiles, golf carts, ATVs, automobile engines, multipurpose engines, outboard motors, unmanned helicopters, powerboats and sailboats (although 47% of their business continues to be motorcycles).

1982 VIRAGO 750: Yamaha, and other Japanese motorcycle makers, flooded the market with bikes in the early 1980s. The 75° V-twin 750 Virago was Yamaha's largest wave, starting in 1981. All Viragos have good peak torque and horsepower, with the larger bikes providing solid power all through the band. Early bikes were general purpose, but lacking in fuel tank capacity. Newer bikes are chromed out, custom, low slung and built to cruise. All have great ergonomics. With a low seat height even on the larger bikes (28 inches on the 1100), small riders should consider Viragos.

Yamaha built the Virago with one word in mind: simplicity. Backyard mechanics will find the bike easy to work on and parts widely available. With so many of them out there, it's easy to find a great $1,000 used Virago. Older bikes have a monoshock suspension that

YAMAHA 1982 VIRAGO 750

Class: cruiser.
Engine: air-cooled 75 degree V-twin 4-stroke.
Displacement: 748cc/46cid.
Valve Arrangement: SOHC 2.
Transmission: 5-speed.
Final Drive: shaft.
Brakes: single disc front, drum rear.
Weight: 496 lbs.
Horsepower: 60.
Torque: 46 lb.ft.
Variations: 700cc, 920cc, 1000cc, 1063cc.

should be upgraded for carrying passengers. Be sure the starter has been replaced, or expect to do it soon.

Some Viragos come with an oil "level" light. This should not be confused with an oil pressure light. This light helped earlier Viragos gain an undeserved reputation for insufficient oil flow to the head. When this light comes on, it is time to add oil, not rebuild the engine.

1989 FZR600: With excellent handling, this is one of the finest road racing bikes around. The FZR600 was one of the best selling and best performing bikes of the 1980s. The bike is powered by the forward angled Genesis engine, which offers good performance across a wide range of r.p.m. The bike is easy to repair and service. Upkeep is inexpensive. Dual headlights on the 1989–90 bikes are well liked and worth the extra margin of safety. Brakes on the 1990 are substantially upgraded. As with other bikes in this class, be cautious. These bikes easily outperform the skills of the average rider. Check insurance first.

1986 YX600 RADIAN: The 600 Radian was constructed from parts bins at Yamaha. Their idea was to make a technologically competent motorcycle at an entry level price. The YX600 did the job marvelously. This is a fun, all-purpose bike that is great in city traffic. It lacks a lot of the raked out, chromed up sizzle of other bikes, but with a very well established engine and parts, the bike has staying power for a used bike buyer. Look for its predecessors, the FZ600 and the FJ600.

YAMAHA 1989 (AND LATER) FZR600

Class: sports.
Engine: liquid-cooled in-line four 4-stroke.
Displacement: 599cc.
Valve Arrangement: DOHC 4.
Transmission: 6-speed.
Final Drive: chain.
Brakes: dual disc front, disc rear.
Weight: 406 lbs.
Horsepower: 74.
Torque: 43 lb.ft.

(Photo courtesy of Yamaha Motor Corporation, USA.)

1985 FJ: Sport riders should look for the 1985 FJ11. This bike had great horsepower and low weight. Sports touring riders should look for the 1184cc FJ12, introduced in 1986. The FJ12 had bigger and better brakes, and a taller and larger fairing. Some newer models have ABS.

The FJ is one of the most reliable motorcycles capable of 130+ m.p.h. Its long history and Yamaha's constant attention to refinement makes this a great thoroughbred. The bike is plush and carries two well. The 72.5 cu. in. engine produces good low r.p.m. torque and high r.p.m. power.

YAMAHA 1986 YX600 RADIAN

Class: commuter-standard.
Engine: air-cooled in-line four 4-stroke.
Displacement: 599cc.
Valve Arrangement: DOHC 2.
Transmission: 6-speed.
Final Drive: chain.
Brakes: dual disc front, drum rear.
Weight: 408 lbs.
Horsepower: 56.
Torque: 35 lb.ft.
Variations: 1986 to 1990.

(Photo courtesy of Yamaha Motor Corporation, USA.)

YAMAHA 1985 (AND LATER) FJ1100 & FJ1200

Class: sports.
Engine: air-cooled in-line four 4-stroke.
Displacement: 1098cc.
Valve Arrangement: DOHC 4.
Transmission: 5-speed.
Final Drive: chain.
Brakes: dual disc front, disc rear.
Weight: 553 lbs.
Horsepower: 102.

(Photo courtesy of Yamaha Motor Corporation, USA.)

YAMAHA 1985 RZ350

Class: sports.
Engine: liquid-cooled twin 2-stroke.
Displacement: 347cc.
Valve Arrangement: n/a.
Transmission: 6-speed.
Final Drive: O-ring chain.
Brakes: dual disc front, rear disc.
Weight: 329 lbs.
Horsepower: 40.
Torque: 26 lb.ft.

FJs have good ergonomics. Given the luxurious seat, rubber-mounted engine, beefy suspension and ergonomically correct relationship between handlebars, seat and footpegs, the bike can be ridden all day without fatigue. Top quality tires are really appreciated on this bike.

1985 RZ350: Two-stroke street bikes became obsolete as the demand for better air quality in cities increased. But Yamaha did not give up. By applying modern technology and catalytic converters, they created a clean two-stroke that could slay many bikes over twice the size. The RZ out of the box can do a quarter mile in under 13 seconds, topping out at over 100 m.p.h. Modifications can shave an entire second off that. And best of all, plenty of inexpensive wheelies live in this puppy. Production lasted only two years.

Yamaha's RD series is also worthy of consideration. The line started in 1973 with the RD350, and ended in 1980 with the RD400. There was also an RD250. All were excellent motorcycles. Powerful front disc brakes, stiff reinforced frame and perfect balance were the hallmarks of these bikes. Some would say that the RZ was nothing more than an RD with a radiator.

DIRT BIKE SPECIALS

A great many excellent off-road motorcycles are manufactured in the world. The problem is that off-road bikes get abused. As such, each used trail bike is much more an individual than a used street bike tends to be, so making a recommendation is more difficult. Technology also plays a keen and interesting role in the dirt bike industry. In the 1970s a dirt bike was often nothing more than a street bike with knobby tires, higher fenders and a spark arresting muffler. Today, dirt bikes are highly specialized machines heaped with technology and amalgam. Before you buy a dirt bike, make a serious and objective evaluation of the riding you are going to do. If you are going to compete, only the newest bikes will get you across the finish line with a competitive time. If you are working in the backwoods where reliability is more important than speed, many mechanically sound two-strokes will do the job. Buy accordingly. A simple 1971 Yamaha 175 Enduro may fit your Sunday riding needs. If you are looking for a relatively recent year bargain, look for the following:

1990 KTM 300E/XC: KTM is a small specialized Austrian manufacturer making some of the most proven competition dirt bikes around. We're talking serious mud slinging here. These bikes get trophies. These bikes can win out of the crate. The E/XCs are the most popular enduro bikes, and the 300 (and its 350 cousin) are the best of breed. This bike comes with all the requirements for racing enduros. It mixes solid power and performance with very light weight. An excellent open class machine, special features include lights, spark arrestor, side stand, White Power suspension, O-ring chain and speedo. You can even trim a few pounds if you want.

Perhaps the best quality of the KTM is its manners. It has an engine you can really wind up. There's lots of good mid-range power. And even though it is an open-class motorcycle, it is as smooth as a four-stroke, and very easy to ride no matter what the terrain. If you are looking for a bike with more low-end torque and a snappier response, take a look at the KTM 250 E/XC supercross. These bikes share the same frame.

1990 ATK 406 CROSS COUNTRY: ATK is a small specialized American manufacturer making some great competition dirt bikes. The 406 is a simple and durable motorcycle. There are no radiators, no water pumps

1990 KTM 300E/XC

Class: dirt.
Engine: liquid-cooled case reed induction single 2-stroke.
Displacement: 297cc.
Transmission: 5-speed.
Final Drive: chain.
Brakes: disc front & rear.
Weight: 216 lbs.
Variations: 1990 through 1992.

(Photo courtesy of KTM Sportmotorcycle USA.)

Class: dirt/enduro.
Engine: air-cooled single reed-valve 2-stroke.
Displacement: 399cc.
Transmission: 6-speed.
Final Drive: chain.
Brakes: disc front and rear.
Weight: 236 lbs.
Variations: 1990 through 1992.

and no hoses to worry about damaging. The air-cooled Rotax engine has no power valves to clean. It does have the excellent ATK patented chain torque eliminator system. This adds up to a simple, enjoyable, low-maintenance dirt bike. Special features include lights, spark arrestor, side stand, White Power suspension, nickel-plated 4130 chrome-moly steel frame and swingarm, stainless-steel and aluminum exhaust, and O-ring chain. The Cross Country has a large 3.7 gallon fuel tank for avoiding the authorities or the commies, whomever you think are coming first.

Note: Also take a look at the 244cc ATK 250 Cross Country. Even with all of the same features (and simplicity) of its big brother, the 250 only weighs 205 pounds.

1987 KAWASAKI KLR650: The KLR650 descends from a fine 600 that was brought into production in 1984. But Kawasaki rethought the entire bike for 1987, and came up with a truly great dual-purpose machine. The 600 was hard to kick over, so in 1987 Kawasaki added an electric start. Nineteen eighty-seven also saw the addition of an extra large steel fuel tank (6 gallons), bigger 650 engine, fairing, hand guards and big cargo rack. This new version also received a new chassis and long travel suspension. If you are stout, this bike can go anywhere you are brave enough to navigate. It is claimed that the bike can do 100 m.p.h. Not bad for a trail bike.

1990 BMW R100GS "PARIS-DAKAR"

Class: dual-purpose.
Engine: air- & oil-cooled opposed twin 4-stroke.
Displacement: 980cc.
Valve Arrangement: SOHC 2.
Transmission: 5-speed.
Final Drive: shaft.
Brakes: front disc, rear drum.
Weight: 443 lbs.
Suspension: rear paralever.

(Photo courtesy of BMW of North America.)

1990 BMW R100GS "PARIS-DAKAR": Introduced in 1981, the BMW GS designation has come to stand for cutting edge, dual purpose technology. The GS models have earned their nicknames, sometimes referred to as UAVs (urban assault vehicles) or "desert panzers." It handles effortlessly and is surprisingly nimble on unpaved road and superslab. The GS is one of the few dual-purpose bikes that truly is as well mannered in sand or on logging roads as it is under good street conditions. It comes fully complemented with engine guards, high rise exhaust, floating front disc brake, tubeless cross-spoke rims and integral torsional damper. It can be fitted with hard luggage creating the quintessential adventure machine.

Five models have been available: R80 G/S, R80 G/S Paris-Dakar, R100GS, R100GS Paris-Dakar (called the R100GS PD due to the trademarking of the Paris-Dakar name by the event organizers) and the R1100GS. Research shows owners do about 70% of their riding on paved road. Recent tire improvements have really enhanced the multisurface characteristics of the bike, and purchase of modern dual-purpose tires for an older bike should be considered.

8

Motorcycle Maintenance

More and more of the service and repairs for modern motorcycles must be done by trained service technicians. But there is still a great deal that can be done by an average owner. As long as you have a good set of tools, a service manual and a solid understanding of basic motorcycle mechanics, you can do plenty of maintenance yourself. In fact, maintaining the bike yourself can keep ownership cost low, double or triple the life of your motorcycle and help you develop the skills required for an emergency roadside repair.

INDIVIDUAL BIKE REQUIREMENTS

Modern motorcycles require some basic care and grooming. Older bikes require even more. The maintenance that your particular bike requires is a function of four things: design, type of use, amount of use and time. Each of these has a particular effect on your motorcycle's maintenance requirements.

Design

Maintenance requirements are designed into the motorcycle. It goes without much debate that a bike with self-adjusting valves requires less valve maintenance than a comparable bike without self-adjusting valves. It is obvious that smaller engines rack up greater r.p.m.s and require more maintenance than larger engines. Less obvious is that body features such as an aerodynamic design can dramatically reduce the work required of the engine, thus reducing the need for maintenance. Similarly, an engine design that encourages heat dispensation may increase the life of the engine oil thus reducing maintenance requirements.

Type of Use

Maintenance requirements are also a function of how the motorcycle is used. A cruiser lumbering along on open road is under little stress, and its maintenance requirements are quite modest. However, fully loaded and pulling a trailer, the cruiser is under considerable stress, and its maintenance requirements increase. Sports bike riders can tour the outer banks and piedmont with little concern about additional maintenance. But that same bike canyon blasting through twisting mountain passes putting maximum pressure on drive train and suspension systems requires additional maintenance. Motorcycle commuters whose daily routes cover freeways and suburban boulevards have low maintenance requirements. That same bike driven in downtown stop and go, high r.p.m., low speed traffic, creating a hot-hot engine and worn brakes requires additional maintenance.

Street bike owners are advised to accelerate the maintenance schedules when the bike is subjected to severe riding conditions. Exactly what are these conditions? They are (1) high humidity conditions (i.e., mud and rain); (2) inordinately dusty conditions; (3) stop and go driving; (4) trips that require excessive amounts of stopping and starting of the engine; (5) extreme temperature conditions (either on the hot or the cold side); and, of course, (6) boulevard drag racing.

Amount of Use

Motorcycles want to be used and need to be used. If you use your bike a lot, you will naturally perform more maintenance over a given period of time than the owner who puts a standard number of miles on his bike each year. However, the owner who rarely rides should perform more maintenance over a given amount of miles than the owner who puts a standard number of miles on his bike each year. This is because bikes age with both time and use! Lack of use is probably harder on a motorcycle than constant use. Without use, contaminants, acids, ozone, ultraviolet rays, oxygen and other environmental corrosives attack the motorcycle. Mobile environmental hazards, such as insects and rodents, find an idle motorcycle the ideal home. Some of these corrosives and hazards are purged from the motorcycle with use.

Time

Everything atrophies. Everything ages. Items such as vinyl accoutrements, tank paint, fiberglass shields, rubber gaskets and synthetic hoses age more with time than use.

FIVE MAINTENANCE SCHEDULES

Standard civilian motorcycles will be on at least one of the following five basic maintenance schedules:

- Break-in Maintenance Schedule—Manufacturers have perfected virtually every piece of the engine and drive train. This has reduced the recommended break-in requirements to virtually nothing. However, following a deliberate break-in procedure and maintenance schedule will ensure that your new bike lives a long and prosperous life.
- New Used Bike Maintenance Routine—Similar to the break-in maintenance schedule, a new used bike (i.e., a used bike you have just purchased) should be taken through the same inspections and fluid changes that a new bike goes through after the first 500 to 800 miles.
- Standard Warranty Maintenance Schedule—To keep a bike under warranty, an owner must perform periodic maintenance at given time or mileage intervals. It is not enough to simply do the maintenance. You must be able to prove you performed the maintenance to keep the warranty valid.
- Trail Bike Maintenance Schedule—While street bike use is measured in miles and months, these metrics have little relevance to the trail bike. A street bike engine might propagate 150,000 revolutions per hour of operation and cover 50 miles. A trail bike might consume twice the number of revolutions per hour and cover only five miles. Trail bike maintenance is therefore predicated on hours or races, rather than miles or months.
- Seasonal Maintenance Schedule—Unless you live in an area with a 12-month riding season, you will be performing special maintenance for the fall, winter and spring.

In addition to the above schedules, every motorcycle is on a daily preride inspection routine. Motorcycles have no secondary or backup systems in case of a major component failure. It behooves the rider to make a habit of performing a basic preride inspection. A preride routine is the most basic form of maintenance.

This chapter covers these maintenance routines in the order that you are most likely to perform them: new break-in maintenance, used break-in maintenance, preride maintenance, standard warranty maintenance, trail bike maintenance and seasonal maintenance.

NEW BIKE BREAK-IN MAINTENANCE ROUTINE

New and rebuilt engines must be "broken in," as prescribed by the manufacturer. Break-in is the process of deliberate riding so that the anomalies and irregularities of machined parts can be worked out (e.g., rings to seat, gears to mesh). Time was when engine break-in was a major production. Owners were required to restrict r.p.m.s and speeds for thousands of miles before full throttle acceleration could be attempted without risk of throwing a bearing or busting a few gears. Modern engines built with alloys and modern machining techniques do not require the same level of pampering as older, pre-1980s engines. Even so, it is best to err on the side of caution when it comes to break-in.

The Objective of Break-In

The objective of a good break-in is to allow parts to properly mate. The engine must be considered. The engine needs the valves to seat, rings to seal, bearings to turn true, cam chains to mate with cam gears, etc. For modern bikes the critical parts are the valves. It used to be that piston and rings were also critical. But piston and ring break-in is needed only for cross-hatched cylinders. Most new engines have smooth bores coated with high-resistant alloys so ring seating is a thing of the past. The piston rings will actually be seated within the first few heat-up/cool-down cycles or after the first full tank of gas has been burned. But this does not mean that you simply take the bike through a couple of warm-up sprints and then go to Daytona.

The transmission must be considered, too. You want to let it "settle in." Transmission gears, shifters, dog faces and such must mesh and mate. Some gears are designed so that the teeth are polished and imperfections are smoothed out during this period. Not enough pressure on the gears may cause them to "glaze" and not mesh properly. Too much pressure can create extremely high load areas on the gear teeth, causing breaks or cracks during full throttle acceleration.

The Break-in Procedure

Read the owner's manual on this one for sure! There will be at least one requirement or caution in the break-in procedure that will surprise you.

The best way to break-in any vehicle is to make sure you vary the operating conditions. The biggest mistake riders make is to get on the turnpike and do 55 m.p.h. to Manhattan and back. You want to vary the r.p.m.s, vary the load, vary the speed and vary the throttle. Varying the engine speed allows the various parts to be "loaded" and "unloaded." That is, pressures and forces are applied, then reduced, allowing the parts to heat, mate and cool.

WOT (wide open throttle) during the break-in period is not only okay, it is good! A few restrictions do apply, however. WOT is good as long as the engine is warm, redline and r.p.m. restrictions (noted in your owner's manual) are observed, and the machine is not continuously operated in full-load conditions. The greatest danger to a new or rebuilt engine is not r.p.m.s; the greatest danger to the engine is lugging the engine or exposing the engine to hard load, low r.p.m. conditions. Lugging puts great pressure on critical areas, particularly the crankshaft. At the same time, the low r.p.m. means less oil is being pumped to those critical pressure areas.

Some engines have an r.p.m. limit that should not be exceeded during break-in. For instance, 4,000 r.p.m.s should not be exceeded during the first 500 miles, 6,000 r.p.m.s should not be exceeded during the next 500 miles, etc. This is not a problem unless the bike is not equipped with a tachometer. Without a tack, you must figure out the maximum allowable speed for each gear, and then never exceed that speed. As a rule of thumb, stay off the throttle for the first tank of gas.

Being too gentle during break-in is just as detrimental as being too severe. Operating the engine at a constant low speed under light load conditions can cause parts to glaze and not seat or mate properly. In addition, oil may not reach engine extremities.

Do some city, do some country, do some hills, do some bayou. Give yourself the opportunity to shift the gears up and down a lot since the transmission is what you are really breaking in. Varying the throttle will make a big difference in the seating of the gears.

Perhaps the best riding, both for street motorcycle break-in and as a pleasurable experience, is to cruise an old highway. Here you will get the city, the country, the burbs and the open stretches. Plus, you will visit a part of America that was once the backbone of a great country. Much of this has given way to strip malls, video parlors and nail boutiques. (Thomas Jefferson once said, "It is hard to build a nation into a superpower on an economic foundation of taco joints and minimarkets.") I recommend Route 1 through New England, the Blue Ridge Parkway through the South, Route 50 through the mid-Atlantic and Appalachian states, Route 66 through the Midwest and Southwest (the parts you can find), 97 and 16 through British Columbia and Route 1 along the Pacific Coast.

Trail bikes are totally different animals when it comes to break-in. Trail bikes must go through a break-in procedure whenever the piston, piston rings, cylinder, crankshaft or crankshaft bearings are replaced. While the principles above apply, the actual procedure is different. Some trail bikes must be processed through a warm-up/cool-down procedure. The actual procedure depends on the bike, but one principle is the same: Let the new engine warm up before doing more than moderate speed. Never ride at more than half throttle at first, and avoid more than ¾ throttle until fully broken in. Never accelerate hard.

Two-strokes often require a lower gasoline:oil fuel mix (i.e., more oil) during break-in. For example, a common operating mixture is 32:1. During break-in, you may run 20:1, reducing the gasoline and increasing the oil in the mix to keep the top end well lubricated and avoiding piston seizure.

A typical break-in/maintenance schedule is presented on the accompanying table.

Opinions about oil changing during break-in vary widely. Some folks just got to get those pesky little metal flakes out of the engine as soon as possible. Others say it makes no difference. The author concurs with BMW. The BMW factory requires the bikes returned after 600 miles to change *all* the fluids (except brake) and filters. Doing this removes all those flakes after only a few days of riding. The next required service comes at 4,500 miles for an oil change. BMW further recommends you change the oil every 1,500 to 2,000 miles if you ride in severe conditions. BMW knows what they are doing because they send every bike out with a three-year unlimited mileage warranty, and they don't have to eat very many. If in doubt, smell the crankcase oil. If you detect a burned smell, change the oil. Oil is cheaper than rings.

NEW USED BIKE MAINTENANCE ROUTINE

The used motorcycle you just purchased instantly becomes your new used motorcycle, and deserves special treatment. The Break-in/Maintenance Table shows a new used bike maintenance routine. You will want to perform all of the maintenance noted there for two reasons. The first is to bring the bike up to grade on its maintenance schedule. No matter what the previous owner told you, you want to be sure that the bike is on a proper maintenance schedule. You must assume that the previous owner did not care one iota for the bike. This might be the case. If it is, the bike might not last long without some tender loving care.

The second reason for performing the new used bike maintenance is to provide peace of mind. You need to know your motorcycle well.

BREAK-IN/MAINTENANCE TABLE

	Break-in Maintenance	New Used Maintenance	Preride Inspection
Chassis Service			
Battery Electrolyte Level—Check	◆	◆	
Brake—Adjust	◆	◆	◆
Brake Fluid—Change		◆	
Brake Fluid—Inspect	◆	◆	◆
Brake Pads/Shoes—Inspect		◆	
Cables—Lube	◆	◆	
Clutch—Adjust	◆	◆	
Clutch Fluid Level—Check	◆	◆	
Electronics—Inspect	◆	◆	◆
Final Bevel Gear Case Oil—Change	◆	◆	
Final Drive Chain—Lube	◆	◆	◆
Final Drive Chain/Belt—Inspect	◆	◆	◆
Fork Oil—Change	◆		
Forks—Inspect	◆	◆	◆
Fuel Filter—Change		◆	
Fuel Lines—Inspect	◆	◆	◆
Fuel Strainer—Service		◆	
Lights—Check	◆		◆
Lights—Replace		◆	
Nuts, Bolts and Fasteners—Tighten	◆	◆	◆
Spoke Tightness—Inspect		◆	
Steering—Inspect		◆	
Swing Arm—Grease		◆	
Tire Pressure—Check	◆	◆	◆
Tire Tread—Inspect	◆	◆	◆
Wheel Bearings—Service		◆	
Engine Service			
Air Cleaner—Replace			
Air Cleaner—Service	◆	◆	
Cam Chain—Adjust		◆	
Carburetors—Adjust	◆	◆	
Coolant—Change	◆	◆	
Coolant—Inspect			◆
Engine Mounts—Inspect	◆	◆	
Engine Oil—Change	◆	◆	
Engine Oil Level—Inspect			◆
Engine Oil Filter—Replace	◆	◆	
Primary Chaincase Lube—Replace	◆	◆	
Primary Drive Chain—Lube	◆	◆	
Spark Plugs—Replace			
Spark Plugs—Service	◆	◆	
Timing—Adjust		◆	
Transmission Fluid—Change	◆		

By performing this intensive maintenance, you will take the bike through another rigorous inspection. If the bike checks out, you can confidently ride it on the road. If not, the bike will be in great shape to sell.

PRERIDE INSPECTION MAINTENANCE ROUTINE

In the chapter on safe riding techniques, a great deal of detail is given to the preride inspection. That detail will not be restated, but riders should be aware that a good preride inspection is a good mechanical inspection. The previous table shows those mechanical inspections that should be performed before hitting the road.

Trail riders should pay special attention to the preride inspection. The constant punishment absorbed by the bike jars parts loose. Tires can be damaged. Shock seals can burst. Brakes can suffer impact and fail. Everything is more at risk on a trail bike. Failure to perform basic preride checks can result in serious engine damage, severe accident, dismemberment and death.

STANDARD MOTORCYCLE MAINTENANCE

All motorcycles have maintenance requirements. For example, each must have its oil changed, tires replaced and filters cleaned or changed. When this must happen is a function of the design of the bike, the size of the engine and how hard the bike is used. The manufacturer's recommended schedule should be followed to keep any warranty valid. If you do not have the schedule, use the generic schedules in this chapter.

Small Motorcycle Maintenance

Small motorcycles (motorcycles under 500cc) put greater demands on chassis, drive train and engine components than do larger motorcycles. In addition, smaller motorcycles are often designed as low cost introductory bikes, meaning they are often made of lesser quality components. Therefore, they must be on a rigorous maintenance schedule. The maintenance schedule for a generic small motorcycle is presented in the accompanying table.

Large Motorcycle Maintenance

The maintenance schedule for a generic large motorcycle (i.e., one with an engine over 500cc) is presented in the table on Large Motorcycle Maintenance on page 151. Some services listed are not appropriate for some motorcycles.

SMALL MOTORCYCLE MAINTENANCE

	Notes	4 1	8 2	12 3	16 4	20 5	24 6	28 7	32 8	36 9	40 10
Months/1,000 Miles											
Chassis Service											
Battery Electrolyte Level—Check	❶	◆	◆	◆	◆	◆	◆	◆	◆	◆	◆
Brake Fluid—Change				◆			◆			◆	
Brake Fluid—Inspect	❶	◆	◆	◆	◆	◆	◆	◆	◆	◆	◆
Brake Pads/Shoes—Inspect		◆	◆	◆	◆	◆	◆	◆	◆	◆	◆
Brakes—Adjust		◆	◆	◆	◆	◆	◆	◆	◆	◆	◆
Cables—Lube				◆			◆			◆	
Clutch—Adjust				◆			◆			◆	
Clutch Fluid Level—Check				◆			◆			◆	
Electronics—Inspect		◆	◆	◆	◆	◆	◆	◆	◆	◆	◆
Final Drive Chain—Lube		◆	◆	◆	◆	◆	◆	◆	◆	◆	◆
Final Drive Chain/Belt—Inspect		◆	◆	◆	◆	◆	◆	◆	◆	◆	◆
Fork Oil—Change							◆				
Forks—Inspect				◆			◆			◆	
Fuel Filter—Change				◆			◆			◆	
Fuel Lines—Inspect				◆			◆			◆	
Fuel Lines—Replace	❹										
Fuel Strainer—Service				◆			◆			◆	
Lights—Check		◆	◆	◆	◆	◆	◆	◆	◆	◆	◆
Lights—Replace	❸						◆				
Nuts, Bolts and Fasteners—Tighten		◆	◆	◆	◆	◆	◆	◆	◆	◆	◆
Spoke Tightness—Inspect				◆			◆			◆	
Steering—Inspect				◆			◆			◆	
Swing Arm—Grease							◆				
Tire Pressure—Check		◆	◆	◆	◆	◆	◆	◆	◆	◆	◆
Tire Tread—Inspect		◆	◆	◆	◆	◆	◆	◆	◆	◆	◆
Wheel Bearings—Service				◆			◆			◆	
Engine Service											
Air Cleaner—Replace							◆				
Air Cleaner—Service				◆						◆	
Cam Chain—Adjust				◆			◆			◆	
Carburetors—Adjust				◆			◆			◆	
Coolant—Change	❸						◆				
Coolant—Inspect		◆	◆	◆	◆	◆	◆	◆	◆	◆	◆
Engine Mounts—Inspect				◆			◆			◆	
Engine Oil—Change	❷			◆			◆			◆	
Engine Oil—Inspect		◆	◆	◆	◆	◆	◆	◆	◆	◆	◆
Engine Oil Filter—Replace	❷			◆			◆			◆	
Spark Plugs—Replace							◆				
Spark Plugs—Service				◆			◆			◆	
Timing—Adjust	❷			◆			◆			◆	
Transmission Fluid—Change	❸						◆				

Notes: ❶ = monthly service ❷ = annual service ❸ = biannual service ❹ = every 4 years ❺ = each race ❻ = as required

Trail Bike Maintenance

Trail bikes are on a totally different maintenance schedule. Service intervals are measured in races raced or hours of operation. The maintenance schedule for a generic two-stroke trail motorcycle is presented in the chart on page 152.

Again, some services listed are not appropriate for some trail motorcycles.

CHASSIS SERVICE MAINTENANCE NOTES

These tables are not without need of explanation. The following notes provide added details about the suggested maintenance.

Battery

Regular maintenance will extend the life of your battery. Make the following checks:

1. Be sure the battery is securely in the battery rack.
2. Be sure the cables are on tight. Loose connections reduce the power the battery can deliver and reduce the charge the battery receives.
3. Keep cables and posts free of deposits. A metal brush or shop rag can be used.
4. Keep the top of the battery clean. Dirt can conduct electricity and drain the battery.
5. Keep the electrolyte at the proper level. Add distilled water until the acid just touches the filler hole stem. The electrolyte should never be so low that battery plates are exposed. Even if the battery is maintenance-free, you should check the acid level if the top of the battery is not sealed. Only use distilled water. (This does not apply to maintenance free batteries.)
6. Put a light coating of petroleum jelly over each terminal to prevent acid from forming. Clean and reapply this coating each time you remove the battery cables.
7. Keep the battery vent tube open, free of debris and venting away from motorcycle parts, especially the final drive chain.

Batteries self-discharge over time at a rate of about .5% to 1% daily. In addition, some motorcycles have electric accessories which continuously draw power. So, even a good battery needs a supplemental charge every 30 days if left idle. But avoid quick charging the battery. A quick charge can damage the battery plates. And cease charging a battery if it gets hot.

LARGE MOTORCYCLE MAINTENANCE

	Notes	Months/1,000 Miles									
		6 / 2.5	12 / 5	18 / 7.5	24 / 10	30 / 12.5	36 / 15	42 / 17.5	48 / 20	54 / 22.5	60 / 25
Chassis Service											
Battery Electrolyte Level—Check	❶	◆	◆	◆	◆	◆	◆	◆	◆	◆	◆
Brake Fluid—Change			◆		◆		◆		◆		◆
Brake Fluid—Check	❶	◆	◆	◆	◆	◆	◆	◆	◆	◆	◆
Brake Pads/Shoes—Inspect			◆	◆	◆	◆	◆	◆	◆	◆	◆
Brakes—Adjust		◆	◆	◆	◆	◆	◆	◆	◆	◆	◆
Cables—Lube			◆		◆		◆		◆		◆
Clutch—Adjust			◆		◆		◆		◆		◆
Clutch Fluid Level—Check			◆		◆		◆		◆		◆
Electronics—Inspect		◆	◆	◆	◆	◆	◆	◆	◆	◆	◆
Final Drive Chain—Lube		◆	◆	◆	◆	◆	◆	◆	◆	◆	◆
Final Drive Chain/Belt—Inspect		◆	◆	◆	◆	◆	◆	◆	◆	◆	◆
Final Drive Gear Case Oil—Change					◆				◆		
Fork Oil—Change					◆				◆		
Forks—Inspect			◆		◆		◆		◆		◆
Fuel Filter—Change			◆		◆		◆		◆		◆
Fuel Lines—Inspect			◆		◆		◆		◆		◆
Fuel Lines—Replace	❹										
Fuel Strainer—Service			◆		◆		◆		◆		◆
Lights—Check		◆	◆	◆	◆	◆	◆	◆	◆	◆	◆
Lights—Replace	❸				◆				◆		
Nuts, Bolts and Fasteners—Tighten		◆	◆	◆	◆	◆	◆	◆	◆	◆	◆
Spoke Tightness—Inspect			◆		◆		◆		◆		◆
Steering—Inspect			◆		◆		◆		◆		◆
Swing Arm—Grease					◆				◆		
Tire Pressure—Check		◆	◆	◆	◆	◆	◆	◆	◆	◆	◆
Tire Tread—Inspect		◆	◆	◆	◆	◆	◆	◆	◆	◆	◆
Wheel Bearings—Service			◆		◆		◆		◆		◆
Engine Service											
Air Cleaner—Replace					◆				◆		
Air Cleaner—Service			◆				◆				◆
Cam Chain—Adjust			◆		◆		◆		◆		◆
Carburetors—Adjust			◆		◆		◆		◆		◆
Coolant—Change	❸				◆				◆		
Coolant—Inspect		◆	◆	◆	◆	◆	◆	◆	◆	◆	◆
Engine Mounts—Inspect			◆		◆		◆		◆		◆
Engine Oil—Change	❷		◆		◆		◆		◆		◆
Engine Oil—Inspect		◆	◆	◆	◆	◆	◆	◆	◆	◆	◆
Engine Oil Filter—Replace	❷		◆		◆		◆		◆		◆
Primary Chaincase Lube—Replace											
Primary Drive Chain—Lube			◆		◆		◆		◆		◆
Spark Plugs—Replace	❺										
Spark Plugs—Service			◆		◆		◆		◆		◆
Timing—Adjust	❷		◆		◆		◆		◆		◆
Transmission Fluid—Change	❸				◆				◆		

Notes: ❶ = monthly service   ❷ = annual service   ❸ = biannual service   ❹ = every 4 years   ❺ = each race   ❻ = as required

Service	Notes	Every Meet or 1.5 Hours	Every 2nd Meet or 2.5 Hours	Every 3rd Meet or 3.5 Hours	Every 5th Meet or 5.5 Hours
Air Filter—Replace	❻				
Air Filter—Service		◆			
Brake Fluid—Inspect		◆			
Brake Fluid—Change	❷				
Brake Hose—Replace	❸				
Brakes—Inspect		◆			
Brakes—Replace	❻				
Cables—Inspect		◆			
Clutch—Adjust		◆			
Clutch Plates—Inspect					◆
Coolant—Change	❸				
Cylinder—Clean					◆
Cylinder Head—Clean					◆
Engine Main Bearing—Replace					◆
Engine Sprocket—Replace					◆
Exhaust O-ring—Replace					◆
Exhaust Valve—Clean					◆
Final Drive Chain—Adjust/Lube		◆			
Final Drive Chain—Replace					◆
Front Fork—Inspect		◆			
Front Fork Oil—Replace				◆	
Fuel Line—Inspect		◆			
Fuel Line—Replace	❹				
Fuel System—Clean		◆			
Fuel Tank—Clean		◆			
Kick Start—Grease	❺	◆			
Muffler—Clean					◆
Nuts, Bolts and Fasteners—Tighten		◆			
Piston—Replace					◆
Piston Rings—Replace			◆		
Radiator—Service	❷				
Radiator Coolant—Replace	❷				
Rear Sprocket—Inspect			◆		
Rear Sprocket—Replace					◆
Spark Plug—Replace	❻				
Spark Plug—Service		◆			
Spokes—Inspect		◆			
Steering—Inspect		◆			
Tire Pressure—Check		◆			
Tire Tread—Inspect		◆			
Transmission Oil—Replace			◆		
Wheel Bearings—Service					◆

Notes: ❶ = monthly service   ❷ = annual service   ❸ = biannual service   ❹ = every 4 years   ❺ = each race   ❻ = as required

Brakes

Brake pads and shoes should be replaced when either the lining or pad thickness, measured at the minimum depth, is 1/16 of an inch (2 millimeters) or less. Disc brake systems generally provide a window of some sort to allow visual inspection of pad thickness. Some pads come with markings that show when they need to be replaced. Those without markings need to be measured with a micrometer.

Drum brakes often have indicator arrows on the arm connected to the brake cam that shows brake shoe wear. Also, you know you have worn the brake shoes down dangerously thin by the amount of cable slack taken up by brake adjustments at the drum and handlebar. Other signs of worn brakes include hearing the drum dragging on the brake shoe pad mounts when the wheel is rotated and seeing black specks around the brake drum.

Brake Fluid

Always use the recommended brake fluid. As with any hydraulic system, be extremely careful to prevent dirt or water from contaminating the brake fluid. Brake fluid naturally absorbs moisture. Moisture is detrimental to hydraulic systems. Store the fluid in a sealed container so neither dirt nor water will contaminate the fluid. Do not substitute power steering fluid for brake fluid. Brake fluid will hurt paint.

Cables

Cables can be lubed with a specially designed commercial pressure oiling tool. Lacking such a device, try attaching a funnel (using aluminum foil, modeling clay or a plastic sandwich bag) to the cable end. Fill the funnel with a little bit of oil and allow the oil to drain through the cable over night. Dry graphite is also a good cable lubricant.

Exhaust

Two agents attack the inside of the exhaust, reducing its effectiveness: carbon and rust. Exhaust carbon build up will reduce engine output. If rust is permitted inside the system, the exhaust pipe, baffles and packing will age rapidly. If you keep the engine tuned and ride the motorcycle enough so water evaporates from the exhaust pipes, neither of these agents should be a problem.

What you look for are signs of leaks where the muffler connects to the cylinder head and damage to the exterior of the muffler. If there are leaks at the head, or if the header gaskets appear damaged, replace the gaskets. If any part of the exhaust system is badly damaged, cracked or rusted, replace the system. Small cracks can be welded closed.

Final Drive Belt Maintenance

Belt failure is problematic. Often there is no sign that the belt is about to fail. They simply haul off and split. This situation is, of course, totally debilitating. You do not want to be riding Route 5 up to the 14,260-foot summit of Mt. Evans when the belt rips. There are only three maintenance tips that may prevent you from being stranded.

First, belts should be adjusted at the 500-mile break-in mark. After this, belts should be adjusted every 5,000 miles. The belt should have between 3/8 and ½ inch play (i.e., deflection) when a force of 10 pounds is applied in the center of the top strand.

Second, belt sprockets should be inspected for nicks and gouges. It is possible, although not very probable, that the sprocket could get spurred by road debris. A spur on the sprocket could chew on the fabric and accelerate belt deterioration.

Third, replace the belt at the recommended interval. It's expensive, but well worth the peace of mind and extra protection. Typically, you do not need to change the sprockets at the same time (as you might with a chain final drive).

Final Drive Chain Maintenance

Lubricate the chain after each ride rather than just before a ride. This technique has three benefits: First, this gives the lube time to work between the links. Second, this removes grit and grime. Third, for O-ring chains, this dissipates water on the chain. The technique is simple. Brush off heavy accumulations of grit. Point the spray into the area between link plates and bushings. This is the area you need to lube. You do not need to lube the roller faces; these faces are designed to contact the sprocket. After the lube sets up, wipe off the excess so it does not collect road kill.

Periodically check the alignment and adjustment of the chain. The chain is not aligned properly if the chain or sprocket teeth show unusual wear. Unusual wear is easy enough to detect. It's those bright shiny spots where as the rest of the chain is dark with oil and grime. The bright spots suggest misalignment of the chain, sprockets, chain guide and/or swingarm. Bright spots may also be suggesting abrasion against some other part of the motorcycle (like the engine case). You should also look for the chain rising on the sprocket.

Standard chains should be checked every 200 miles for proper tension on a street bike, or before every ride on a dirt bike. A properly tightened chain will have three-quarters to one inch of play (measured in the middle of the bottom chain run) on a street bike. On a monoshock dirt bike, play can vary up to two inches.

Battery acid corrosion of the chain is a major problem for motorcycles that have a battery vent tube discharging near the chain. A drop of acid on a modern case hardened chain link will visually damage the link in minutes and destroy the link within 24 hours. Acid will etch grooves into the chain and create black discoloration. Other signs of acid corrosion include flecks of rust or oxidation around the battery, frame or swingarm. Be sure the battery vent tube is discharging close to the ground and away from the chain.

Final Drive Chain Lubrication

Only use a high-grade oil of suitable viscosity on a chain. Motorcycle dealerships sell a variety of these products. Never use heavy oil, low-grade products, impure oil, grease, kerosene or used oil. These lubricants will not lubricate the chain effectively and will reduce service life.

O-ring chains require different lubes than standard chains. Standard chains need lube that will dissipate heat, absorb shock and prevent corrosion. O-rings only require lube that dissipates water. Motorcycle dealers sell lubricants specially designed for use on motorcycle chains. These lubricants are several dollars more expensive per can than household spray lubricants, but only a fraction of a penny more expensive per use. (Do not use lubricant on an O-ring chain that is not designed for this use!)

Special motorcycle chain lubricants offer several key properties. First, the lubes are generally formulated with extreme pressure aluminum complex grease containing molybdenum disulfide antiwear additives that have greater lubricating properties. Second, the lubes penetrate pins and rollers, resist water washout and will not damage O-rings. Third, the lube stays where you spray it. Motorcycle chain lube has tackiness agents so the lube hangs on the chain, and the spray nozzle is designed to spray on a chain, instead of over a wide swath.

Final Drive Gear Oil

Final drives for shaft drive motorcycles generally require little attention. SAE 90 weight hypoid gear oil that is API rated GL-5 is often used. Cold temperature riders may want to run SAE 80.

Lights

Check the operation of all lights before each ride. Bulbs become weak and dull with use. As a safety measure, replace bulbs every two years. If you replace bulbs yourself, be sure not to touch the glass of the bulb. This can cloud the glass with dirt and oil, and result in premature failure of high temperature halogen bulbs.

Check the headlight adjustment every year. The owner's manual will have the proper adjustment measurements. To properly adjust the headlight on an average large motorcycle, park the motorcycle on a level surface twenty-five feet from a wall. With a rider on the bike, the headlight beam should shine straight ahead, approximately 35 inches above the floor. Or, on open road with a rider on the bike, the low beam should intersect with the road 150 to 200 feet directly ahead.

Spokes

Broken spokes should be replaced immediately. A missing spoke puts extra strain on the remaining spokes and leads to more spoke failures. Spokes stretch during use, so check the tightness. Standard torque specifications can be found in your motorcycle manual. The wheel may need to be trued—to make perfectly round—if there are a considerable number of loose spokes.

Steering and Steering Bearings

Steering should be tight but not prevent you from turning the handlebars quickly. To check steering tightness, put the motorcycle on its center stand so that the front wheel is off the ground. Push the handlebar lightly to one side. If the wheel continues moving, steering is not too tight. Check if the steering is too loose by grabbing the lower ends of the forks at the axle. If play is felt when pushing back and forth, the steering is too loose.

Steering stem bearings should be free of cracks and excessive wear.

Suspension Adjustment

Motorcycles that place great demands on the suspension generally offer several fork and shock adjustments. There are two basic rules of thumb for suspension adjustments. First, both the front and back suspension should work in harmony. This means that they are set for the same riding and the same load level. Second, the suspension should be set to work within the first third of suspension travel for normal trip conditions. If the suspension travels more than a third when loaded and on open road, it needs to be adjusted. You need at least two-thirds of the travel for when you hit unexpected hazards like potholes and opossums.

There is an extensive number of ways to adjust the rebound and stiffness of modern shocks. Fork oil can be changed, fork springs replaced, air pressure setting adjusted, etc. Consult your owner's manual.

Tire Inspection and Inflation

Tires should be replaced after suffering a major gash or contusion, or when the tread depth is less than 3/32 for a front tire, and 2/32 for a rear tire. Always replace the tube when you replace a tubed tire.

The correct tire inflation for average, fully loaded use will be stamped on the side of the tire. This will be measured in pounds per square inch (p.s.i.). Use this as a general guide for maximum tire inflation. Solo riding does not require the maximum p.s.i., and you will get a more comfortable ride at a lower inflation (approximately four pounds less than maximum p.s.i.). However, you may need to increase the p.s.i. if you are riding with two passengers, fully loading the bike or pulling a trailer. Under no conditions should you exceed the maximum cold p.s.i. Ask your tire dealer or manufacturer for correct inflation pressures based on your riding needs.

Wheel Bearings

Replace wheel bearings if there is noticeable side-to-side play. Sometimes a high pitch whining sound represents a bearing that is burning out. A burned out bearing will eventually seize. Incidences have been recorded of burned bearings actually catching fire.

ENGINE SERVICE MAINTENANCE NOTES

Air Cleaner

Air cleaners come in disposable paper element and reusable plastic foam element types. Paper element filters can be cleaned by applying air pressure from a compressor to the inside of the element. This will force some dirt out of the filter. Never use the air hose on the outside of the air cleaner element, or dirt will be forced deeper into the filter, restricting air flow.

Foam elements are cleaned with either soap and hot water, or in a bath of high flash-point solvent. Some require that the filter be oiled with foam filter oil, others do not. Consult your owner's manual for proper foam element care.

Coolant

Radiator maintenance is often overlooked because the drain intervals are two years apart. However, motorcycles use aluminum and alloys in their cooling systems that are highly susceptible to corrosion. Consequently, a 50/50 mix of coolant and distilled water must be maintained.

Some folks believe that if a 50/50 mixture is good, 100% straight coolant must be twice as good. This is not true. Running at concentrations above 60% actually increases the freeze point of the mixture and reduces its capability to remove heat from the block. Also, at higher concentrations of antifreeze the coolant mixture can jell at low temperature, offering almost no cooling capability. Running a mixture that is less than 30% coolant will not provide the necessary rust and corrosion inhibiting protection. This can result in rapid corrosion of the aluminum radiator.

The use of distilled water is critical. Tap water contains minerals that can clog the system and may rust and corrode the aluminum radiator.

The procedure is simple. Drain the system. Recover the used antifreeze for recycling. Refill the system with water. Run the motorcycle until the engine reaches operating temperature. Drain the system again. Repeat this process until the drained water is colorless. Refill the system with coolant and distilled water. Do not open the radiator cap when the engine is hot. Hot vapor or coolant can escape and burn you.

Engine Oil

Change your motorcycle's oil as recommended by the manufacturer. It is better to err on the conservative side and change the oil more often. But remember that, from a financial, trade surplus and environmental standpoint, it is best to get the maximum use out of each quart of oil. Use it up, wear it out, make it do, or do without.

Experts say you do not need to change the filter with every oil change. Experts say to change the filter every other oil change. Results from our poll of Joe Backyard mechanics, representing over 2,000,000 miles of driving and 20 rebuilt engines, show that 100% say to change the filter every time you change the oil.

Do not substitute a spin-on car filter for a spin-on motorcycle filter unless you are sure the filter is rated for motorcycle use. Some car filters have no by-pass valve. On others the by-pass valves are set for greater pressures than that of a motorcycle filter.

Using a quality mineral/synthetic-blend automobile oil in your motorcycle is fine.

Spark Plugs

Spark plugs are cheap, but that does not mean they should be needlessly tossed out instead of serviced. Most backyard mechanics replace, rather than clean, an old plug. This is rarely necessary. Unless the plug is totally dead, the insulation cracked or the electrodes burned away to a shadow of their former selves, cleaning and regapping will restore them.

Spark plug service is a lost art. It involves three steps. First, inspect the plug. Spark plug conditions that indicate problems include:

- Wet Black Shine—This is probably a plug fouled from excess oil due to worn rings, worn piston, worn or loose valves, wrong oil ratio or faulty ignition.

- Coated Electrode—Plug electrodes coated with a dry black soot indicate a fuel mixture that is too rich.

- Glassy Electrode—Plug electrodes covered with a light brown, glassy deposit have overheated. These plugs may also have cracked insulators or eroded electrodes. If the plug is of the correct temperature range, the condition may be caused by a fuel mixture that is too lean, an engine that is running too hot, improper ignition timing or poorly seated valves.

A normal plug will have a white, yellow, light tan or rusty brown powdery deposit on the electrode. If the plug is fouled, corroded, burned or cracked, you have some other problem on your hands that a new plug is not going to fix.

Second, clean the plug electrode. Most plugs will last for ages with a simple light cleaning of solvent and a little (very little) light filing. Some shops have a sandblasting tool for cleaning plugs. Note that a plug with sharp electrode edges requires 25% to 40% less firing voltage than one with rounded electrode edges.

Third, gap the plug. A properly gapped plug results in hotter spark, crisper throttle response and better top-end performance. Fuel economy is also improved. Check the plug gap with a wire feeler gauge. The flat metal feeler gauges used for ignition points and valves will not be as accurate as a wire gauge.

When reinstalling the plug, do not coat the threads with antiseize compound or oil. This will reduce the thermal transfer through the plug. Gasketed spark plugs are put in finger tight, then turned one quarter turn further, no more. Tapered seat plugs get only an additional sixteenth of a turn after finger tight. Always use the correct heat range plug as recommended by the manufacturer. Be sure that the cap is tightly seated to the top of the plug.

Transmission Lubricant

Most four-stroke motorcycles use the same oil for the gear box as for the crankcase. This puts an extra burden on the engine oil. Some motorcycles, most notably Harleys, Triumphs and two-strokes, use separate lubrication for transmission and engine. Follow the manufacturer's specifications for these bikes.

SEASONAL MAINTENANCE

If we all lived in tropical climates (or cared less about the cold), we might all ride our motorcycles every day. But for the most part, even the most fanatic rider hangs it up for some part of the year. Any time you are going to leave the bike in storage you should take it through a proper storage maintenance procedure. This helps prevent corrosion, preserve the battery and reduce gum and varnish build-up in the fuel system. Therefore, for the average rider living any place but where there is a 12-month riding season, there is significant fall, winter and spring maintenance to be performed.

Fall Maintenance

Sometime in the fall you will be forced to put the bike into storage. A good storage maintenance routine can be the difference between a bike that is ready to ride and a bike that must be towed to the shop in the spring. It makes the difference between a bike that looks like hell in three years or a bike that shines up showroom pretty when 10 years old. When it comes time each year to put the bike into long-term storage, the following steps should be taken:

- Detail the Motorcycle—Clean the bike of all road grit and grime. Cover all plastics, rubber, vinyl and metal with waxes, protectants and preservatives.
- Stabilize the Gasoline—Gasoline stabilizer is sold at motorcycle stores and auto retail outlets. The gasoline must be stabilized to prevent gum and varnish from building up in the fuel line and carburetors. Follow the directions on the can. Fill the tank to the top with fuel. This reduces the condensation inside the tank that can cause rust. Add the amount of gasoline stabilizer recommended.

   Purge all fuel from the system if it contains any alcohol. This becomes more important as more metropolitan service areas are required to sell oxygenated fuels (a.k.a. gasohol). These fuels collect water into the fuel system, corroding the gas tank, fuel lines and carburetors.

   Alternatively, you can drain all gas from the tank and the carburetor float bowls, coat the float bowls with light oil and treat the tank interior with a rust preventative. The stabilizer seems so much easier.
- Change the Oil—There is big debate over this issue. Some experts say to change the oil in the spring, some say the fall. Some say spring and fall. Some experts say change the oil in the fall but not the filter. The author's opinion is to change the oil and filter in the fall, but just the oil in the spring.

Changing the oil may seem like a waste of money, but it is not. The old oil in the engine contains acids. These acids corrode the oil and engine parts when the bike is not in operation. Changing the oil minimizes the acids left in the engine.

- Change the Coolant—If a coolant change will come due during storage, change the coolant. This keeps the cooling system from rusting and corroding over the winter.

- Run the Engine—This may seem surprising to many, but this is a very sound practice. Running the engine after detailing the bike, adding gas stabilizer, changing the oil and changing the coolant makes sense. You want to run the bike long enough so that any water that has accumulated in the mufflers has a chance to evaporate. At the same time you need to allow the stabilized gasoline to fill the entire fuel and carburation system. Running the motorcycle after changing the oil dilutes the acids in the oil lines to the lowest possible level.

- Add Extra Lubrication to the Cylinders—Once you have run the bike for the last time, remove the spark plugs. Pour two tablespoons of fresh engine oil directly into the spark plug ports. Use a major brand SAE 30. Install the plugs (but not the caps) and kick the bike over once or twice. This gets extra lubrication to the upper cylinder which prevents rusting. There are also special antirust coatings available for this. Follow the directions on the can.

- Prepare the Battery—Proper battery storage prevents battery sulfation, which is a major reason motorcycles "eat" batteries. Be sure the battery is in good shape before storage. Top off each cell with distilled water. Charge the battery if it is not fully charged. Disconnect the leads from the motorcycle. Connect a trickle charger. If the bike will be kept in an unheated space, consider storing the battery someplace else where it will not suffer freezing temperatures. Battery self-discharge is minimized if the battery is stored in a cool, dry location.

  A trickle charger keeps the battery at a given state of charge. It does not increase the charge. Unless the battery is fully charged before storage, the danger of sulfation will still exist even if a trickle charger is used. In addition, during extreme cold the electrolyte can freeze. The weaker the charge, the more likely the electrolyte is to freeze, expand and crack the battery case.

- Lubricate and Grease—Lube and grease all lubed and greased parts such as the chain, cables, swingarm, etc. Apply a light film of oil to exposed unpainted surfaces.

- Get the Tires Off the Ground—Tires should be inflated to proper p.s.i. If the motorcycle is to be stored for any extended period of time, securely support the motorcycle under the frame so that all weight is off the tires.

- Cover the Motorcycle—Close off the intake and exhaust orifices. This prevents moisture from entering the system. It also keeps critters out of the bike, such as rodents and insects. Cover the bike with a cover designed for motorcycle storage. Use a material which breaths, such as light canvas. The cover should not promote condensation.

These steps are over and above standard maintenance and assume that you are also keeping the bike on a regular maintenance schedule.

Winter Maintenance

If you are a home mechanic and have a protected repair area, winter is the perfect time to get all of those long and involved repairs done so you have maximum riding time the rest of the year. Take a strategic planning perspective. Review the upcoming season's agenda and maintenance schedule. If your tires, brakes, valves or other major components need repair, get them done now. If you are not handy with tools, get the bike to a shop during the off season. You will avoid the long spring and summer repair lines.

If there are no major repairs to perform, put the bike into storage and forget it. Starting it up periodically can do as much harm as good.

If you do not have a trickle charger hooked up to the battery, perform a monthly recharge. Charge the battery at a rate (ampere) of 1/10 of its capacity.

Spring Maintenance

Bringing a motorcycle out of storage has as rigorous a maintenance routine as putting it into storage. The goal is to be sure that the bike has not suffered during its winter hibernation.

If you went through a rigorous storage procedure in the fall, you still have some work ahead of you. Perform the following services:

- Uncover the Motorcycle—Remove all of the protective coverings, especially those covering the air box intake and the exhaust.
- Check the Battery—The battery should be in top shape, although it may have lost some electrolyte during the winter. Fill each cell to the recommended level with distilled water. Recharge the battery.
- Change the Oil—Even without the engine being run, acids were at work breaking down the oil in the sump. Change the oil.
- Check Air Pressures—Air has been leaking from shocks and tires all winter.

- Perform Regular Maintenance—Keep your bike on its routine maintenance schedule by performing all regular maintenance at this time.
- Detail the Bike—All of those protectants, preservatives and waxes have evaporated away by now. Clean and polish the motorcycle again.

If you did not go through a rigorous storage procedure in the fall, shame on you! Perform the following services in addition to those noted above:

- Drain the Fuel System—Get all of the old fuel out of the system. Drain the carburetor bowls, the fuel lines and the tank. Replenish with fresh fuel. If the carburetor floats, jets, needle valves or throttle slides have gummed up during the winter, you may be in for a carburetor rebuild.
- Check the Fuel Tank for Rust—Small flakes of rust can get from the tank, past the filters, to the carburetors where jets can become clogged. If the tank has rusted out, you will need to clean and seal the tank before using it.
- Charge the Battery—If there is any life in the battery at all, it might get you through another summer. Top off the cells with distilled water and properly charge the battery to its full state.
- Lube the Cylinders—Follow the same procedure performed before storage. Pour two tablespoons of fresh engine oil directly into the spark plug ports. This gets extra oil to the upper cylinder area where it has been missing for months. Although you will not get the benefit of the rust protection, starting the bike after months of sitting only makes matters worse if you do not lube the upper cylinder.

There are several tricks you can use to help lubricate the cylinder. For bikes with a kick start, kick the bike over several times with the ignition off. For bikes without an on/off switch, or for bikes where the ignition and kill switch must be on to turn the bike over, put the bike in second or third gear. Then rock the bike back and forth with the throttle wide open. This will force gas into the cylinder, which also helps lubricate. This technique is quite common at racetracks, and especially important for two-strokes.

9

SAFE RIDING

If you remember only three postulates about motorcycle safety, let them be the following:

- Wear a helmet
- Don't drink and drive
- Take a motorcycle safety course

Postulates, however, do not tell the whole story; the devil is in the details. The details are in this chapter.

This chapter begins with basic information about the physics governing motorcycles. Preride preparation is covered next, which involves all those little steps you must perform before you ride if you want to stay in one piece. The remaining chapter covers on-bike riding technique for street, trail and special situations.

THE PHYSICS OF RIDING

Two-wheel transportation is not intuitively natural. There seems no reason for a motorcycle to be stable in motion when it is unstable while standing still. Motorcycles are stable in motion through the observance of several physical principles that govern their operation. These are the principles of gyroscopic forces and of friction. The motorcyclist should be acquainted with these principles. Violation of these principles often results in some sort of mishap.

Gyroscopic Principles

Two-wheeled vehicles stay upright through gyroscopic force. A gyroscope is nothing more than a spinning wheel on a movable axis. The motorcycle's wheels are gyroscopes.

Gyroscopes have interesting properties that do not seem to agree with common sense. First, a gyroscope will maintain its axis of spin. Once a gyroscope is started spinning, it will resist moving off its original plane. You start the bike upright. The gyroscopic force of the wheels keeps the bike upright. The faster the spin, the greater the gyroscopic force. The greater the gyroscopic force, the more stable the motorcycle. Ergo, if other forces such as aerodynamics were not at work on the bike, the faster the bike, the more stable the bike.

Second, if force is applied to turn the axis of a gyroscope, the gyroscope leans as well as turns. If force is applied to lean the gyroscope, the gyroscope turns as well as leans. This property is known as gyroscopic procession. This is how motorcycles are turned at speed. Try this experiment on a bicycle. Have one person hold the bike up. Another spins the front wheel. A third turns the handlebars left. Note how the wheel wants to lean and twist the bicycle frame to one side. This action can also be demonstrated on a moving motorcycle. If you quickly push the handlebar right (or left), you will have changed the axis slightly. According to gyroscopic principles, the bike will lean and go right (or left). This is why you will often hear this statement in a motorcycle safety course, "Push left, go left. Push right, go right."

Third, gyroscopes want to return to their original axis of spin. Once the leaning or turning force applied to the axis is removed, the gyroscope will return to its original plane of spin. This is the force that brings a motorcycle upright coming out of a turn. This is also why, in a turn, you "slow in, accelerate out." In other words, you reduce the forces that keep the bike stable and upright as you go into a turn. As you pull out of the turn, you increase the upright forces.

Principles of Friction

All motorcycle navigation is achieved by controlling the forces at work on the wheel, tire and riding surface. The critical point is the friction point, or "contact patch," where tire meets road. If not for the contact patch, you would have no leverage to manipulate the gyroscopic forces, no ability to force the bike forward and no ability to bring the bike to a stop.

The first systematic analyses of the laws of friction were made by Leonardo da Vinci in the 15th century. The French physicist Charles de Coulomb further advanced da Vinci's work in the 1780s. Friction, as defined by Coulomb in classical mechanics theory, is the resistance to motion which occurs when an attempt is made to slide one surface over another, such as a motorcycle tire over a roadway. The amount of surface adhesion (i.e., friction, traction or "grip") available at the contact patch is numerically stated as the coefficient of traction. When the coefficient of traction is exceeded, the tire slips over the roadway rather than grips it.

Three applied forces work on a tire: driving force, braking force and side force. Driving force is force used to move the bike forward, and is only applied to the rear wheel. Braking force is the force applied to slow the motorcycle. Side force is the force used for turning. Unused traction is the difference between the force applied and the total force that could be applied as dictated by the coefficient of traction. Unused traction is called the "traction reserve." When the bike is at rest and no forces are acting on the tire, the traction reserve equals 100% of the coefficient of traction. As forces are applied, the reserve is reduced as traction is consumed for turning, driving and braking.

The traction reserve is the margin of safety available to make an emergency maneuver. When the traction reserve is equal to zero, adding any additional side, driving or braking force will cause the tires to slip rather than grip, as in these examples:

- When too much acceleration force is applied to the rear wheel, and the coefficient of traction is exceeded, and by definition the traction reserve is reduced to zero, you have what is known in motorcycle vernacular as a "peel out," a "burnout" or "burned rubber." The rear tire slips, spins excessively and smokes, laying down a patch of black rubber on the pavement.
- When too much braking force is applied to either wheel, you have a situation known as a "lock-up." The tires in this situation stop spinning all together and slip over the pavement. Again, a patch of black rubber is often laid on the road.
- When too much turning force is applied, the tires slip out from under the motorcycle in a classic low-side or "wipe out."

In all three situations, however, the rider has lost control of the bike by reducing the traction reserve to zero, or conversely stated, exceeding the coefficient of traction available at the contact patch.

The coefficient of traction varies with the design of the tire and the road surface. Normal street riding on a good tire has a coefficient of approximately 1.0. This means that if a tire is carrying 200 pounds, the amount of force that can be exerted before the tire loses grip on the road is 200×1, or 200 pounds. Mud has a coefficient of about 0.2. Therefore, the amount of force that can be exerted in mud is 200×0.2 = 40 pounds.

So, how are the laws of friction and the coefficient of traction related to the laws of gyroscopic forces? Well, even at very slow speeds, a motorcycle is really never "steered" like a car with the front tire pointing where you want to go. Motorcycles are turned through leaning, and leaning is controlled by a technique called "countersteering." Countersteering is the principle behind "push right, lean right, go right," or "push left, lean left, go left." Although it is true that you move your body and shift your weight to get the motorcycle to lean, without help this amount of force is too small to create anything but a very lazy wide turn. The best way to understand countersteering is to dissect the "push right, lean right, go right" formula.

- Push Right—With the bike going straight ahead, this means push forward on the right handlebar grip. The front tire turns left. Pressing harder will make the motorcycle lean more quickly or at a greater angle, respectively.
- Lean Right—The rest of the motorcycle wants to continue moving straight ahead. Turning the tire to the left also has the effect, using the momentum of the bike, to roll the motorcycle around its center of gravity. This results in the bike leaning to the right.
- Go Right—Gyroscopic procession is the property of a gyroscope that causes it to tilt when an attempt is made to turn its axis, as you have done by pushing right. Steering trail concerns the amount of "rake," or angle, in the steering geometry. As the motorcycle leans, steering trail and gyroscopic procession will force the tire back to the right to follow the geometry of the turn being created by the lean.

Of course, none of this could happen without leverage, and what you leverage against is the contact patch.

STRATEGIC PRERIDE PREPARATION

Motorcycle riders make lots of decisions that affect their riding well before they mount the beast and kick it over. Good decisions, made with full knowledge, make riding safe and enjoyable. Poor decisions, based on folklore and old wives' tales, make riding perilous and agonizing. The marketplace of ideas is full of folklore. Here is what every rider needs to do before riding.

Get Proper Training

Most riders get their training, quite literally, at the school of hard knocks. Training, however, should be under the direction of motorcycle experts. Every motorcycle rider should take a beginning and experienced rider safety class, taught by a certified riding expert. You can find the location of such classes from your local motorcycle dealer, insurance agent, community college or police department. If all else fails, call the Motorcycle Safety Foundation in Irvine, California.

In a beginning riding class, you will learn the basics of motorcycle operation and control. Often, small specially designed motorcycles are provided. A riding course is set up for you to try out various stopping, turning and emergency techniques. You will learn about the local laws governing motorcycle use. The experienced class covers the same material, but more time is spent on the riding course and riders use their own motorcycles.

Aside from your own safety, there's another reason for taking these courses—they can lower your insurance premiums. With premiums commonly over $1,000, the payback can result in substantial savings.

Every time you purchase a motorcycle, review the training material supplied in your rider safety course. Studies show that it is not just new or inexperienced riders who are at high risk, but also those experienced riders with recently acquired (thus unfamiliar) motorcycles.

Helmets

Whenever you are on a bike, wear a helmet. Studies show that helmets reduce head injuries threefold: (1) the hard outer shell resists penetration and abrasion; (2) the inner liner absorbs shock; and (3) most helmets offer some form of shield for eye protection.

The debate concerning mandatory helmet use has raged for years. It centers on the conflict between individual freedom and the cost society pays for disabilities resulting from motorcycle riders who fail to protect their heads. Those against mandatory helmet laws often claim that helmets reduce vision and hearing, which leads to more accidents, and cause spine and neck injuries. The University of Southern California Hurt Report of 1981 (considered the authoritative source by safety experts) concluded that wearing a helmet does not increase the probability of an accident. Hurt also concludes that wearing a helmet does not reduce vision or hearing, or increase the possibility of neck and spine injury in case of an accident.

Although persuasive, the Hurt Report was not conclusive. More recent findings published by Daniel Sosin in the *Journal of the American Medical Association* in 1992 are conclusive. The findings come from a survey of deaths due to motorcycle-associated accidents in the United States between 1979 and 1986. The survey found that:

- Motorcycle deaths resulted primarily from head injuries.
- States with full helmet use laws had fewer deaths resulting from head injuries (47% compared to 56%).
- States that change their laws from full to partial helmet use show significant increases in death due to head injuries. States that change their laws from partial to full helmet use decreased these deaths.

The survey also found that individuals who died in motorcycle accidents had five to six times higher risk of death from a head injury than those who died in other types of motor vehicle accidents. The survey concluded that use of motorcycle helmets decreases the severity of nonfatal head injuries and incidence of fatal head injuries. Helmeted riders have fewer injuries, have less serious injuries, are less likely to have spine and neck injuries and are less likely to die in a motorcycle accident. The use of helmets was strongly recommended.

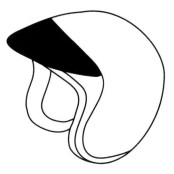

This is not to say that a free society should force motorcycle riders to wear helmets. There is a lot of destructive activity out in the populace that costs society far more than motorcycle riders who do not wear helmets. Alcohol, tobacco and drug abuse are the classic examples. This is only to say that the research implies that wearing a helmet will reduce your injuries if you are in an accident. So, no matter what the laws, wear a helmet. If it happens that you are a Jeffersonian Constitutionalist and you live in a state with a mandatory helmet law, work for its repeal.

The best helmets meet U.S. Department of Transportation (DOT), Snell Memorial Foundation and/or American National Standards Institute (ANSI) standards. DOT sets the minimum standards for helmets sold in the United States. DOT standards cover impact resistance and penetration resistance, chin strap strength and available peripheral vision.

The Snell foundation was established in 1969 to certify full-face helmets. At that time there were no DOT standards for these helmets. Since then both DOT and Snell standards have been broadened and updated. Snell testing attempts to simulate more realistic motorcycle hazards. For example, Snell employs a different penetration test than does DOT. Snell also tests the chin bar in full-face helmets.

ANSI standards were developed by a committee of representatives from consumer groups, helmet manufacturers, testing organizations and the Department of Defense. The standards they developed, ANSI z90.1, are more stringent than the DOT standards but less demanding than the Snell standards.

Helmets come in full-faced, three-quarter, skullcap, "shorty" and motocross varieties. Full-faced and motocross helmets offer the most protection. Full-faced helmets have the advantage of incorporating a

SHORTY HELMET

FULL-FACE MOTOCROSS HELMET

face shield and chin bar. Motocross helmets incorporate the chin bar but are designed to be used with goggles, although motocross helmets with face shields are becoming popular.

A helmet that fits properly is snug, but comfortable. Cheek pads should fit tightly to your face. There should be no gaps at the temples or the brow. A new helmet will fit much tighter than a helmet that has been broken in, so buy a tight helmet. Why do you need a snug fit? The answer is simple: so it won't shake loose while you are riding or if you are in an accident. Your head and helmet should move as one.

If you are in an accident and the helmet is loose, it is almost like having no helmet at all. Take the situation where a Buick Roadmaster pulls out from a blind alley without looking and broadsides you into a telephone pole. Your helmet, if loose, will impact the pole at, say, 40 m.p.h., and then fractions of a second later, your head will impact the helmet at 40 m.p.h. All of the impact protection and most of the impact absorption features of the helmet will be spent at the moment the helmet makes impact with the telephone pole, not at the moment your head makes impact. You might as well have been wearing no helmet at all. Your head and helmet must be one.

A helmet should not exert too much pressure on your skull, causing a "hot spot." These pressure points can be quite painful and cause headaches. If your helmet is causing a hot spot, either you need a larger helmet or a small adjustment needs to be made to the lining. You might place a thin padding of some sort—a folded washcloth or soft sponge —in the top of the helmet. It is also possible to compress the internal liner with a spoon very slightly if there is only one small area giving you a problem. But do very little of this. Too much adjusting can compromise the integrity of the liner.

Helmet sizes are measured several ways: in inches, centimeters, hat size or helmet size. Use the helmet sizing table below to properly fit a helmet. The inch and centimeter measurements are taken around the head one inch above the eyebrows and across the largest portion of the back of the head. Note that different manufacturers use different helmet size systems, so it is best to use head or hat size measurements. But the only way to truly know if a helmet fits right is to try it on.

HELMET SIZE CHART								
Inches	20.5	21.25	22	22.75	23.5	24.5	25.25	26
Centimeters	52	54	56	58	60	62	64	66
Hat Size	6.5	6.75	7	7.25	7.5	7.75	8	8.25
Helmet Size	XXS	XS	S	M	L	XL	XXL	XXXL

The Snell Memorial Foundation makes the following recommendations: (1) always use the chin strap; (2) have the helmet inspected if it ever receives a severe blow; (3) never wear a helmet tilted back; (4) never ride with the helmet strapped to the helmet holder; (5) never hang the helmet on a projection, such as a bike's sissy bar or rearview mirrors, which will damage the soft liner; (6) use only warm water and a few drops of mild cleaner to clean the helmet; (7) replace a helmet that has been damaged.

Helmets need to be replaced about every two to four years because the padding wears out and/or shell integrity is compromised through normal use. Replace any helmet that may have been damaged in an accident or through simple abuse (such as falling off your motorcycle and rolling 120 feet downhill coming to rest under Uncle Phil's Studebaker Superhawk). Unseen cracks developing from these small episodes of abuse can compromise the integrity of the helmet.

Dressing for the Road

The clothes you wear should do four things: (1) protect you from the elements; (2) protect you in a fall; (3) make you more visible; and (4) help you enjoy riding. The following figure shows a well-dressed rider.

Eye Protection—It is wise to use two or more devices for eye protection. A fairing provides good protection. Adjusted correctly it can send rain and bugs over and around you. However, turbulence behind the fairing can direct road grit and bugs to your mouth and eyes. A full-face helmet or a three-quarters helmet with face shield is good protection, but without a fairing or goggles, dirt and insects can still be blown into an eye. Goggles, made with impact-resistant lenses, provide good eye protection, but used alone they do not cover the entire face. Impact-resistant glasses, lacking side protection, are barely adequate but better than nothing.

Jacket & Pants—Despite the season, all skin should be covered by abrasion resistant clothing. That means expensive leather or synthetics made for motorcycle riding. Denim without Kevlar reinforcement is not a good substitute. Denim offers almost no protection against abrasion. But denim is affordable. Sturdy work denim (not fashion denim) is the best of what is available at your local discount department store.

Whatever you wear, the fit should be snug and let you move freely. You want a snug fit so that cool air is not leaking in. You want to move freely so that you can manipulate all of the bike's controls. For this reason, clothing designed for motorcycle riding is a good value for the serious rider. It is designed to fit right, and it offers features for the motorcycle environment. Motorcycle clothing is cut longer in the arms and legs for full protection in the riding position. It offers flaps and adjustments that keep the rain and wind out. It's made of the right materials, and it looks great!

Some motorcycle clothing has special retroreflective stripes or fabric for night riding. These fabrics increase your visibility in daylight, too. It is recommended that you wear over 70 inches of retroreflective material. One of the best high-tech articles of clothing is a lightweight vest with two-inch stripes of retroreflective material running front to back on each side. These vests offer over 100 square inches of reflector and can be worn over any riding apparel.

WELL-DRESSED RIDER

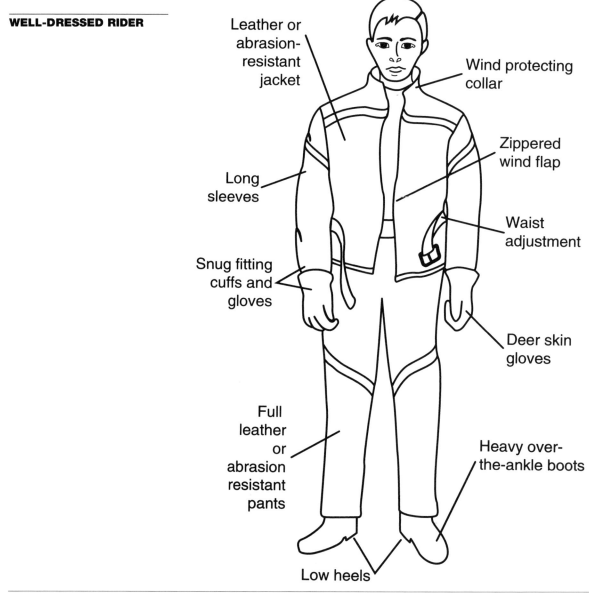

Leather or abrasion-resistant jacket

Wind protecting collar

Long sleeves

Zippered wind flap

Waist adjustment

Snug fitting cuffs and gloves

Deer skin gloves

Full leather or abrasion resistant pants

Heavy over-the-ankle boots

Low heels

A warm, dry rider is much more alert than a cold, wet one. Therefore, in inclement weather, you need clothing that is windproof, waterproof, visible and insulated. Wind- and waterproofing means not only that the elements will not penetrate the fabric, but also that the zippers, cuffs, collars and waistband prevent wind and rain from leaking in. If you do any significant wet weather riding, invest in a rainsuit. These are usually made out of brightly colored PVC plastic or nylon. Not only do rainsuits keep you dry, but their emergency orange or yellow color enhances safety in low visibility weather.

Gloves—Gloves should fit well and be designed specifically for motorcycle riding. This means (1) the stitching will not abrade; (2) the lining will not bunch when the hand is clenching the handle grips; (3) extra leather, studs or other protection devices are strategically placed in the areas most likely to suffer abrasion or impact (e.g., knuckles, palms, topside of fingers); and (4) padding is added to absorb vibration. No gloves should be so bulky that you have trouble operating the controls. Gloves should not contribute to numbness in the fingers or hands, often caused by the glove reducing blood circulation. If you ride in the Yukon, New England or elsewhere in the cold North, you'll need two pairs of gloves, one for summer and one for winter riding. Although high-tech fabric alternatives are widely available, I recommend you buy gloves made out of deer skin or other leather.

Boots—Boots must protect your ankles and shins from road or trail debris, from burns caused by contacting the engine or muffler and from rain and cold. Boots should be waterproof with a steel toe and shank. Get lined boots for cold weather riding. The sole should provide some traction even in oily conditions (such as when you stop at a toll booth). The heel should be short so that it does not catch on road debris or the motorcycle's footpegs. Stilettos are out, ladies.

Packing Loads

No matter how short the trip or small the load, pack properly. Know your bike's rated load capacity, the tires' rated load capacity and how to properly secure a load. The bike's load capacity can be found in your owner's manual. The load capacity of a tire is stamped on the side of the tire. These ratings may not be the same. Never exceed the lesser of the two. Be sure to adjust the suspension (if your bike has adjustable suspension) and tire pressure for the extra weight.

Properly packing the load will ensure that you and the cargo arrive in one piece. It also ensures that a shifting load does not interfere with riding the bike. Load the bike with these rules in mind:

- Pack bags so that contents cannot shift.

- Put the load as close to the rider as possible. Tank bags are good for this.
- Keep loads low, such as with saddlebags.
- Maintain the normal weight distribution. Maintain the normal center of gravity.
- Balance the load. Each side of the bike should carry about the same weight.
- Let the bike do the work. Backpacks should be secured to the bike, not the back of the operator. It is better to let the bike carry the load so that the operator is free to maneuver and is not fatigued by carrying the weight.
- Secure the load. Everything is firmly held in place. Use bungee cords and elastic netting.

Take it slow every time you ride with an extra load. The extra weight can change the handling characteristics of the bike. Increase your margins of safety: ride slower, brake sooner and allow more space between vehicles.

Preparing Passengers

Most states require that your bike be equipped with a passenger seat and buddy pegs to ride two-up. To carry a passenger a long distance, your bike should also have a backrest for the passenger. Inexperienced passengers should be briefed on what to expect, how to ride on the back and how to communicate with the rider. Here are some things passengers should know before mounting the bike:

- Passengers should be properly dressed.
- Do not mount the bike until instructed by the driver.
- Hold firmly onto the driver's waist, hip or belt.
- Keep both feet on the buddy pegs.
- Legs and feet must be kept away from hot components, the drive chain and wheel spokes.
- Lean with the driver, never more or less. A passenger's torso should always line up with the driver's.
- Avoid sudden motions. Even simple arm waving can influence the path of the motorcycle.
- The passenger's helmet can be in the way when the driver looks to his blind spots. The driver is more likely to need to check his left blind spot, so the passenger should favor looking over the driver's right shoulder. If the driver looks left, the passenger should move

his head right. If the driver looks right, the passenger should move his head left.

- Communication with the driver is limited unless you are using an intercom. Work out some rules for communication. This may take a few rides to iron out, but some simple hand signals and an understanding of what is important is sufficient.

Do not take a passenger on your bike until you are adept at solo riding. Passengers change the riding characteristics of the bike. Passengers can also take control of the bike away from you, especially large ones. Further, never carry an intoxicated passenger.

Motorcycle Preride Eight-Point Inspection

Motorcycles are less forgiving than cars when something goes wrong. It is therefore wise to perform a bike safety inspection before each ride. Minor technical failures can be lethal on a motorcycle. Conduct the following eight-point inspection before each ride:

- Lights—Operate all lights. This includes the low beam, high beam, turn signals, taillight, brake light and running lights. When you flip the ignition switch on, be sure all "idiot" lights come on. If one fails to light, it generally means the bulb is blown. Clean any dirty lenses.
- Horn—Sound the horn. Many motorcycles have ineffective, weak horns that are worthless getting someone's attention. If your bike has one of these, replace it.
- Mirrors—Adjust the mirrors so you can see behind you, and as much of each lane next to you, as possible. When properly adjusted a mirror may show the edge of your arm or shoulder. Clean any dirty mirrors.
- Throttle, Clutch and Brakes—Check the action of the levers and pedals. They should operate smoothly. Test the operation of the throttle. Worn throttles may have weak springs that cannot return the throttle from open to closed. These are euphemistically known as "suicide" throttles, with good reason. If you have one, don't ride until it's been fixed.
- Wheels and Tires—Inspect tires for damage, worn tread and invasive foreign objects such as glass and nails. Do this visually and by lightly running your hand over the surface. Check the air pressure. Inspect wheel rims for damage and loose or broken spokes.
- Final Drive—Belts and pulleys on belt drives should be checked for wear and missing teeth. Chains should be inspected for proper lubrication and worn links. Sprockets should be checked for worn or missing teeth.

- Fluids—Check for gas, oil or other fluid leaks. Leaking fluids may accumulate on the ground or on various components of the motorcycle. This could be a sign of trouble. Keep the oil, antifreeze and hydraulic fluids to recommended levels.
- Loose Fittings—Everything on a bike should be held tightly in place. Anything that might fall off or snag could lead to trouble.

Unfamiliar Motorcycle Preride Inspection

As noted in previous chapters, motorcycles have varied designs and characteristics, and what may enhance the skill of one rider may detract from the abilities of another. For example:

- The seat height may be high, making it difficult for a short-legged rider to stop.
- The distance between the footpegs and seat may be short, making the bike difficult for a long-legged rider to turn and uncomfortable on a long run.
- The handlebars may be high and chopped, making steering for anyone but a 6'4" weightlifter difficult.

There are many other examples. Therefore, in addition to making the regular preride inspection, you should acquaint yourself with an unfamiliar bike before hitting the road. The last thing you want to discover on the road is that you don't know where a particular control is located. Or that you can't reach it. Or that you don't know how it works. Or that it takes more strength than you have to operate.

Sit on the bike and observe how the controls are laid out. Study the instrumentation and "idiot" lights. Check the location and operation of the horn, high beam switch, turn signals, engine kill button (i.e., ignition cutoff switch), compression release and ignition. Note the position and action of any options you may use, such as a CB, intercom, cruise control or stereo.

Find the fuel petcock and discover how to move the petcock to reserve. Note the location and action of the front brake lever, clutch lever and rear break pedal. Look for the optional decompression valve lever if you are on a bike with a two-stroke engine. Practice using and adjusting these controls, until you're able to do so without looking.

THE STRATEGY OF ROAD RIDING

Understanding the physics of riding is not enough. Knowing how to properly prepare to ride is not enough. It is important for all motorcycle riders to be familiar with basic safe riding concepts. The following strategies have been tried and tested by professionals. They will work for the average rider if properly followed. However, the following strategies cannot make up for an unsafe motorcycle. Nor can the following strategies make up for the stupidity of the rider. It is best to supplement these strategies with a motorcycle safety course!

The SIPDE Technique

SIPDE is the acronym for Scan, Identify, Predict, Decide, Execute. SIPDE is the mental process suggested by the Motorcycle Safety Foundation for making judgments and taking action when riding a motorcycle.

Scan—Always be looking. Your eyes should follow a standard three-point rotation checking mirrors, controls and ahead. Your eyes should constantly patrol all areas for potential hazards and opportunities.

Scan your rearview mirrors often. Check your mirrors whenever there is the potential for changing speed or lane position. When coming to a stop always scan your mirrors for a driver who may not recognize you are slowing.

Most riders look ahead to where they will be in four or five seconds. This distance is known as your "visual lead." But a four or five second visual lead is not enough. Take a defensive posture and increase your visual lead to 12 or 15 seconds. If, due to twists and bends in the road, you cannot see 12 seconds ahead, slow down. Increase your visual lead in situations that offer few escape routes or present added hazards.

Scan ahead for approaching opportunities, too. Opportunities include areas to pass (or to let people pass you), rest and, in isolated areas, buy gas. Monitoring your fuel supply can be crucial, even in areas that are not isolated. Some motorcycles have less than 100 miles range. When you are in the boondocks, start thinking about gas whenever your tank goes below half full.

Identify—Identify the situation ahead. Does it represent a hazard or an opportunity? The Motorcycle Safety Foundation recommends dividing these hazards into three categories: other vehicles sharing the road, pedestrians and animals, and stationary objects. Each category presents its own unique challenges to the motorcyclist.

Predict—Anticipate the hazard or opportunity. What is the situation going to be like when you come to it? Predict what might happen and visualize escape routes.

Decide—Select a course of action from the available alternatives. Actions include communicating your presence, adjusting your speed, adjusting your course or some combination of the three. These actions are limited by road conditions, the condition of the bike and your skill level.

Execute—Do it. Take the action necessary to avoid the potential hazard. In general, responding to a potential hazard means creating a larger "envelope of safety" around your motorcycle, increasing your visual lead and scanning behind you more often. The "envelope of safety" is the space between you and all vehicles around you. Normal driving conditions require a 2–3 second following distance. This "envelope of safety" should be expanded to 4–5 seconds when following large vehicles, and to at least 6 seconds if the roads are wet. Avoid situations where you find yourself surrounded by truck traffic. Yield to road hogs, hot heads, youth gone wild, blue hairs and other drivers who put you in jeopardy.

Accelerating and Shifting

In physics, acceleration is the rate of change of velocity with respect to time. Torque is defined as the force that produces rotation about an axis. Thus, engine torque is the measurement of the power that creates acceleration. Engines achieve different useful and peak torque levels at different r.p.m. Shifting is how you keep the engine operating in the useful torque range. You must have a "feel" for the torque curve of the motorcycle for efficient and effective accelerating and shifting.

Acceleration from a dead stop requires coordinating the transfer of power from the engine, through the clutch, to the drive train and rear wheel. Too much engine (i.e., excessive throttle) with too much clutch may cause the bike to jump or the rear tire to spin out. Too much engine with too little clutch will burn out the clutch. Too little engine with too much clutch will kill the engine. Incorrect acceleration of any type is very hard on the engine and drive train. Control the flow of power by balancing the engine's r.p.m.s with the degree to which the clutch is engaged. Keep the throttle even, increasing the throttle as the clutch engages.

In general, you want to shift so that you keep the engine's speed high on the ascending side of the torque curve. This is the engine's "sweet spot." This is where there is a good deal of available power at both lower and higher r.p.m.s. If you are running at an engine speed where you still have power for powering out of a bad situation, but also have power if you lose a thousand r.p.m. or two, you are running in the engine's "sweet spot."

Everyone has their own idea of when to shift up and down. Upshifting too early (i.e., at too low a rate of r.p.m.) "lugs" the engine and contributes to overheated valves. Upshifting too late wastes fuel. Upshifting way too late can cause major engine damage (e.g., thrown rods, scored bearings, busted gear teeth) if r.p.m.s reach redline. Within these guidelines rests most of the tachometer and torque curve, so you should never commit these sins.

Downshifting is a bit trickier than upshifting because the throttle action is different. When downshifting, you actually increase the throttle as you release the clutch so not to subject the drive train and engine to a power surge from the rear wheel. This power surge can cause massive bearing failure in large mass engines (mostly older European and American bikes). It is for this reason that downshift points are at lower r.p.m.s than upshift points. For example, you might upshift into fifth at 3,000 r.p.m., but downshift out of fifth at 2,000 r.p.m.

Cornering and Curves

Curves are inherently more dangerous because: (1) the roadway is often obscured; (2) the chosen path through the turn limits escape options; and (3) some traction reserve that would be available for braking or accelerating in a straightaway is being used for turning. It is therefore important to learn proper cornering technique before plowing into a hairpin curve at high speed.

Cornering is deceptively complex. Decide as soon as possible the line (a.k.a route) you will take through the curve. Then "set up" the turn by taking the best position from which to attack the curve. Setting up a turn involves moving the bike to the right side of the lane on a left-hand turn, and the left side of the lane on a right-hand turn. This gives the best view of what is ahead and puts you at the best angle from which to assault the curve.

Once in the turn, you want to follow a path with the greatest possible radius for the smoothest possible turn. In a constant-radius turn, the apex is at midpoint of the turn. For example, on a right turn, move to the left of the lane, come in to the right side of the lane as you reach the middle of the turn, and then move back to the left as you complete the turn. In an increasing-radius turn, where the turn starts tight but opens up, the apex is before the midpoint of the turn. In a decreasing-radius turn, a turn that become tighter as it progresses, the apex is after the midpoint of the turn. When in the turn, always look ahead to where you want to go. This is known as "looking through the turn."

A good rule of thumb is: slow in, accelerate out. Reduce your speed before going into the turn. Gradually accelerate as you come out of the turn. Deceleration while in the turn can destabilize the motorcycle.

Another good rule of thumb is: start wide, go in close, come out wide. As you go into the turn start on the outside of the curve, or "wide." Lean the motorcycle inside, bringing the bike "close" to the apex of the turn. Exit the turn by moving to the outside and accelerating.

Remember to lean. Motorcycles are cornered primarily by leaning, not steering. Push right, lean right, go right. Push left, lean left, go left. The tighter the turn or the faster your speed, the more you must lean. Lean your entire body with the motorcycle in a fast turn. Lean only the motorcycle in slow turns, keeping your body upright.

One of the most common errors riders make is giving up on a turn too early. Modern motorcycle tires offer a tremendous amount of cornering capability. Usually you will be scraping a footpeg before you have the bike leaning beyond the traction reserve of the tires. In other words, if you find that you have taken a turn much too fast, hang in there and lean the bike harder. Push the tires to the limits of the bike's capability and the limits of your skill. You will find that trusting the technology can get you out of bad situations. Of course, you must later reconsider how you got into a bad situation in the first place, and avoid making that mistake again.

A quick series of two or three turns in order to avoid an impediment or hazard is called a "swerve." For example, push hard right, go hard right. Then quickly push hard left, and go hard left. Swerving is a good skill to learn since this is how you avoid many sudden road hazards.

Braking

You will often hear heroic stories of the dare devil motorcyclist who says, "Car pulled out in front of me so I had to put it down!" These riders are talking about putting the entire side of the motorcycle down on the pavement to stop the bike before it collides with a car. They often command a good deal of folk hero status among motorcycle buffs and groupies, but in fact these guys are dimwits. Think about it. What is going to stop faster? Metal on asphalt or rubber on asphalt? Rubber will win out every time. Straight-line stopping using good braking techniques will slow the bike faster and bring it to a stop in a shorter distance than any other technique. Anyone who "puts the bike down" hits whatever they hit needlessly or at greater speed than if they simply kept the bike up and applied good braking technique.

Slowing the bike is accomplished by increasing the drag on the front and rear wheel. Drag can be increased by allowing the engine's natural drag to transfer to the rear wheel (through deceleration and downshifting) and by applying the front and rear brakes.

Engine drag is best used when only moderate slowing is required or on long downhills where the brakes can overheat. Four-stroke engines are not harmed by this action. Two-strokes, however, should only be used in this manner for very short periods if not equipped with a decompression valve.

There is international disagreement about how to brake in an emergency. Some countries teach that you apply the rear brake first to stretch and lower the suspension. The U.S. method is to apply the front brake just a quarter count before the rear wheel. Slowly reduce pressure as you come to a stop. The direction of force when braking increases front tire grip, so the front brake has about 70% of the total stopping power of the motorcycle.

Don't lock up either wheel. Locking a wheel can be a major emergency on a motorcycle. The proper reaction to a front wheel lockup is totally different from a rear wheel lockup. Locking the front wheel reduces the bike's navigation capacity to zero. If the front wheel locks, instantly disengage and re-engage the brake quickly and repeatedly.

A rear wheel lockup is more common and not nearly as dangerous as it may seem. The tail of the bike will fishtail left and right when the rear tire is locked. Ride it out. A firm grip on the handlebars will allow you to keep the bike under control and in a straight line. Do not release the rear brake! Releasing the rear brake frees the rear wheel to roll. The rear wheel will roll in the direction it faces, which, during fishtailing, most likely is not in the same direction as the front wheel. The bike will jackknife, sending the motorcycle end-over-end.

Locking a wheel is more common in a turn since less traction reserve is available for stopping. There are also fewer opportunities to make corrective action while turning, so a lockup is extremely dangerous. Be cautious when braking during a turn. Avoid braking while swerving. Brake immediately before and after a swerve.

BRAKING DISTANCE

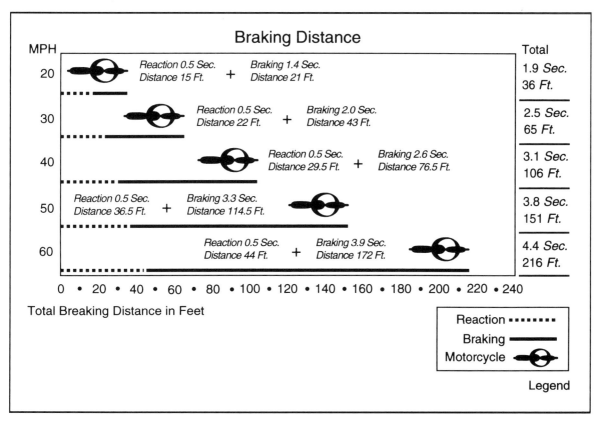

Braking with only the rear wheel may be necessary under certain conditions. For example, when the front wheel is not straight, applying the front brake may cause the front wheel to skid. Another example is when loose gravel covers the road but you must slow rapidly.

The chart on the preceding page shows the average braking distance for a well-maintained bike at a given speed. But road conditions can increase these distances; for example, wet road conditions can increase braking distances 300%. Water on the road reduces the coefficient of traction, so you cannot apply your brakes as hard as when the surface is dry. Water also increases braking distances if the water gets on the brake pads. Just as there is less friction on a wet road, there is less friction on a wet brake rotor. Water can be purged from the disc by periodically applying the brake delicately.

Lane Positioning

Traffic lanes are about 12 feet wide. From a motorcyclist's perspective, the lane is divided into three sections each four feet wide: left, middle and right. The following illustrates these sections. The middle third is that meaty third of the roadway generally designated by an oil slick created from years of dripping fluids from passing vehicles.

There is some debate about lane positioning among the experts. Some say that, all things being equal, a motorcyclist should ride in the left third. Others advocate riding in the middle third just left of the oil slick. But there is agreement that a rider should keep to the left when given a choice.

THREE LANE SECTIONS

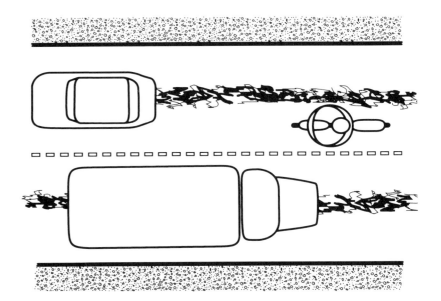

There are many reasons for riding on the left, whether in the middle of the left third of the lane, or left of the middle in the middle third of the lane. First, this is where you can see the most. Second, this is where you can most easily be seen. Third, this offers you the greatest number of avenues for escape since you have paved areas to both your left and right. Fourth, this is where you have the most time to react to hazards (such as bicyclists or small, yappy black dogs) coming from either curb.

But you will not always ride in the left position. You will move from the left position to set up a turn, view something up the road that represents a potential hazard, let another driver see you or avoid a hazard. For example, a car driver entering from the right may not notice you behind a van. If you can make yourself known to the car driver by moving right for a brief period, do so. Or, if an oncoming Freightliner is plowing a huge wake of wind, you can avoid the worst of the blast by moving right.

Respect, but do not fear the oil slick. Dangerous oil buildup is rare. In dry weather, the slick itself provides sufficient traction and can be ridden on safely in most instances.

Significant oil and grease accumulations occur where traffic stops, such as at intersections and toll booths. Be extremely cautious at toll booths! Often large, deep lakes of oil can be seen. The oil slick is also wide, virtually the entire width of the lane. When stopping to pay the toll, you may not find the traction you expect when you put your foot down. When you leave the booth, drive away slowly and cautiously. You may find that the tires have received a coating of oil and do not grip as well as they should. You may also find that your soles are coated with oil and do not grip the footpegs, brake lever or road surface well.

Passing

Passing is a four-step procedure. First, establish your pre-pass position in the left third of the lane, scan in front and check your rearview mirror. Second, identify a good passing opportunity. Third, when the opportunity arises, signal your intentions, check your mirror and left blind spot, and move into the middle of the left lane while accelerating. Fourth, after passing the vehicle, signal right, check your right blind spot and return the original lane.

Not all motorcycles are capable of passing at high speeds. Some smaller motorcycles are not capable of even low speed passing. The Passing figure illustrates the distances covered for both a high speed and low speed pass. For this example, a high speed pass is defined as a pass where the initial speed is 50 m.p.h. and the terminal speed is 80 m.p.h. How your motorcycle performs depends on many things, such as your motorcycle's ability to go from 50 m.p.h. to 80 m.p.h. But, for the purposes of this example, assuming an average 350cc motorcycle, and

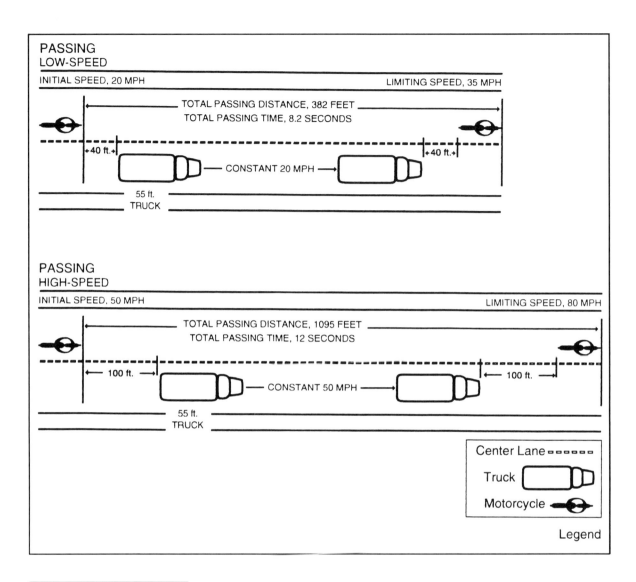

PASSING
LOW-SPEED

INITIAL SPEED, 20 MPH

LIMITING SPEED, 35 MPH

TOTAL PASSING DISTANCE, 382 FEET
TOTAL PASSING TIME, 8.2 SECONDS

40 ft.

40 ft.

CONSTANT 20 MPH

55 ft.
TRUCK

PASSING
HIGH-SPEED

INITIAL SPEED, 50 MPH

LIMITING SPEED, 80 MPH

TOTAL PASSING DISTANCE, 1095 FEET
TOTAL PASSING TIME, 12 SECONDS

100 ft.

100 ft.

CONSTANT 50 MPH

55 ft.
TRUCK

Center Lane

Truck

Motorcycle

Legend

PASSING

an average passing speed of 65 m.p.h., a high speed pass will cover about 1,100 feet and require about 12 seconds to complete. A low speed pass is defined as a pass where the initial speed is 20 m.p.h. and the terminal speed is 35 m.p.h. Assuming that the motorcycle is a typical 125cc bike, a low speed pass covers about 400 feet and takes about 8 seconds to execute.

When passing or being passed, there is generally a large wake of air turbulence being plowed by many large vehicles. This turbulence is strong enough to push even small cars out of the lane. Anticipate the wake.

ADVERSE RIDING CONDITIONS

Motorcyclists face many more adverse riding conditions than motorists. A full list is impossible to compile, but night riding, inclement weather, long downhills, intersections, older drivers, and animals represent six unique situations for the motorcyclist. The general rules about adverse riding conditions apply to any situation that represents increased riding risk. These are:

- Reduce speed
- Expand the envelope of safety
- Increase your visual lead

Above and beyond these general rules, here are some suggestions for handling the dark, the storms, the long inclined plane, intersections, blue hairs and Rover.

Night Riding

Night riding is the most enjoyable riding around. There is less traffic. The sights are glorious. The air seems cleaner, more aromatic. The sounds are thick and sensuous. You make better time. But night riding offers four additional risks not present during the daytime:

First, and most obvious, you can see less due to reduced natural light. Contrasts are less obvious, making road debris and other hazards difficult if not impossible to see. Even with your headlight, your ability to see is cut by up to 50%.

Second, your visual lead is cut. Headlights illuminate about 220 feet in front of the motorcycle. It is very easy to override the visual lead provided by your headlight. Under prefect conditions going 60 m.p.h., you need 220 feet to stop. Anything beyond 220 feet will not be visible to you. This means that you will just barely have enough time to react should an emergency situation develop, if you instantly SIPDE.

Third, it is easy for an oncoming driver to lose your headlight or tail lamp among the other night lights. So, you do not want to rely solely on your lights to make yourself visible and obvious to other drivers. Always ride with brightly colored and retroreflective clothing at night.

Finally, there are other hazards at night. More fatigued drivers are on the road. More drunk drivers are on the road. Road grime on fairings and goggles can make seeing into lights more difficult. The list goes on.

Inclement Weather

Rain, wind and cold weather present unique hazards to the motorcyclist, as noted below:

WIND CHILL CHART

Wind Speed (m.p.h.)	Actual Thermometer Reading Fahrenheit											
	50	40	35	30	25	20	15	10	5	0	−5	−10
	Equivalent Temperature Fahrenheit "Wind Chill Factor"											
calm	50	40	35	30	25	20	15	10	5	0	−5	−10
5	48	37	30	27	20	16	10	6	0	−5	−10	−15
10	40	28	20	16	10	4	0	−9	−15	−21	−25	−33
15	36	22	15	9	0	−5	−10	−18	−25	−36	−40	−45
20	32	18	10	4	0	−10	−15	−25	−30	−39	−45	−53
25	30	16	10	0	−5	−15	−20	−29	−35	−44	−50	−59
30	28	13	5	−2	−10	−18	−25	−33	−40	−48	−55	−63
35	27	11	5	−4	−10	−20	−30	−35	−40	−49	−60	−67
40	26	10	0	−6	−15	−21	−30	−37	−45	−53	−60	−69
Wind speeds greater than 40 m.p.h. have little added effect	Little danger for properly clothed rider						Increasing danger—exposed flesh may freeze within one minute.					

Rain—Rain reduces the traction coefficient of the road surface, tripling braking distances. The first few minutes of a rainstorm are the most dangerous. Rain lifts and spreads accumulated road oil. Until this oil is washed away, the entire road surface is one massive oil slick. Rain makes markings painted on the road as slick as ice. It makes railroad tracks, which are a trick to cross in good weather, as slick as wet painted roadway markings. Periodically check your brakes in wet weather. This means lightly applying them to be sure they still grip. Do this especially after going through a large puddle or stream.

Wind—Sudden wind, like the air blast from an oncoming truck, can toss a motorcycle from side-to-side. A really strong blast can put you in the ditch!

Cold—Cold weather also creates surface hazards. Bridge surfaces often collect moisture that freezes before roadway surfaces.

But perhaps the greatest danger of rain, wind and cold weather is hypothermia. Hypothermia is the condition when human body temperature drops so low the body can no longer warm itself. Hypothermia is insidious. It quickly results in the loss of coordination. Conditions need not be extreme for hypothermia to develop. The same air that cools the engine also cools your body. This cooling effect of air passing over a warm body, whether the body be an engine or a human, is called "wind chill." Wind chill is one measurement of the danger represented by wind and cold. There is a direct relationship between wind chill and hypothermia. Unhealthy wind chill conditions increase the chance of a rider suffering from hypothermia.

The chart on the facing page shows the wind chill equivalents for a given wind speed and temperature. For example, when riding in 50°F weather at a speed of 40 m.p.h., the wind chill equivalent is 26°. This means that your body is losing heat riding at the same rate it would lose standing still in 26°F. If you do any significant cold weather riding, consider buying a riding suit designed to protect from wind chill.

Wet weather exacerbates wind chill conditions. Water conducts heat 25 times faster than air. Most cold weather clothing relies on trapped air pockets for insulation. If water replaces the air, the insulating properties of the clothing is lost and heat is conducted rapidly from the body.

Long Downhills

Long and/or steep grades present hazards to motorcycles operating under full load conditions. Roadside warning diamonds often mark these grades. The warning diamond tells you two things: the grade, expressed in percent and the length of the grade.

The grade percent on the warning diamond tells you how fast the slope is falling. A 5% grade falls five feet for every 100 feet you drive. Grades less than 5% are generally not marked on well-designed roads like freeways, unless the grade is extremely long. A 10% grade, which is extremely steep, falls 10 feet for every 100 feet you drive. Roads with grades greater than 10% can feel unnatural to drive, such as the famous streets of San Francisco, some of which have grades that exceed 20%.

These factors create the potential for building up excessive speed. Controlling this speed can cause excessive heat to build-up in the brakes. When overheated, brake pads and shoes can fade, losing their ability to slow the motorcycle. Severely overheated brakes can fail totally. To reduce the chance of brake fading or failure, use engine drag on long downhills to slow the motorcycle. Shifting to third or lower and periodically braking should be enough to control your motorcycle's speed.

In a brake fading emergency caused by overheating, pump the brakes to regain braking power. Pumping the brakes helps to cool the brakes while still slowing the motorcycle. Fading brakes often recover if cooled. Brakes that have totally failed will not recover by pumping since total failure is usually due to the pad or shoe coming unglued. If your brakes have failed, try downshifting further. If the bike has an engine "kill" switch, turn the switch off to increase engine drag. In a worse case scenario, many mountain roads have runaway truck ramps that you can use. However, these ramps are often filled with gravel. Gravel is good for stopping trucks, but crummy for stopping motorcycles.

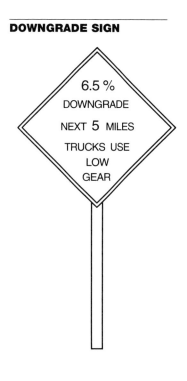

DOWNGRADE SIGN

6.5 %
DOWNGRADE
NEXT 5 MILES
TRUCKS USE
LOW
GEAR

Intersections

Sixty-six percent of accidents involving motorcycles colliding with other vehicles are the fault of the other vehicles. Car drivers contribute to another 10% of motorcycle accidents by unintentionally forcing a motorcycle out of its lane. Intersections are where most of this action takes place.

The most common car/motorcycle accidents happen at in-town intersections where a car turns left in front of a motorcycle (known as "T-boning" in motorcyclist vernacular). As the more vulnerable, a motorcyclist must pay special attention at intersections and in situations when cars are turning or changing lanes. Be sure the other drivers see you! Wear bright clothes, run with the high beam on during daylight and select a lane position where other drivers can see you.

Blue Hairs and Q-tips

We will all be old and gray some day. Lord help us to meet the challenges of old age with grace and dignity. But the reality of the older driver is this: Older eyes have a difficult time focusing and adjusting from near to far. For example, it takes older eyes an extra second after scanning the speedometer to see and interpret road conditions near and then road conditions in the distance. It also takes an older driver an extra second to interpret the scene when scanning from one side to the other. These second delays, along with reduced physical reaction capabilities, make older drivers more dangerous to the motorcycle rider. Watch for older drivers. Give them a wide berth and pleasant smile. Help them along their way in a courteous manner. Treat them with the respect any tribal elder deserves. And, as with any other driver, when they mess up, let them know it.

Animals of Field and Air

Animals represent a unique problem to the motorcyclist. Some animals panic when they hear your motorcycle and run into your path. At night, some animals become hypnotized by headlights and will not move out of your path. Some animals are attracted to the motorcycle, such as dogs. If a small animal is in your path, and you cannot avoid it without endangering human life, it is better to hit the small animal. However, it can be fatal to hit a larger animal, such as deer, moose, cow or water buffalo.

Dogs are of special concern given their large number and disquieting temperament. Some dogs simply must attack any two-wheeled vehicle. It's a karma thing, their purpose in life. The best stratagem is to feint and throttle. Go slowly and steer slightly toward the animal, changing the dog's line of attack away from your intended course of travel. As you reach the perpetrator, turn and speed away.

Do not attempt to kick or strike an animal that is threatening you. This is quite dangerous. Not only might the animal inflict some harm to your arm or leg, you may lose control of the motorcycle. It is also bad public relations. Citizens have a low enough opinion of motorcyclists without believing that motorcyclists are out to kill Benji or Lassie (or Flipper or Bambi).

TOURING AND GROUP RIDING TECHNIQUES

Motorcycle touring along the back routes and old highways is a great way to get to know a land and its people. Motorcycle touring is nothing like car touring. Motorcycle touring is a vastly more rich and robust experience. On a motorcycle, you experience the land and environment. You see much more of it. You feel and smell it. In a car, you are separated from the land—cramped, enclosed and isolated from the outside world.

Touring

Planning and preparation are key to any motorcycling situation. If you have a destination in mind, establish a detailed route plan and timetable. Your route plan should include important road markers before, at and after important junctions. This will not only help you know where to turn in advance, it will help you know when you have gone too far. Your timetable should include planned rest stops, gas stops and breaks for roadside attractions. The timetable should also take daylight hours into consideration. If the roads are poorly maintained or the weather threatening, you may want to avoid driving at night.

Even if you have not planned a destination or picked a route, you still must plan for the conditions you expect to encounter. In some outland areas the weather can change in a matter of minutes from sunshine to rain, fog or blizzard. If severe conditions are possible, take along provisions that would be necessary if you get stranded, such as blankets and food.

Part of your plan should be to start out fresh. Do not drive when tired or fatigued. You must be alert and observant when driving in new territory. To start out fresh, pack the night before. To stay fresh, take a 15-minute off-the-bike break every two hours or whenever you gas up.

Many people plan too much riding on their trips. We have all heard about the "Iron Butt" awards for guys who try to go 1,000 miles in a day. It is hard on the body and spirit to average over 45 m.p.h when touring, unless you are on interstate highways the entire way. But even on the interstates it is hard to average more than 55 m.p.h. Plan accordingly.

Group Riding

Touring is even more fun in a group. When touring in a group, stagger your riding position, as shown in the next figure. The first rider leads the group by riding in the left section of the lane. The second rider takes the right section of the lane. The third rider rides in the left section again, providing a two second riding cushion between himself and the first rider.

This staggered technique does two things. First, compared to riding in single file, it allows the riders in the back to see farther up the road without the riders in the front totally obstructing the view. Second, compared to riding two abreast, this technique provides each rider with the most area for emergency maneuvers.

Never bunch up. Never ride two abreast. Always leave yourself and the other guy a full lane to use if an obstacle or hazard must be avoided. This has special significance when passing other vehicles. When in the staggered formation, the lead motorcycle should be about two seconds riding time behind the vehicle to be passed. After the lead rider passes, the riders behind the vehicle he just passed move up one position in the riding formation. Bikes that were on the outside of the lane (in the right third of the lane) now move over to the inside of the lane (the left third) and the inside riders move outside. The new lead bike establishes a position two seconds behind the vehicle to be passed, and makes his pass when safely possible. As he falls in behind the first rider, he takes proper group riding position in the right third of the lane. This procession continues until all riders have passed the vehicle.

STAGGERED RIDING

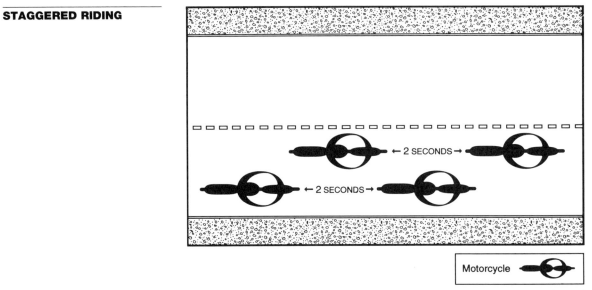

Legend

It is critical to treat any motorcycle like any other vehicle you might pass. Do not assume that the motorcycle rider you are passing sees you. Never pass him on the right third of the lane.

TRAIL RIDING STRATEGIES

Trail riding requires all of the skills that street riding requires, and more. Here are some pointers for trail riding.

Keep Your Equipment in Top Shape

It is obvious that the bike should be in top shape with no questionable running characteristics or weak links. Breaking down along the AlCan highway or deep in the Sierras may mean abandoning the bike . . . forever. And nothing destroys your buddy's Saturday fun more than when your bike breaks down.

Trail bikes require much more attention to maintenance and repair since they are subject to so much more punishment than street bikes. (Hard ridden bikes need engine rebuilds and suspension rebuilds after only a half dozen races.) Do not wait for the bike to show signs of fatigue, failure or wear. Clock your hours trail riding and replace or repair parts accordingly. Since you will never be any better rider or any safer rider than the bike allows, always keep the bike in top shape.

Keep Your Body in Top Shape

It should be obvious that trail riding is physically brutal. If you ride correctly, your bike, and not your body, will take the pounding of the trail. On the trail you will constantly stand on the bike's footpegs. Your arms and legs will manhandle the bike and prevent the shock of the trail from reaching your body and brain. You must often lift the front tire on the approach to a hazard, toss or bounce the bike left or right around a hazard, and hang on for dear life or lose control of the bike. Therefore, you must be in good physical shape.

Keep Your Mind in Top Shape

The mental demands of trail riding are just as great as the physical demands. Hundreds of snap decisions are made over each mile. Your brain is constantly SIPDEing. Be rested. Be sober.

Dress for the Trail

Not all trail riders wear proper protective gear. This is foolish. Safe riding is also more enjoyable riding. At a minimum you must wear the following:

- Helmet—preferably a full-face trail helmet
- Eye protection—goggles are the only acceptable protection. More debris is thrown at your face during one day on the trail than one year on the street. This debris comes from all directions and it all seems to be aimed at your eyes. Odds are, one or two of these projectiles will be bull's-eyes.
- Boots—all leather, steel shank and steel toe
- Gloves—leather with brush protection devices sewn on

TRAIL DRESS

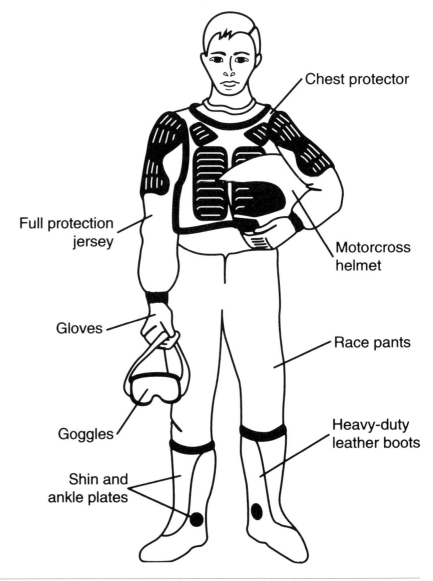

Chest protector

Full protection jersey

Motorcross helmet

Gloves

Race pants

Goggles

Heavy-duty leather boots

Shin and ankle plates

- Jersey and jeans—long sleeve jersey and sturdy jeans. No shorts.
- Chest protector—flexible body armor.

Good Trail Technique

Trail riding requires the constant shifting of weight from front-to-back and side-to-side. Radical terrain requires adjusting the traction applied at each tire while minimizing the impact and danger of each obstacle. Here are a few tips for riding the range:

Keep the r.p.m.s up—In most situations you want to be able to harvest instant power from the engine. This means knowing the bike's power curve and keeping the engine operating within its "sweet spot." If this means downshifting, downshift! If this means running for long periods in second gear, run long periods in second gear. Trail bikes are designed for high r.p.m., low speed riding.

Sand and mud—In sand and mud you need to maintain momentum and power. Often your momentum helps lift you on top of and through sand and mud. Smaller bikes may not have the power to go through large mud holes or sand pits, so you will need to either go around or walk out (which is very humiliating).

Ruts—Riding over a rut or a series of ruts is made easier on the rider by lifting the front wheel before the rough spot and carrying the wheel over the rut. For a series of ruts, get up on the pegs and shift your weight to the rear wheel. If you get in a rut, ride it out. Trying to cut up the side of a rut can be difficult to impossible. The front tire often gets out, but not the back, causing the bike to sidewind and buck.

Water—Many a trail rider has lost his bike to unfamiliar water. Inspect any new water situation before attempting to cross. Slow water often runs deep. Fast moving water is often the most shallow. You may have to ride along the bank until you find a spot providing a good straight crossing with good access and exit.

Experts say the best way to cross short water is to wheelie across. This keeps water off the rider and keeps the front brake dry. If it's too great a distance, it's best to transfer weight to the rear wheel and keep a constant pace while crossing.

Obstacles—Items such as rocks and logs should be avoided. If you cannot avoid them, try to lift the front wheel over the obstacle and power the back wheel over. If you must hit the item, hit it square and near the middle so you are less likely to be tossed from the bike and the object is less likely to snap up and hit you.

Good Trail Etiquette

Trail riding is under increased scrutiny as the sport grows and land for the sport diminishes. It is important that trail riders follow some basic rules. Disregard for these rules by trail riders has tarnished the off-road sport, and resulted in further restrictions on areas where outdoor recreation vehicles (ORVs) can be used. If this keeps up, no land will be available for dirt riding. Tread lightly and follow these tips.

Travel only where permitted—Take your bike only into areas where ORVs are permitted. Be aware that some areas may be open only certain times of the year. Some areas may be closed temporarily due to environmental damage, fire hazard or industrial operations (e.g., logging, mining). Do not assume that an area that was open to you last spring is still open to you today. Check it out with local authorities, first.

Use a proper muffler—The muffler should limit the exhaust noise to 105 decibels measured 20 inches from the exhaust. Many riders do not want a muffler. They still believe the old wives' tale that a muffler hurts performance. This is no longer true. Modern motorcycles work best when back pressure is controlled. A straight pipe, or simply louder pipes, will not improve stock performance. Straight pipes are very annoying to other riders and other users of the forest. Loud motorcycles also traumatize wildlife and farm animals. The stress brought on by their fear of your motorcycle can kill them.

Use a proper spark arrestor—Most trail bikes incorporate a Forest Service–approved spark arrestor. Exhaust sparks are bits of super-heated carbon that, when ejected from the tail pipe, can start a fire. Given that the lives of so many animals and the livelihoods of so many people depend on the forest, never ride without a spark arrestor. They do not reduce power! Factory-equipped enduro bikes come with spark arrestors. Bikes designed for competition motocross do not.

Pack it out empty—It is an old woodsman's saying that if you can pack it in full, you can pack it out empty. Take your trash out of the forest when you leave. Maybe take out trash left by some slob from last week, too.

Respect public and private land—Unless you personally have permission from the owner to ride on private land—don't! If you do have permission, respect the owner and the land. If it is public land, know that you are not the only "owner." Treat the land as if it belongs to someone else. It does. ORV owners have for a long time taken the attitude that public land is for them to use as they please. The result has been an onslaught of legislation restricting ORV access to public lands.

Ride at a safe speed—Keep speeds below 25 m.p.h.

Lights—Run with your lights on at all times, if your bike is so equipped.

Be "trail legal"—Some states require that your motorcycle have certain equipment, such as spark arrestors, mufflers, lights and a trail permit (different from a license to ride on public roads) to legally ride on their trails. Note that some Forest Service and park roads are public roads. Your motorcycle must be street legal to use these roads!

Stay out of environmentally fragile areas—Staying on the main trail is the best way to reduce your impact on the environment. The best way to stay on the main trail is to consult a topographical map of the area. But a map is not required to recognize areas that are environmentally sensitive and where you should not ride. Avoid running over young trees, shrubs and grasses. Cross streams only at designated areas. Stay off soft roads and trails. Travel around (not through) meadows, steep hillsides, stream banks, spawning grounds, lakeshores, wetlands and estuaries. Do not bushwhack new trails or short circuit switchbacks. Obey regulatory signs. Obey gate closures. Do no vandalism. Stay out of wilderness areas; these areas are closed to all vehicles. Repairing the damage is expensive, and the taxpayer takes note of this.

Respect the rights of other users—Hikers, skiers, campers and others have just as much right to the outdoors as you do. Respect their rights. Their love for their land is as great as yours, and they vote. When you meet others on the trail, do the courteous thing and yield the right-of-way to them. Pull off and stop your engine. This is particularly true for horseback riders.

Purchase your ORV tags—Even if your bike does not need to be street legal, your state may operate an off-road vehicle tag program. The program helps pay for the maintenance and development of off-road vehicle parks and education programs. Buy your tags.

Violating any of these rules may not have any consequences. On the other hand, it may result in a hefty ticket from a state trooper or local sheriff. It may result in ORV riders losing the right to ride in certain areas through legislative action taken by irate campers and nature lovers. Violating these rules may also result in confiscation of your bike by an irate private landowner wielding a two-barrel shot gun filled with rock salt.

Preparing for Hitting the Trail

Proper preparation for the day's riding can make a big difference between having a good time or having a life-threatening experience. Here are some preparation tips:

Prepare for the day—Check the weather. Know the riding conditions. Know the terrain and plan the route. Let the home folks know your ride plan. Make sure your riding buddies know this information as well.

Go in a group—Do not ride alone. Trail riding is inherently risky. You don't want to be alone 12 miles into the wilderness with a flat tire or broken femur. At least one member of the group should be trained in standard first aid and adult cardiopulmonary resuscitation.

Know the route—If you are going into new territory, plan a slower ride. Take time to get to know the area your first time through.

Prepare for the worst—Carry enough tools and spare parts to handle common mechanical failures. Take along a few emergency supplies in the event you must stay the night in the wilderness. This means a small shelter device, tools to make a fire and a first aid kit.

Perform a preride inspection—Inspect your machine before you leave home, as noted in this chapter. Inspect it again at the trail head. Make sure everything works. Check your fuel supply.

RIDING IMPAIRMENTS

The three most common impairments to safe riding are alcohol, drugs and fatigue. They result in the vast majority of fatal accidents, and are all within your control.

Alcohol

Alcohol's primary effect on the body is to distort judgment. Secondly, it impairs vision and small muscle movement. These impairments make riding a motorcycle safely virtually impossible. It is little wonder then that 50% of all fatal motorcycle accidents involve alcohol.

In most states, a person with a blood alcohol content of .10% is legally intoxicated. Some states put this limit at .08%. But your riding capabilities will be affected long before you are legally intoxicated. Even low levels of alcohol will reduce your ability to scan the environment. Alcohol reduces night vision. It reduces your ability to recognize moving objects. It interferes with your coordination, inhibits your sense of balance and slows your reaction times.

Drugs

Drugs, legal and illicit, also impair a rider's ability. Over-the-counter and prescription drugs often come with user warnings against operating machinery when taking the medication. Follow this advice. Even drugs considered by some to be "harmless" (e.g., marijuana, antihistamines) can impair visual cognition and reduce reaction time.

Fatigue

There are more collisions during evening rush hour traffic than during the comparable morning rush hour. This may be due to fatigue. A fatigued driver is less alert, more irritable and more likely to make rash decisions. If you are tired, take it slow. If you are exhausted, stop and get some rest.

10

THE SIX MOST COMMON PURCHASES

Every time you buy something for your motorcycle, whether it's gasoline, chain lube or #1 white carnauba paste wax, you are making a decision that makes a big difference in terms of bike cost, performance and life expectancy. Knowing what you are buying will maximize your enjoyment and minimize the cost of owning a motorcycle. The most common purchases are gas, oil, tires, roller chains, spark plugs and batteries.

This chapter provides the motorcycle consumer with the knowledge to make better purchases. The intent is not to detail every step for performing a specific task. Maintenance and repairs performed by the uninitiated or uninformed can result in financial loss, injury or death. If you plan to do your own repairs:

- Buy a repair manual
- Purchase the right tools
- Purchase high-quality American tools
- Read the directions

If in doubt, pay a pro to do the job right the first time.

GASOLINE

Given that gasoline is purchased almost daily, a great deal of attention should be given to this purchase. Some motorcycles run well on any fuel. (My grandfather ran a 1963 step-through Honda Trail 90 on turpentine.) Others will spit and sputter on all but the most expensive hi-test. When purchasing gasoline, you should be concerned about:

- Detergents
- Alcohol
- Volatility
- Octane
- Lead
- Contaminants

Gasoline Detergents

Detergents in gasoline bond with contaminants, preventing the dirt from bonding to the engine or fuel system components. The critical areas where dirt is likely to build up are at the fuel injector nozzle and carburetor jets. To prevent dirt build up, detergents are added to gasoline.

Not all gasolines have enough detergent agents to prevent clogged fuel injectors or carburetors. The only current standard for testing gasoline detergents is the BMW valve test. This test measures the deposits on engine valves after 10,000 miles. If the gasoline passes the BMW valve test, it has plenty of detergents in it. The only way to know is to ask at the service station.

Gasoline Alcohol

To reduce the amount of imported oil, and to increase octane, refineries blend gasoline with alcohol. For years this fuel has been called gasohol. Now there is a new alcohol fuel being sold in metropolitan areas suffering significant air pollution problems. This fuel is called "oxygenated" fuel to distinguish it from gasohol.

Oxygenated fuel is gasoline mixed with either ethanol or methyl tertiary butyl ether (MTBE). The major difference between gasohol and oxygenated fuel is that oxygenated fuel has no more than 10% alcohol content, while fuel sold as gasohol may have up to 40% alcohol content. Many motorcycles run well on gasohol fuels while others get cranky and pout.

Alcohol: (1) increases the octane rating of the fuel, reducing knock and ping; (2) adds oxygen to the combustion formula, causing cleaner combustion; (3) vaporizes earlier; (4) requires a lower air/fuel ratio than gasoline; (5) acts as a fuel system cleaning agent; and (6) removes water from the fuel system.

These qualities are good for some motorcycles, bad for others. As a cleaner and solvent alcohol can be too effective. Gasohol can strip the protective liner off a gas tank, put so much crud into the fuel filter that it clogs, and dissolve some gasket materials in the fuel system. If you take care of your motorcycle, your fuel system should not be so dirty that a clogged fuel line becomes a problem. If your bike was manufactured after 1975, it has no organic-based hoses, float-needle tips or plastic floats to dissolve. (Organic materials were replaced by 1975 to make way for higher levels of certain additives to resolve knocking problems brought on by unleaded gasoline.)

Alcohol's propensity to collect water will work against you if there is too much water in the system. Water occurs naturally in gasoline, but too much causes the gas, water and alcohol to separate. The engine will first burn gasoline that is waterless (not good). The engine will then try to burn water and alcohol (also not good). Methyl alcohol is the biggest water absorber. Ethyl alcohol at less than 10% concentrations and MTBE are supposed to be free of this water separation problem.

Incidentally, alcohol's tendency to collect water means death to a two-stroke engine. Racers recommend avoiding gasohol at concentrations above 10% at all costs.

Oxygenated fuels introduce more oxygen into the combustion mix, resulting in more carbon dioxide and less carbon monoxide exhaust gases. All motorcycles will run leaner. If your motorcycle is running lean already, you may experience a small power loss (under 5%). Older bikes with naturally rich fuel mixtures may see performance improvements.

Gasoline Volatility

Gasoline is a mix of high and low volatility hydrocarbons. Volatility is defined as the propensity to vaporize. Gasoline must vaporize at a certain rate to burn efficiently in your motorcycle engine. Volatility is critical when you are trying to start a motorcycle. When you choke your bike during your cold engine start-up routine, you are increasing the amount of highly volatile hydrocarbons reaching the cylinder by increasing the total amount of hydrocarbons reaching the cylinder. This is a tricky act. You want enough highly volatile hydrocarbons to start the bike, but at the same time you are dumping large quantities of low volatility hydrocarbons into the cylinder as well. You are betting that the high volatility hydrocarbons get the engine started before the low volatility hydrocarbons drown the spark plug, known as "flooding" the engine.

Volatility is measured in pounds per square inch (p.s.i.). Gasoline p.s.i. is changed depending on whether the fuel is for winter or summer use. Oil refineries produce winter grade fuel at 12 p.s.i., and summer grade fuel at 9 p.s.i. Increased temperatures in the summer help gasoline vaporize. Summer gas, therefore, does not need to be as volatile and has additives that reduce volatility. If summer gas were as volatile as winter gas, it would tend to vaporize in the fuel line, causing "vapor lock." Fuel can't move through the fuel line if there is a vapor lock.

The lower temperatures in the winter inhibit gasoline vaporization. In winter the fuel must be more volatile or your motorcycle would never start. If the gas does not vaporize, the fuel mixture will not be ignited by the spark and the engine will flood. Therefore, summer additives are not used. You do not have to worry if the gas you buy is for the right season. The refining companies seasonally change their product.

Motorcycle manufacturers design motorcycles to tolerate some variations in the p.s.i. If the p.s.i. is too far from the norm, the air/fuel ratio will be wrong and the engine will run rough. There are four ways that you might get fuel with the wrong p.s.i. First, you might have a tank of winter fuel, yet experience summer conditions, such as in the spring. Second, you might have a tank of summer fuel, but experience winter conditions, such as in the fall. Third, you might buy gas from a less than reputable dealer who has tampered with the fuel mix. Or, fourth, the fuel may have come from a less than reputable refinery. For example, a refinery may add butane to the fuel. Adding butane is a cheap way to increase octane, but this also increases p.s.i.

Gasoline Octane

An internal combustion engine is powered by exploding a fuel vapor at high compression. When ignited, the fuel vapor does not burn all at once. Ideally, the spark sets off an even burn sequence with the flame front traveling away from the plug consuming unburned vapor. Gasoline that burns unevenly in the cylinder causes "knock."

Knock is the uncontrolled explosion or detonation of gasoline. Violent knocking is not good for a motorcycle, although some periodic knocking in newer motorcycles is expected. To create an even flame front, gasoline comes with additives called octanes. The octane rating is a measure of the antiknock properties of liquid motor fuel.

The octane number is a measurement of the gasoline's ability to resist spontaneous detonation due to factors other than the ignition spark. There are two octane rating systems. One system is the Research Octane Number (RON). The other is the Motor Octane Number (MON). RON is a good indication of low speed antiknock performance. MON is a good indication of high speed antiknock performance.

The octane rating on the fuel pump is an average of RON and MON. The higher the octane number, the less likely the fuel is to knock.

Engine design can affect the engine's propensity to knock. High compression engine designs increase the likelihood of gas detonating violently in the cylinder. Special head domes and piston faces, highly advanced timing or the spark plug position also affect the gas burn and can increase the likelihood of knock.

Engine condition can influence knock. Specifically, knock is more likely to occur in an engine with carbon buildup. When this carbon is super heated, it can act like a diesel engine glow-plug, igniting the fuel. The term "dieseling" was coined for engines that continue to run after the ignition is turned off.

Engine temperature can also induce knock. In hot weather or when pulling a large load you may want to run high octane fuel.

The difference between regular and premium gasoline is the octane rating. Premium costs more because it is refined to increase the percentage of octanes that resist knock. High octane numbers do not equate to high quality in other key areas of gasoline performance, such as detergency. A high octane rating means only one thing: high octane gasoline. It does not mean more additives or better quality compared to lower octane fuel.

Running high octane gas will do nothing for the performance of the motorcycle alone. In fact, you may find—especially at high altitudes—that higher octane fuel hurts your bike's performance. The only way to get better performance from premium fuel is to tune the motorcycle for premium fuel. Some bikes come from the factory this way. Others need modification.

You can buy race gasoline that has octane ratings as high as 102. This is a waste of money unless the bike is ported and tuned for the higher octane fuel. You might also have heard about "avgas," or gasoline refined for aviation. Avgas is for high altitude, fixed-throttle, cold temperature environments. It is unlikely that any motorcycle rider ever encountered these conditions. Don't waste your money.

Gasoline Lead

Lead (tetraethyl lead) is a highly toxic fuel additive used to improve gasoline octane ratings and to lubricate the intake and exhaust valves. Some states still sell leaded fuel, which is often cheaper than unleaded fuel. Do not buy leaded fuel unless your valves require it. Two-strokes do not need leaded fuel. Only really old four-strokes demand it. Even if it is cheaper at the pump, leaded fuel is more expensive in the long run. Mufflers and other components last longer if leaded fuel is avoided. Burning leaded fuel also poisons the air we breath.

Gasoline Contaminants

Contaminants are found in gasoline that is improperly shipped or stored, so how the local gas station handles the fuel is as important as the fuel itself. Low margin service stations that pump lots of gas often cut corners to save a buck. Corners cut include:

- Not cleaning the storage tanks regularly. Water and dirt accumulate in the storage tanks of all service stations. Dealers must clean their tanks periodically to ensure that the dirt and crud do not build up and get pumped into your motorcycle.
- Allowing the storage tank to be pumped too low. Gasoline, water, dirt and crud exist in layers in the storage tank. The gas is the middle layer. As long as the storage tank is maintained at no less than about 10% of capacity, the pumps will be pumping from this middle layer of gasoline, and you will not get water or dirt pumped into your motorcycle.
- Not replacing tanks. In the past they made tanks of metal that rust over time. Small, pinhole size openings in a tank allow contaminants to leach into the tank.
- Handling gasohol improperly. If the service station does not maintain its tanks, the first load of gasohol will collect every bit of rust, metal flake and gunk it finds and send it right out the hose into your tank.
- Deliberately buying trash gas and mixing it with good gas. Yes, this happens.

Recommendation

Buy the lowest octane fuel your bike will tolerate, following manufacturer recommendations and your own proven experience. For two-stroke engines, this means 92 octane fuel. For street bikes, you should get by on 86 octane fuel. Always buy from a reputable service station. When you find a fuel and dealer you like, stay with them.

If you receive bad gas, drain the tank.

MOTORCYCLE ENGINE OIL

Oil performs three tasks in an engine. It lubricates; it prevents rust, corrosion and deposit buildup; and it cools the engine.

Motor oils come in various "grades" or "weights," rated for compression ignition (diesel), spark ignition (gasoline) or both. Oils can have detergents or not. They can be multigrade (e.g., 10W-40) or single grade (e.g., 30). Oils can be specifically designed for motorcycles or for general automotive use. Finally, oil can be natural or synthetic.

Oil Grades

The American Petroleum Institute (API) developed a service rating system to identify the qualities and characteristics of the oil and appropriate uses for that oil. That rating can be found on the oil container, as shown in the figure. Oil suitable for use in spark ignition engines is labeled "S." Oil formulated for vehicles built in 1988 or later is marked "G." Oil formulated for 1994 vehicles or later is marked "H." "J" is the current standard. The "C" indicates that the oil is suitable for compression engines, meaning diesels. The "D" is a classification for diesel engines.

SAE stands for the Society of Automotive Engineers. The SAE rating specifies the oil viscosity. Viscosity is a fluid's resistance to flow. It is easier to understand this rating system by first understanding how a single grade oil is rated. A SAE 20 oil is lighter than SAE 30. Lighter means it flows faster at any given temperature. Both oils thin and flow faster when heated.

Multigrade refers to the two number designation, like 10W-40. (The "W" means winter, a redundant bit of information.) Additives, called viscosity index improvers, are mixed with the oil so that when the oil is cold it flows like an SAE 10 oil. When the oil is hot, the oil flows like a heavier SAE 40. This means that the oil has thinned less over the temperature range.

"Energy Conserving" oils have additives that increase gas mileage.

"Detergent" oils have additives called dispersants (alkaline earth salts) that adhere to dirt and contaminants such as combustion by-products, carbon particles, unspent fuel and acids. Detergents suspend these contaminants in the oil so they do not block oil passages or adhere to engine parts. Non-detergent oils were used in older motorcycles because these by-products were important for breaking in a new engine. Left unchecked, lacquer developed from the by-products. This lacquer filled gaps between bearings, rods and cranks, making up for the lack of extremely high-precision engine parts. Today's manufacturing techniques are extremely high precision. Lacquer is now the enemy.

Motorcycle Specific Oils

Motorcycles have unique lubrication, corrosion protection and cooling requirements. Motorcycle engines run at high r.p.m.; use the same oil for engine, transmission and clutch; and often operate at extreme temperatures. This puts a greater strain on the oil compared to machines where these components are lubricated independently with their own special lube stock. (Cars, for instance, usually have separate lubrication for transmission and engine.) This requires oil with highly compounded metallic detergents (magnesium and calcium), greater antiwear/anti-

OIL LABEL

scuff agents (zinc and phosphorus) and greater shear pressure protection additives than required by automobile engines.

Automobile oils are not designed for the punishment associated with motorcycle engines and transmissions. The antiwear additives in car oils are rapidly destroyed by the shearing of gears in a motorcycle transmission. Motorcycle oils are designed to perform the lubrication of clutch, transmission and engine. Is the added expense worth it? Only if you do not keep your bike on its maintenance schedule or if you operate the bike under punishing conditions.

Mineral vs. Synthetic Oils

Mineral oil hydrocarbon molecules (esters and polyalphaolefins) vary greatly in structure and lubricating properties. Some of these molecules become too thick when cold, boil off too quickly when hot or oxidize too soon. Synthetic oils are hydrocarbon molecules engineered by man that do not vary in structure or lubrication properties. Compared to mineral oils, synthetics flow better in cold temperatures, are more stable under high temperatures, do not break down as easily and require fewer additives so there is more of the all important base stock.

Two-Stroke Oils

Two-stroke oil must perform additional duties not required of four-stroke oil. First, it must provide greater corrosion and off-season rust protection. Second, it must prevent piston seizure and scuffing. Finally, it must prevent spark plug fouling.

Two-stroke oils come in three types: mineral, synthetic and synthetic biodegradable. Like four-stroke synthetics, two-stroke synthetics offer greater protection over a wider range of temperatures and conditions than do mineral oils. Biodegradable oil breaks down after being released into the environment several times faster than mineral oil.

Two-stroke oils also come blended for specific applications. For example, chain saw oil is specially designed for chain saws. Outboard oil is designed for marine two-strokes. A motorcycle is not very much like a chain saw or a boat. Only use two-stroke oil designed for motorcycles in motorcycles.

One selects an oil based on how it is delivered to the fuel system. Some two-strokes have no automatic delivery system for putting oil in the gas. These motorcycles must have the gas and oil mixed by the rider. Special oils are designed for this. Other two-strokes have automatic oil injection systems. These systems require oil designed for injection. The injection pump varies the gas to oil ratio from 20:1 to 100:1. The oil must be designed to provide adequate lubrication at the higher ratios while having low smoke and fouling characteristics at the lower ratios.

The best way to match the oil to the bike is to find the recommendation in the owner's manual. Lacking this information, most two-strokes start with a 32:1 gas:oil ratio. You can experiment (at your own risk) with different ratios until the proper ratio for your type of riding is achieved. It is best to follow the manufacturer's recommendation.

Recommendation

If you maintain your bike according to schedule, a high-quality motorcycle oil is preferable. Mineral/synthetic blend automotive oil is acceptable.

Use 100% synthetic motorcycle oil under three conditions. First, if you plan to subject the bike to extra stress, such as a summer vacation tour through the high desert, or pull a trailer or any activity that will create additional heat buildup, use a synthetic. Synthetic oil is most beneficial when the engine runs temporarily hotter than usual.

Second, if you cannot follow the maintenance schedule, and can only find time to change the oil once or twice a year, better run the most expensive synthetic available.

Third, use a 100% synthetic if you ride your bike short distances such that it often runs at less than operating temperature. This condition will affect more motorcycles than one would think. It takes a great deal of time for a motorcycle to warm up. Under these conditions, water and acids build up rapidly in the crankcase.

Do not use a synthetic in an older engine that has not experienced synthetic before. Synthetic oils will break down the sludge and varnish that has built up in the engine over time. Some of this buildup may actually be performing a useful function, such as keeping the worn bearing tolerances within spec or plugging a gap in a gasket. Freeing these buildups might also send the sludge coursing around the oil system, where it might plug up something vital, such as an oil line.

Unless there are rare circumstances relating to your motorcycle, run a multiweight detergent oil. It just makes sense. The price difference between a multigrade and a single grade oil is only a few nickels. This is insignificant compared to the price of a blown engine. However, the wider the multigrade range, the greater the percentage of additives. Additives break down faster than the base stock oil, so keep the range as small as possible. If you can run 10W-40, do so and shun running 10W-50.

Run biodegradable oils in two-strokes.

MOTORCYCLE CHAINS

Motorcycle final drives come in three varieties: chain, shaft and belt. Shaft and belt drives have been touted as superior to chain drive. Yet

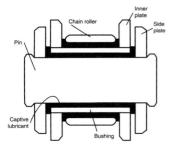

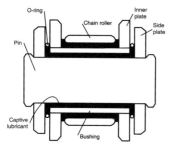

still we have chains. Why? Basically because chains have characteristics that prevent shaft and belt drive from totally replacing them. Low cost, high efficiency and low weight are three of these characteristics. But chains wear out faster than belts or shafts and require more maintenance.

Types of Chains

As with most motorcycle components, chains have gone through a technological revolution in the last 20 years. There are three basic types of chains: common roller chain, lubricant impregnated chain and O-ring chain. OEM chain is often common roller chain. Roller chains are made of five components: pin, pin link plate, roller link plate, roller and bushing (see the accompanying figure).

Lubricant impregnated chains have the additional feature of lubricant impregnated bushings. O-ring chains have two additional components: lubricant (lithium grease) and O-rings that seal the lubricant into the bushings.

Replacing Chains

An improperly adjusted chain is the motorcycle owner's nemesis. It needs replacing more often and absorbs energy that should be going to the rear wheel. A chain should be replaced if you notice unusual wear on the chain or sprockets. Unusual wear is easy to spot. Look for bright worn "polished" spots on the chain and sprocket.

A worn out chain needs replacing. The only way to know if the chain is worn out is to remove the chain from the motorcycle and measure it. If it is more than 3% longer than a new chain, it has been stretched to its limits and needs replacing.

Motorcycles come with frame guides to help you tighten the chain and keep the rear wheel axle at right angles. Unfortunately, these guides are not sufficient proof of properly aligned sprockets and chain. Over time bike components can become misaligned. For example, engines can move in the cradle (especially rubber-mounted engines). A good second check for proper alignment is to look. The rear sprocket should be directly in line with the front sprocket. This can be checked using a straight edge or string.

Chains and sprockets tend to eat each other when not aligned or maintained properly. A worn sprocket will destroy a new chain lickety-split. A worn chain will destroy a new sprocket just as fast. One rule of thumb is that sprockets should be replaced every third chain. However, if you do not replace the sprocket, you must be sure the reason for chain failure is only due to age. Most often misalignment has played some role. Unless you are certain that the sprockets are in top shape, replacing the sprockets and chain simultaneously is a wise investment.

Recommendation

Buy the best chain you can afford. A broken chain is not only a major inconvenience, it can also be a major heartache. Engine cases, drive line components, plastic motorcycle panels and fleshy human body parts can be damaged when a chain link bursts apart. A broken chain can also lock up the real wheel or drive sprocket!

Replace the chain with, at a minimum, the same OEM type, size and quality. (Size is often stamped on each link.) Your motorcycle owner's manual should be consulted since there are often warnings about the type of chain that can be used. Using the wrong chain can void the motorcycle warranty. If your motorcycle came with an O-ring chain, replace it with an O-ring chain. If your bike came with a standard chain, you may have the option to upgrade. The decision to move to an O-ring depends largely on how well you maintain the chain. If you are conscientious about chain lubrication, alignment and adjustment, an O-ring chain only offers a bit more life and peace of mind. If you tend to forget chain maintenance, an O-ring chain will last twice as long as a standard chain.

MOTORCYCLE TIRES

The previous chapter on mechanisms discusses motorcycle tires as components of a motorcycle. Below is detail about buying tires.

Tire Sizes

There are several motorcycle sizing and rating systems. Before the 1980s, tire manufacturers used a simple number scheme, such as 3.25x16, which means that this tire has a section width of 3.25 inches and fits a wheel with 16-inch rim diameter.

Currently, a tire measured in inches will have a size code such as 4.00S18. The first digit refers to the width of the tire in inches. The second and third digits are code for the aspect ratio of the tire. Aspect ratio is the height versus width of the tire (see figure). Dividing the section height by the section width produces the aspect ratio. If the number is 10 through 19, or in the sixties, the profile is about 90%, which is a low profile tire. If the number is 25, 50, or 00, the tire is a

TIRE ASPECT RATIO

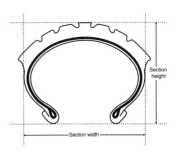

STREET TIRE SIZE INCH DESIGNATION	
5.00 H16 4PR	
Section width (inches)	5.00
Speed rating	H
Rim diameter	16
Casting strength (ply rating)	4PR

ALPHA TIRE CODES	
STREET TIRE SIZE ALPHABETICAL DESIGNATIONS **MT90-16B**	
Motorcycle code	M
Tire width code	T
Aspect ratio (90%)	90
Rim Diameter (inches)	16
Load range	Load Range B
Load Rating—a numerical code that corresponds to the total load carrying capacity at the speed indicated by the speed symbol.	

METRIC TIRE CODES	
STREET TIRE SIZE METRIC DESIGNATIONS **130/90-16 67H**	
Section width (mm)	130
Aspect ratio (90%)	90
Rim Diameter (inches)	16
Load rating	67
Speed rating	H
$Aspect\ Ratio = \dfrac{Section\ height}{Section\ width}$	

higher profile tire, with an aspect ratio over 94%. The letter refers to the speed rating. The final two digits are the wheel rim size.

Street tires are sometimes designated with an alphabetic code such as MT90-16 B (see Alpha Tire Codes). The "M" is the motorcycle code. The "T" is a tire width code. The "90" is the aspect ratio, or the height of the tire. This tire's height is 90% of its width. The "16" is the rim diameter in inches, and "B" is the load range.

Today it is more common for the tire to be measured in metric scale, as shown in the accompanying figure. A metrically measured tire will have a code on it such as 130/90VR16. The first three digits are the tire's width in millimeters. (100 millimeters is approximately four inches.) The second set of numbers (90 in the example) refers to the aspect ratio. The 16 refers to the wheel diameter (i.e., rim size) in inches.

Several different sizes may fit your motorcycle. Then again, only one size might fit your bike. Just because a tire fits the rim does not mean it will fit your motorcycle. A tire must also fit the frame. Given the small clearances between fenders and forks, a tire can be too wide or too tall to fit your bike. Haphazardly playing around with tire sizes is dangerous. The motorcycle and rim dimension limits mean that the size of the tire cannot be increased too dramatically and still fit the unmodified bike. A dealer will know what will and will not fit. To some degree you can resolve the anxiety of tire size selection by buying the same size tire as is currently on the bike.

Tire Ratings

Tires are rated by speed and load range. Ratings are assigned based on controlled indoor testing. A speed rating indicates the top speed at which the manufacturer believes the tire can be continuously run safely. A tire may have an "N," "S," "H," "V" and "Z" speed rating. "N" rated tires are good for sustained speeds up to 93 m.p.h. "S," "H" and "V" tires are good for sustained speeds up to 112, 130 and 149 m.p.h. respectively. "Z" rated tires are recommended for applications where speeds above 149 m.p.h. are sustained. Tires at the higher speed ratings dissipate heat better, although they may accomplish this by sacrificing tread life. Never install a tire with less than the speed rating required in the owner's manual.

Load range ratings are generally either "B" or "C." "B" is the lesser range, and should never be used on bikes requiring "C" range tires. "C" range tires can be used on all motorcycles.

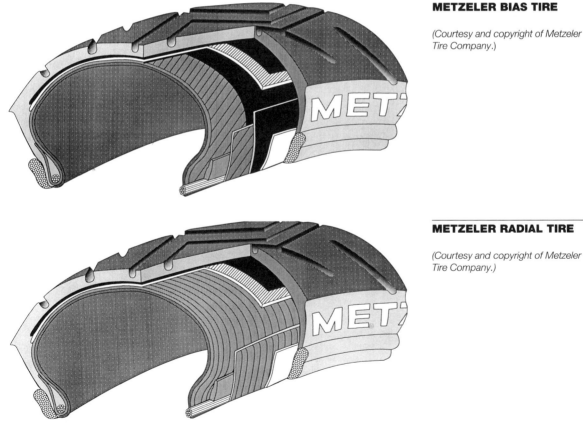

METZELER BIAS TIRE

(Courtesy and copyright of Metzeler Tire Company.)

METZELER RADIAL TIRE

(Courtesy and copyright of Metzeler Tire Company.)

Bias, Radial and Belted Tires

The tire measurement may also include a "B" or "R," indicating a bias or radial tire. Bias and radial refers to the way the cords of the tire run through the tire carcass. Bias tires have a firm sidewall, which makes them better for low-speed comfort and bashing into curbs.

Radial tires have cords that run the radius of the tire. The major difference between a radial and a bias tire is that radials have softer sidewalls, which helps them hold a firmer contact patch. To compensate for soft sidewalls, radial tires are designed with less sidewall and are mounted on special wider rims. A weak sidewall is good for road racing, but is a liability for touring applications. Radials also have the benefits of being lighter and running cooler.

Do not run radial tires without checking with the manufacturer or dealer. There is a difference to how radials work, and your bike may be unable to use them.

Belted tires are constructed with extra Kevlar, fiberglass or rayon belts to increase carcass strength. These belts do not extend down to the sidewalls, so they do not offer greater sidewall strength. Belts stabilize the tread surface and improve the tire's characteristics.

Matched Sets

All but the smallest motorcycles require different tire designs for front and rear. Tires have turning and riding characteristics that must match, front and rear. Tire and motorcycle manufacturers work together to match tires. Tires that can be put on the same bike are known as matched sets. Two great tires can be deadly when put on the same bike if their characteristics are not compatible. Always buy matching tires. This does not mean, for most riders, that you must buy two tires every time one needs replacing. It does mean that the replacement tire must be designed to match the characteristics of the older tire. For performance riders, always replace both tires at the same time.

Tubed Tires

Tires come tubed or tubeless. You can use tubeless tires only if the wheel rim is designed for them. Tubeless tires are safer since their design resists immediate blow-out if punctured. Always replace the tube when you replace a tubed tire.

Recommendation

Replace your tires often, and put good money into them. Ninety percent of all tire failure happens during the last 10% of tire life. Buy a tire that honestly matches the driving you do. If you don't ride at 100 m.p.h. hour after hour, you don't need high-speed tires. Do not replace bias tires with radials unless the manufacturer says it is acceptable.

New tires must be broken in. The tires come with a protective coating that must be worn off. This coating reduces the tire's grip. Tires also need time for their cords and belts to stretch. Do not put your new tires to speed or cornering tests until you have ridden several hundred miles.

Always have your tires balanced.

SPARK PLUGS

Spark plugs ignite the air/fuel mixture in the combustion chamber. Simple in design, spark plugs consist of only five to seven parts. The design is really ingenious. Every feature of the plug performs several critical functions. For example, the ceramic insulator (the white part of the plug) not only keeps the spark from grounding out before reaching the spark gap, it prevents flashover and helps control the heat range of the plug.

Spark plugs are engineered to match the engine exactly. If the plug is too short, the electrode will not be deep enough into the combustion chamber, resulting in poor idle and uneven running. If the plug is too long, the plug may be struck by the piston or valves.

Heat range refers to the temperature of the electrode when at operating temperature. A "cold" plug is a plug that dissipates heat faster than a "hot" plug. A colder plug may be needed if the engine is burdened for a long time under a full load. A hotter plug may be needed if the engine is run for long periods at partial throttle. Changing to a colder or hotter plug must be done with great care. If the plug runs too hot, preignition will result. It is also possible to damage the pistons and valves when the plug runs too hot. If the plug runs cold, deposits will build up, resulting in fouling.

Some spark plugs come with a resistor element. This element reduces radio interference originating in the motorcycle ignition system. If the bike has lots of radio equipment, or if it has electronic ignition, use a resistor plug.

Spark plugs are often thrown away needlessly. Unless the plug is dead, the insulation cracked or the electrodes burned away, the plug can be cleaned, regapped and used again.

MOTORCYCLE BATTERIES

A battery performs three critical functions. First, it supplies electricity for starting your motorcycle's engine. Second, it supplies additional power when the alternator is unable to meet electrical demands. Third, it acts as a capacitor absorbing high-voltage peaks that could damage electrical components. Given its critical role, the right battery makes a great deal of difference.

Any rider will tell you that motorcycles eat batteries. This is because:

SPARK PLUG

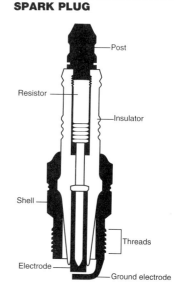

BATTERY

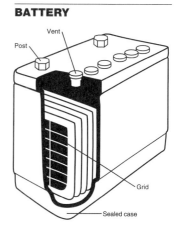

- Most motorcycles are designed with alternators that barely meet the bike's requirements. This means that the battery is not receiving a good charge every time you ride.
- The battery loses 1% of its power every day it sits idle, such as in winter storage.
- Vibration shakes the plates (i.e., grid) in the battery apart.

The low charge and high losses create ideal conditions for sulfation, which is the destruction of the battery grid. Vibration damage adds to the destruction. This is why the average life for a motorcycle battery is about two winters.

It may appear that there are endless numbers of replacement batteries for your motorcycle. This is not so. There are only a few possible replacement choices.

Battery Types

Just like car batteries, motorcycle batteries are rated by size, amps, volts and reserve capacity. Size refers to the physical dimensions of the battery case. Size is important because the battery must fit properly into the battery tray of your bike. A battery that cannot be secured in the tray will bounce around and suffer damage. Size is not directly related to the amount of power a battery holds.

Amp rating refers to the amount of cold cranking power the battery delivers. A higher rating means more power for cold weather starts. Reserve capacity gives you a general idea of how long the battery could power every critical system if the alternator failed.

But motorcycles, unlike cars, have few replacement choices. Motorcycle and battery manufacturers work closely to design batteries that exactly meet the requirements of a particular motorcycle. You must replace your battery with one that is virtually identical to the OEM battery. Not only must the physical size of the battery match the battery tray, but the terminals (including their polarity), terminal leads (if included) and vent tube must match the OEM.

You may have the option of upgrading to a high-capacity lead antimony battery, lead calcium battery or a maintenance-free battery. In fact, if you have a bike with lots of electrical accessories, or if you have modified the engine with high-lift cams, high-compression components or exotic carburetion, you should consider upgrading the battery.

Batteries and Cold Weather

Cold weather makes starting difficult. Cold temperatures reduce the chemical activity of the battery, which results in less power. Cold weather also makes the engine more difficult to crank or to turn over.

Compared to starting the engine at 80°F, a cold weather start at 32°F requires 65% more power. Unfortunately, at 32° the battery can supply only 80% of peak output. On the first really cold day of fall all those neglected batteries that were fine for summer are worthless.

Recommendation

To save money some folks mail order batteries, others like to buy batteries at the shop and install them personally. If you buy mail order, know that the battery does not come with acid, and the acid will cost you about $5. Also know that you need to charge the battery at one-tenth its amp hour rating (generally less than one amp) which probably means the investment in a small trickle charger. If you want to save money, and you know that your present battery is dead because of age, buy a battery at a battery store instead of a motorcycle shop. You can save as much as 50%. If you do not know why the battery failed, it could be that there is another electrical problem. Best take the bike to an expert.

Be careful when working around batteries. Batteries produce explosive gases and can leak acid. Never smoke or create sparks around a battery and always keep the battery upright.

ADDITIVES AND MAINTENANCE FLUIDS

Additives are made for oil, gas, batteries and tires. Some work, most do little or nothing for you.

Oil Additives

Oil additive products generally are concentrations of additives already found in motorcycle oil. These additives include sulfur, chlorine, phosphates, teflon (i.e., PTFE), kerosene and zinc. These additives do have important qualities. The question is whether you need more of these additives than provided by motorcycle oil.

The oil additive industry has not done a good job providing convincing evidence that these additives are worth the cost. You are better off using a high-grade motorcycle oil than buying a low-grade oil and adding an additive package. (In fact, some additives contain solids that can clog filters and screens.) It is best to follow the recommendation of the motorcycle manufacturer.

Gas Additives

Motorcycles have smaller carburetor jets and ports than cars. Using automobile gas additives can clog these jets and ports. However, gas stabilizer is one additive that should be used. Gas stabilizer is available for those of us who put the motorcycle up for long winter storage but refuse to drain the fuel system.

Battery Additives

Battery additives boost the charge of a low battery. This is a quick fix to what may be a major problem. It is very tempting, given the outrageous cost of motorcycle batteries. Do not do it. It is better to discover why the bike is having battery trouble than to attempt to solve the problem with an additive.

By the way, don't add straight sulfuric acid to a battery. Adding sulfuric acid solution to a battery will make the electrolyte solution too strong. The battery will be ruined in a short time.

Tire Additives

There are two types of products that can be squirted into the tire's air chamber: tire balancing agents and flat guards. The former balances the tire, keeps the tire running cooler and can temporarily seal a small puncture. These are generally used by backyard mechanics who replace their own tires. They work.

Flat guards are designed to stop the vast majority of small punctures a tire may suffer. Their intended purpose is to provide you with just enough range so that you can limp your bike to the shop for a repair or replacement tire. Some are put into the tire after a puncture has occurred. Some are designed to go into the tire before you ride. The author has had good experience with these additives, although you should inspect your tires frequently for nails, glass and other punctures when using them. They only keep air from leaking out of the tire. They do not restore the structural integrity of the tire carcass.

RECYCLING THE MOST COMMON PURCHASES

Oil, tires and batteries represent major disposal problems and should be recycled. Used oils, and the plastic quart or gallon containers new oils come in, are valuable resources and should be recycled. Many communities offer curbside pickup of oil. Many gas stations offer a used oil collection service free to home mechanics. Be sure to keep the oil free from contaminants such as antifreeze or other chemicals.

If you replace your own tires, recycle them. Tires represent a major solid waste disposal problem in landfills, yet they can be incinerated or recycled into other oil products. Your tire dealer should take your old carcasses for a buck or two.

Batteries represent a real solid waste hazard if not disposed of properly. An average automobile battery contains twenty pounds of recyclable lead and three pounds of recyclable plastic. Several states require that batteries be recycled. Usually you can return an old battery to any store selling batteries for recycling. Some even offer a dollar or two for old batteries.

11

WOMEN RIDERS

According to the Motorcycle Industry Council's 1998 Motorcycle Owner's Survey, the profile of the average motorcycle rider in the United States has changed quite a bit in the last 15 years. Then, the average rider was single, under 30 years of age, with some high school education and probably a high school diploma. Only 9% of riders earned over $35,000 a year. Today's profile is considerably different. Today's average rider is married (59%), 38 years of age, and has completed high school (89%). Forty-eight percent have some college education, a college degree, or post-graduate degree. Median income for this group is over $44,000. On average, motorcycle riders as a group are better educated and earn more money than the average American.

The sport, however, is still dominated by men. In 1980, 92.1% of the motorcycle owners were male. In 1990, 92.7% of the owners were male. The 1998 survey shows that 91% of the owners are male. Although recent trends show that women are joining the motorcycle ownership ranks in record numbers—reflecting the larger social trend of women undertaking more active lifestyles—only about 500,000 American women own motorcycles.

Therefore, motorcycles and motorcycle riding products are produced first and foremost for men. Only recently have manufacturers been making a line or two of motorcycle apparel in women's sizes. While the author wishes to avoid sexist stereotypes, the fact is that the sport does not make itself as available to women as it does to men. These statistics demonstrate why a female rider may find the sport less accessible and more difficult to enjoy than her male counterpart.

For these reasons, this chapter covers some of the issues faced by the female rider. It borrows heavily from American Motorcyclist Association and Motorcycle Industry Council surveys. But it is also supported by independent surveys of women riders coast to coast representing a total of more than 300 years of motorcycling experience.

FINANCIAL GENDER DIFFERENCES

According to the MIC survey, the average female rider tends to be better educated and have a higher income than her male counterpart. Fifty-six percent of women riders have completed some college or have graduate degrees. Thirty-four percent are in white-collar jobs, compared to 31% for men. Women riders' median household income was nearly $3,000 higher ($47,300) than male riders' median income. Female riders also tend more to be married (64% vs. 59%) and older (39 vs. 38 years old) compared to male riders.

ANATOMICAL GENDER DIFFERENCES

The average female is smaller in mass, height, weight, leg length and total surface area than the average male. The average female has a lower center of gravity and greater tendon laxity than the average male. Compared to the average male, the average female is different in the following ways:

- Three to four inches shorter
- 25 to 30 pounds lighter
- 20% less mass
- 33% less lean body mass
- Smaller bones
- Leg length 51% compared to 56% in a man
- 10 to 15 pounds more fat
- 40% to 45% less fat-free weight
- 18% less surface area

None of these factors should be looked on as an advantage or disadvantage, because they make little difference in motorcycle riding, positive or negative.

The big difference is simply in the numbers: There are significantly fewer women riders than men riders. This fact has implications.

GETTING STARTED IMPLICATIONS

One might think that the average female rider started riding after her husband or boyfriend raised her interest. Not so. While this scenario does happen, it is just as likely that a woman decided on her own to get into the sport without influence from anyone, male or female. Advice provided to female novices from the surveys includes:

- The decisions must be your own. You will not enjoy the sport if coerced.
- Take the Motorcycle Safety Foundation course. (In fact, nearly a third of all participants are women!) Do not try to learn from a companion unless the companion is a saint.
- Build up your skill level. Start out on a small, light bike. Buy used.
- Learn to take care of the simple things on your bike. This is an amazing confidence builder.
- Seek information from a variety of sources: fellow women riders, men riders, magazines, sale reps, motorcycle club members, anyone and everyone.
- Just do it! Attitude is everything. Go for it!
- Ride your own ride.

No doubt current riders already think riding is great. But there are clear benefits to taking up riding. Survey respondents stated four consistent themes:

- Learning to ride and care for a motorcycle increases self-confidence.
- The feeling of freedom is rich and wondrous on a bike.
- You meet many great people.
- The world is experienced more intensely when enjoyed from the vantage point of a motorcycle.

OUTFITTING IMPLICATIONS

Despite the low number of women currently in motorcycle riding, indications are that women's ownership of motorcycles and participation in motorcycle sports is rising. In fact, women riders tend to start riding later in life, which translates into more economic clout and financial sophistication than the average male rider. And the industry is taking note.

Regardless, there are important outfitting and riding considerations that female riders need to keep in mind. In particular, there are four critical measurements to which attention must be paid: seat height, front wheel angularity, control access and weight distribution.

Seat Height

Seat height is no mystery. If your feet cannot reach the macadam when you sit on the bike, you're going to lay that bike down a lot. The humiliation is tremendous. The damage to the motorcycle great. The damage to your body of significant concern. It is preferable that new riders be able to safely get the whole foot down on the pavement—heel and toes. This can be critical for dismounting and in slick environments like toll booths, parking lots and gas stations. Experienced riders can usually control the bike with just the ball of the foot on the ground. Not many motorcycles allow even average-sized riders a full foot on the runway, so some compromise may be required.

Front Wheel Angularity

Front wheel angularity is called wheel caster. Caster is the steering angle that places the weight of the bike behind the vertical centerline of the front wheel. It is euphemistically called "trail," "rake," or "chop." Exaggerated rake is the prominent feature of a "chopper."

The significance of front wheel angularity is that greater positive caster makes the bike more stable in motion but more difficult to turn. Touring bikes, for example, have greater positive caster to take advantage of the stabilizing effects. Too much caster makes the bike extremely stable at speed, but too difficult to turn at speed and less stable in a low speed turn.

Less positive caster makes the bike more nimble. Sport bikes, for example, need to respond quickly and so have minimal rake. Too little caster makes the bike unstable at high speed and more difficult to control.

Both situations can be dealt with if you are physically strong. Individuals with less muscle mass might want to look for a motorcycle with moderate caster.

Control Access

Access to controls is a concern for those with short arms and small hands. You must be able to reach all controls that need adjusting while riding. Not that folks with longer arms don't need to reach the controls, too. It's just not an issue for them.

It goes without saying that you need to be able to reach the clutch, brakes (front and back), shift lever and lights. But do not think that controls used less frequently are somehow less important to reach. These include the turn signals, horn, ignition switch, cutoff switch, radio and fuel petcock switch. (Some fuel petcocks tend to be in less than easy-to-reach positions. Many are very difficult to switch when riding.)

Control access also means the ability to properly manipulate the control. Of particular importance are brake and clutch controls. Some of these controls (and Harley comes to mind here) take a great deal of hand strength to engage. Repetitive engagement of these controls can lead to hand fatigue, a hazardous condition for a motorcycle rider.

Weight

There are two weight issues—total weight and weight distribution (how top-heavy the bike is).

The total weight of a bike, its passengers and its cargo must be within the smaller rider's capacity to control. The more the bike weighs, the more important it is to keep the bike vertical. Total weight becomes more of an issue in low speed situations. Anyone can tilt a 250-pound bike well over to the left or right and still hold it up and recover to a full upright position. But this is not so true of a 900-pound full dresser. In a parking lot situation where you need to turn the steering sharp left or right, the bike will naturally lean away from the vertical. It is under these conditions that total weight really makes a difference. Get a huge bike just a little past vertical and it really wants to go down. You've got to be strong to hold that big bike up.

Weight distribution can exacerbate the total weight problem. Top-heavy bikes are more difficult to control than bikes with a low center of gravity. If you do not have much muscle mass, buy a bike with a low center of gravity. Finding such a bike is difficult since manufacturers do not advertise whether a bike is top-heavy or not. (Being top-heavy is not considered a feature by the manufacturers.) To find a bike with a low center of gravity, try out a variety of motorcycles. Ask around. Women riders will gladly give you their advice. At the dealer, insist on riding a new bike first if you are unsure. And ride it with a full tank of gas! A full five-gallon tank (a gallon weighs about eight pounds) perched way up high can do a lot to make a bike top-heavy.

Otherwise, small people are no less able to handle heavy bikes than large people. The author does not believe in formulas that say if you weigh only X than you should have a bike with no more than Y displacement that weighs no more than Z. However, your riding strategy must be somewhat different. Smaller people may not be able to manhandle a bike out of a dangerous situation as quickly, or in the same manner, as a larger person. No matter what your sex, all beginners should start out on a smaller bike (both in weight and displacement). What you finally end up with after a few years riding is your choice.

Buying the Right Gear
In the past, women riders had no choice but to buy small sizes of men's riding apparel since no manufacturers made a separate line of women's riding gear. This has changed, but given the limited number of female riders, the selection is still not great. Women who want top quality and a perfect fit have two choices. The first is to get custom-designed clothing. This may be expensive, but nothing makes riding more enjoyable than perfectly fitting gear. The second is to be patient and look around. What you want is out there, but it takes some hunting down. There are several small start-up companies designing motorcycle clothes just for women.

Surveyed riders universally agreed that the right gear makes all the difference. It is extremely important to find apparel that fits properly, especially when buying cold weather riding gear. Given the greater possibility of hypothermia (see below), female riders should seek and demand only the best. Other comments from the surveys included:

- Don't be cheap with the basics. Buy good gloves, boots, jacket and helmet.
- Safety rules. It is not a fashion show.
- Shoot the wad if you need warm stuff.
- Check pawn shops and club newsletters.
- You can get by with carefully selected cheap stuff.

Custom Fitting a Motorcycle
It is possible to adjust a motorcycle to better fit a smaller rider. Most motorcycles can be lowered as much as two inches if you have the desire and money.

Before you do anything, consider changing your boots. Good motorcycle boots can be purchased with soles that add up to a half inch to your reach. Since you are only trying to get the ball of your foot down (for an experienced rider), this is the least expensive modification you can make.

Here are five possibilities for lowering a bike. But first, three cautionary notes. Any of these adjustments may significantly change the bike's performance and handling characteristics. These changes may be good or bad. Second, lowering the bike may change the bike's relationship to its side stand. You may have to have that modified, too.

Third, lowering a bike can reduce clearances. Your lean angle may be reduced. Your suspension travel may also be reduced causing the bike to bottom out more easily and limiting its load capacity. And your ground clearance may be reduced. Be cautious with a newly modified motorcycle until you fully understand the effects of the reengineering. Take it easy the first few times out.

1. Cut down and narrow the seat. Several companies, such as Corbin, specialize in making custom motorcycle seats using the current seat pan from your motorcycle. You can also check with other riders for a local upholstery shop that does this type of work. Cutting down the seat reduces its width so that your foot can get closer to the ground. Even if you do not cut it down, a custom seat is a great investment and highly recommended.

2. Mount lower profile tires. Get the advice of your motorcycle tire expert before doing this. A lower profile tire is generally a radial tire and can certainly lower the entire bike. But adding a radial to a bike can have a major impact on bike performance and safety. The tire must match the specifications of the manufacturer, since an incorrect tire can cause "head shake," severe vibration around the steering crown. Be particularly careful with older bikes and sports bikes. Older bikes were not designed for radial tires, and most sport bikes were designed specifically for only one type of radial.

3. Adjust or replace forks, shocks and springs. This also needs to be expertly handled. Check your owner's manual for ways to adjust the forks, shocks and springs currently on your motorcycle. Usually there is an option to soften the suspension, which often lowers the bike. If that is not enough, there are many after-market companies that sell suspension kits, different shocks or other components designed to lower the bike. Again, be careful. It is important to maintain the geometric relationship between the forks, shocks and frame. Changing the angles reduces the capability of the components to absorb shock and can lead to quicker failure of the parts.

4. If the reach to the handlebars is the problem, you can get totally new bars that are more swept back, bars that adjust forward or back, or brackets that move the bars closer to you. These changes may also require that you purchase new cables and hydraulic lines.

5. Finally, almost any lever, control or peddle can be custom machined, relocated or modified. It might cost a bit and it may take time finding someone who will do the work, but the benefits and improved safety make it worth it.

GENDER RIDING IMPLICATIONS

Accidents

Here is an interesting fact from the Hurt report: Women are overrepresented in accident statistics. There are several theories on why women should be more likely to be involved in an accident, although none of this is backed up by facts. Women may tend to buy motorcycles of a lower quality. Just walk into a large motorcycle dealer and look at the pastel colored bikes marketed for the college coed. More likely, however, is the fact that sometimes the only thing that can pull a rider out of a bad situation is a power maneuver that requires strength. With only two seconds to make several combined course maneuvers, the strong have a better opportunity to survive. Men have, on average, more muscle mass than women and therefore a better chance to muscle a bike out of a bad situation.

Cold Weather Riding

Generally speaking, women have a higher fat percentage than men. In other animals, fat is a survival device for conserving body warmth in cold weather. So one might think that women would be warmer than men when riding. Nope! Given the overall structure of the human skeleton, fat is not a survival device for homo sapiens. Heat loss in humans is more a function of the ratio of exposed surface area to relative weight or body mass. Women have more curves than their male counterparts and therefore have a higher ratio of surface area to mass, especially slender women.

The conclusion that can be reached is one that many women have known for years. Women tend to lose significant amounts of body heat when exposed to a cold environment. They tend to feel the cold sooner than their male counterparts. It is more than just perception. Women are at higher risk of hypothermia in a wind chill situation such as cold weather motorcycle riding.

Carrying Loads and Passengers

In the riding skills section of this book I discussed carrying cargo and passengers. Read that section. The author reiterates here that large passengers and heavy loads present an added danger factor for any motorcycle rider. Large passengers can actually take control of the bike away from you by leaning incorrectly. This problem is of greater concern for smaller motorcyclists.

Raising a Fallen Bike

At some point in your life you are going to face the humiliation and anger of needing to right a bike that has toppled over. It may have gone over because the kickstand sank into the parking lot asphalt on a hot day. Or maybe your foot slipped in a pool of oil when you stopped at a toll booth. Maybe you hit some unseen gravel, or you were going at a very slow speed and lost balance. In any event, sooner or later all motorcycle riders need to pick up a fallen motorcycle.

Although this is an issue with all riders, women seem more willing to talk about it.

As with lifting anything, you want to lift with your legs, not your back. A smaller bike can usually be addressed with a straight back from the squat position and put right side up. A really big bike, such as a full dresser, needs a special technique to bring it up. Here are the steps:

1. Inspect the situation. If you went down with the bike, make sure you are okay. Inspect the bike for dangerous spills, such as battery acid or gasoline. You may have to figure out some way to deal with leaking fluids before dealing with the fallen bike.
2. Prepare the bike. If on a hill, orient the bike so it is facing up or down hill. If the bike is down on its right side, put the kickstand down so it might catch the bike should you push it past the upright position and cause it to tumble over to the other side. Put the bike in gear.
3. Grip the bike. With your back to the seat, grab the lowest handlebar grip with one hand and pull up, turning the front wheel as far as possible. Find a good sturdy gripping location for the other hand.
4. Assume the lifting position. Tuck your butt into the saddle. Keep your back straight up and your legs straight and out.
5. Right the bike. Slowly, taking small baby steps, walk the bike back to the upright position. If the bike was down on its left side, once you get the bike up and balanced, put down the kickstand with one free foot. If the bike was down on its right side, rest the bike on its kickstand, which you put out before trying to right the bike.
6. Finally, perform a preride inspection on the bike to be sure all systems are operational, or at least to know what is not.

You will be happy you bought case guards in this situation. Not only will they keep your bike's engine cases from being punctured (an expensive proposition), they will also keep the bike more upright after it has tipped over, making it easier to recover.

SAFETY IMPLICATIONS

How safe is it to be a female motorcycle rider? No matter what gender you are, you are safer riding with a buddy than riding alone. If something goes wrong, you have a pal to assist or get help. If someone threatens your stuff, you have a buddy to outflank the intruder. Otherwise, female riders have made it clear to the author that, in their view, riding solo presents no more danger to a female rider than to a male rider. Comments include:

- It is as safe as you make it.
- Dumb question!
- How safe is it to be female?
- How safe is it to be male?
- As safe as any other motorsport or hobby.
- A woman on a bike can travel anywhere she wants.
- Safer than being a man . . . they're more "fragile."
- Safer than being a man . . . we do not ride beyond our capabilities to prove how "macho" we are.
- Safer than being a man . . . we do not suffer from testosterone poisoning.
- It is as safe as going shopping.
- I carry a cell phone.
- I do not carry a gun or any other obvious weapon. Many of my couple riding friends do not leave home without one. I am unwilling to shoot to kill, the only appropriate self-protection use of a weapon under dire circumstances. I avoid these circumstances.

The author is skeptical. Too much weird stuff is going down on the roads these days. Let's be careful out there.

MALE IMPLICATIONS

The attitude of males toward female riders is a big topic. The surveys point out that the attitude of the vast majority of men toward motorcycle women is positive and most men in the sport are supportive of women in the sport. There are, however, a significant number of "just don't get it" men out there. And many of them seem to have the job of motorcycle salesman.

It should go without saying that you do not let your husband, boyfriend or father pick out a bike for you. In particular, do not let them talk you out of the bike you want in favor of the bike they want. Experience shows that a man will probably suggest a bike to his female soul mate more in line with what he would purchase as a second bike to round out his collection. A male will make a major display of anger, hurt and anguish if you do not take his advice. This can result in actions not unlike a tantrum. Ignore it just as you would the tantrum of any other child.

Make your own choices and get something that you are comfortable with. You'll never ride that bike unless you are physically and mentally comfortable with it. Your enjoyment of the bike will be diminished if you are not satisfied with its quality, performance, fit, finish, fashion and social statement. Keep in mind that there are many after-market products that can make your bike perfect. If you buy the bike your boyfriend wants and there is something wrong with it, you are never going to even attempt to correct the problem because you don't even really like the beast (the bike, not him)! Take the advice of one survey respondent who wrote, "Choose and own your own bike. If the first choice isn't right, sell and try again."

Dealers, on the other hand, got blasted in the surveys with comments such as:

- If a woman is with a man, the salespeople talk to the man. If she is alone, they ignore her.
- Some are helpful, some don't bother with you. None carry enough gear.
- They assume we could not be riders, let alone operators.
- "You have to buy it to test-ride it," said one salesman to a potential female customer.
- "Go home and get your hubby."
- Many think you are invisible or stupid or that all women are perpetual beginners.
- Most will try to sell to men the big machines. But they will say to women, "Don't you like this pretty bike and here are the pretty accessories."
- They assume you can't do your own repairs, or can't make a decision about parts or service.

Most of the people surveyed echoed the following advice: "If you walk into a place and they ignore you, take your business someplace else. Don't deal with a shop that has an attitude."

TOP PICKS

The following motorcycles have proven to be top sellers as new bike purchases among women riders.

KAWASAKI VULCAN 500 LTD

Class: cruiser.
Engine: liquid-cooled, in-line twin 4-stroke.
Displacement: 498cc.
Valve Arrangement: DOHC 4 valves per cylinder.
Transmission: 6-speed.
Final Drive: chain.
Brakes: disc front, drum rear.
Weight: 439 lbs.
Seat Height: 28 in.

(Photo courtesy of Kawasaki Motors Corp., USA.)

HARLEY SPORTSTER

Class: Harley.
Engine: air-cooled, 45° V-twin 4-stroke.
Displacement: 1200cc/73 cid.
Valve Arrangement: OHV 2 valves per cylinder.
Transmission: 5-speed.
Final Drive: belt.
Brakes: disc front & rear.
Weight: 491 lbs.
Seat Height: 23 in.
Torque: 71 lb.ft.

(Photo courtesy Harley-Davidson Motor Company.)

BMW F650

Class: dual sport.
Engine: water-cooled,
single 4-stroke.
Displacement: 652cc.
Valve Arrangement: DOHC 4
valves per cylinder.
Transmission: 5-speed.
Final Drive: chain.
Brakes: disc front & rear.
Weight: 421 lbs.
Seat Height: 31.5 in.
Torque: 41 lb.ft.
Horsepower: 48.

*(Photo courtesy of BMW of North
America.)*

YAMAHA V-STAR

Class: cruiser.
Engine: air-cooled,
V-twin 4-stroke.
Displacement: 649cc.
Valve Arrangement: SOHC 2
valves per cylinder.
Transmission: 5-speed.
Final Drive: shaft.
Brakes: front disc, drum rear.
Weight: 496 lbs.
Seat Height: 28 in.

*(Photo courtesy of Yamaha Motor
Corp., USA.)*

SUZUKI KATANA 600

Class: sports.
Engine: oil-cooled, 4-cylinder 4-stroke.
Displacement: 599cc.
Valve Arrangement: DOHC.
Transmission: 6-speed.
Final Drive: chain.
Brakes: disc front & rear.
Weight: 441 lbs.
Seat Height: 30.9 in.

(Photo courtesy of American Suzuki Motor Corp.)

CMC SUSAN

Class: custom.
Engine: air-cooled, S&S V-twin 4-stroke.
Displacement: 88 cid.
Valve Arrangement: OHV 2 valves per cylinder.
Transmission: 5-speed.
Final Drive: belt.
Brakes: disc front & rear.
Weight: 630 lbs.
Seat Height: 24 in.
Torque: 77 lb.ft.
Horsepower: 75.

(Photo courtesy of California Motorcycle Company.)

HONDA SHADOW VT600C VLX

Class: cruiser.
Engine: liquid-cooled,
52° V-twin 4-stroke.
Displacement: 583 cc.
Valve Arrangement: SOHC
3 valves per cylinder.
Transmission: 4-speed.
Final Drive: chain.
Brakes: disc front, drum rear.
Weight: 445 lbs.
Seat Height: 27 in.

(Photo courtesy of American Honda Motor Company.)

12

WHAT EVERY MOTORIST NEEDS TO KNOW ABOUT SHARING THE ROAD WITH MOTORCYCLES

Motorcyclists and motorists (a.k.a. car drivers) seem to have a difficult time getting along on the road. Motorcyclists are often viewed as outlaw hooligans or irresponsible speed freaks by the public. Although some motorcyclists fall into these categories, the vast majority are law abiding citizens no different from the average automobile driver.

Motorcyclists view motorists as inattentive adversaries who crowd them out and cut them off. Statistics support this view. According to the National Highway Traffic Safety Administration, 66% of accidents involving motorcycles colliding with other vehicles are the fault of the other vehicles. Motorists contributed to another 10% of motorcycle accidents by unintentionally forcing a motorcycle out of its lane.

This chapter is for motorists to read. Please lend this book to your automotive friends so they might learn something about the danger they present to motorcycles.

THE PROBLEM PRESENTED BY MOTORCYCLES

Visibility is the big issue. Motorcycles have smaller profiles and are harder to see in traffic. This problem is exacerbated if the rider is not wearing brightly colored clothing or running with the headlight on. A motorcycle only a few hundred feet away occupies less of a driver's field of vision than does a pencil held at arm's length. Obviously, the smaller profile means that a motorcycle can more easily be:

- Hidden in a driver's blind spots
- Obscured by other traffic or roadside structures
- Camouflaged in the background, or "visual noise," of urban traffic

The small profile also means that there is no reference scale for the motorist. The lack of reference scale can lead a driver to:

- Misjudge the distance between the car and motorcycle
- Misjudge the speed of the oncoming motorcycle

Motorcycles can also accelerate much faster than cars, so the time it takes the motorcycle to close any distance can be much less than what a motorist expects. Motorists often conclude that a motorcycle is farther away and traveling slower than it really is.

WHAT MOTORISTS MUST DO TO SHARE THE ROAD

In a typical car/motorcycle accident scenario, a motorcyclist has 1.9 seconds to avoid an accident. This is not much time. Therefore, prevention and circumvention, by the motorist, are key. Motorists should take the following six defensive driving steps to avoid an accident with a motorcycle.

Look for Motorcycles

Studies show that drivers most often see what they look for and what they expect to see. Motorists must make a conscious effort to look for motorcycles. Motorists must mentally think about motorcycles in advance. The most critical time is when a driver, either of the motorcycle or car, changes speed or position of the vehicle. Scan 20 seconds ahead (about a quarter-mile at 50 m.p.h.), check to the side and your rearview mirrors often and perform a shoulder check when changing lanes.

For older drivers this is even more important. Studies show that the older we get, the longer it takes for our brains to recognize what it is we are looking at when the scene changes. This cognitive convergence problem can only be addressed by older drivers who take their time and deliberately look for motorcycles.

Communicate

The National Highway Traffic Safety Administration recommends that drivers always signal turns, even if there are no other vehicles in the area. There may be a motorcycle in the vicinity the driver does not see. Signaling alerts the motorcycle rider to the motorist's location and intentions.

Pay Special Attention

Pay special attention at intersections, when turning or when changing lanes. The most common car/motorcycle accidents happen at in-town intersections where a car turns left in front of a motorcycle (known as T-boning in motorcyclist vernacular). If you cannot determine the speed of the oncoming motorcycle, allow the motorcycle to pass before proceeding.

The next most common accident is a car cutting off a motorcycle in a left or right lane. Be sure to check your blind spots when changing lanes. Don't rely on a simple mirror check. Look over your shoulder as well. This is critical in states such as California that allow lane splitting, which is the practice of driving a motorcycle along the white lines of a freeway.

Treat the Motorcycle Like a Car

Legally, motorists must provide the same right-of-way and privilege to a motorcycle as to any other vehicle. Although the motorcycle does not physically take up the entire lane, the motorcyclist needs this space to maneuver around road hazards. Do not crowd the motorcyclist.

Allow at least a two-second cushion between your car and the motorcycle when traveling under 40 m.p.h. Increase this cushion to at least four seconds when traveling faster.

When passing a motorcycle, use your turn signals and move entirely into the passing lane. Do not return to the right lane until you can see the motorcycle in your rearview mirror. In congested traffic, suppress the urge to make a lane change by forcing your car into the motor-cylist's space.

View the Road from a Motorcyclist's Perspective

The motorcyclist is confronted with far more road hazards than a motorist. Many road situations that are inconsequential to the automobile driver are potentially fatal to the motorcyclist.

All things being equal, the motorcyclist will ride to the left of a lane's middle oil slick. This is where the motorcyclist can see the most and is the most easily seen. But the motorcycle faces far more hazards on the road than a car, so all things are rarely equal. Road oil, potholes, railroad tracks, pavement seams, road debris, merging traffic, large trucks and turning vehicles represent situations that may require special maneuvering. Weather, such as strong wind gusts or high glare situations, have a greater impact on a motorcycle.

Not only does the motorcycle rider face more hazards on the road, the motorcyclist does not take the same preventative action as a motorist. Motorcyclists react differently to hazards because of the limitations and nature of their machines. It takes an average motorcycle, traveling at 50 m.p.h., about 3.8 seconds (about 150 feet) to stop under good conditions. Bad conditions such as greasy wet pavement can triple a motorcycle's braking distances. Threats such as gravel, manhole covers and steel plates, which present little threat to a braking car, may make braking hazardous for the motorcycle. In such cases some motor-cyclists will "power-out" of the hazard. Some motorcycles, especially mopeds and scooters, have no torque to "power-out" of a bad situation. The only option for these bikes is to maneuver around a hazard. And this option may not be available from a poorly maintained or over-loaded motorcycle. Therefore, the motorist must give the motorcyclist room so that all of the possible escape actions are available.

The only way for a motorist to be sure he is not taking away any of the possible escape actions is to (1) scan around and beyond the motorcycle to get a good view of what the motorcyclist sees and (2) give the motorcyclist room to react.

Avoid the Young and the Restless

Many of today's motorcycles can go from zero to 100 m.p.h. in under 10 seconds with top speeds nearing 150 m.p.h. Very few motorcyclists have skills equal to the capabilities of these machines.

One of the most influential research studies on motorcycle safety is the 1981 Hurt Report by the University of Southern California Traffic Safety Center. This report notes that, not unexpectedly, inexperienced or incapable motorcycle riders are hurt most often. For example:

- More than 26% of all crashes involved riders with less than one year's experience on their motorcycle
- Ninety-two percent of riders in reportable accidents were essentially without training (i.e., self-taught or learned from family or friends)
- Motorcycle riders between the ages of 16 and 24 are significantly over represented in accidents; riders between the ages of 30 and 50 are significantly under represented.

And here is one more critical fact:

- Twelve percent of all motorcycle accidents show alcohol involvement. However, almost half the fatal motorcycle accidents show alcohol involvement.

Inexperience is the single most important factor in the cause of motorcycle accidents, followed closely by alcohol use. It makes everyone angry when a motorcyclist is riding like the road is his own private speedway. However, if you are near a motorcyclist who is young, driving recklessly or riding a poorly maintained motorcycle, the best course of action is to give that rider a wide berth.

Know How to Drive

Studies show that the typical driver thinks his or her driving is pretty darn good. This typical driver also thinks that most other drivers' driving is pretty darn bad. The truth is, none of us are really that good 100% of the time. Most of us are ignorant about what "good" driving really is. And, most of us are not aware of how our driving skills and habits change with age.

"Good" driving was probably defined for most of us in high school when either our folks taught us how to drive or we took a safe driving course. What our folks taught us was probably not "good" driving. What the safe driving course taught us, if we remember any of it, has probably been radically updated. It is beyond the scope of this text to describe "good" driving. The only logical course of action is have every driver take a student driving course every five or ten years, because our driving habits and skills change with age. This knowledge will help any driver understand just what the heck it is he is doing, and what he is up against, out there on the big macadam of life.

Young Motorists—Young drivers lack experience and a healthy respect for death. Therefore, young drivers tend to take unnecessary risks. However, young drivers do possess the best physical skills. Their eyesight is keen. Their mental and physical capabilities are fast. These skills allow them to process far more information far faster, and take action faster, than older drivers.

Experienced Younger Motorists—Motorists between the ages of 25 and 35 have acquired the necessary experience to drive safely, and still have good physical, visual and mental skills. They have seen enough disaster and tragedy in their lives to respect the destructive power of the automobile or motorcycle. These drivers are the lowest insurance risk of any age group.

Middle-Aged Motorists—By age 40, our bodies have degenerated enough to affect our driving. The most significant change is with our vision. Eyes become more light sensitive. Eyes do not adjust from light to dark as well. Eyes do not focus as well, and because eyes need ever increasing amounts of light to see, night driving becomes more difficult. Driving into and out of shadows is troublesome. Many details are not seen in low light situations. And, compared to younger drivers, our mental abilities have declined. Motorists in this category still have relatively good physical skills for driving, and so compensate for their diminished skills by driving slower.

Senior Motorists—Motorists over the age of 55 face a continuing decline of visual and physical skills, although mental skills will remain good enough to drive as long as illness does not impair brain functions. Peripheral vision is significantly diminished. Objects that are not moving are often not visually recognized. Night vision continues to deteriorate. Reaction times increase.

Automobile drivers and motorcycle riders alike should take a realistic appraisal of their skills. Ask your friends and family. If you do not trust them (or if you trained them), get an expert's opinion of your driving skills. Hang up the keys if you are too young, too old or too immature to drive safely.

GLOSSARY

ABS	Antilock brake system. System that senses when a tire is about to lose traction during braking and decreases braking force, preventing tire lock-up.
Accelerator pump	Extra pump in carburetor to temporarily increase the amount of fuel delivered to the air stream.
Air	4/5 nitrogen, about 4/5 oxygen, some carbonic gas and minor trace elements.
Air-cooling	Mechanism used to keep the engine at operating temperature by using air flowing over heat sinks to disperse excess heat into the environment directly.
Air filter	Fabric, foam or paper element used to remove dirt, contaminants and abrasive particles from the air before entering the carburetor or engine.
Air fuel ratio	Proportions in which air and fuel are mixed to form a combustible gas.
Air lock	Similar to a vapor lock, a pocket of air develops that blocks the normal flow of a fluid, such as in a hydraulic brake line. Common in two-strokes when oil injection system is allowed to run dry.
Alloy	A solid or homogenous solution that is a mixture of two or more metals to create a combined metal with better characteristics for a specific purpose.
Alternator	Modern replacement for the dynamo (generator), producing large quantities of alternating current (even at low r.p.m.) to run the electrical systems of a motorcycle.
Ammeter	Gauge that measures amps in electrical circuit.
Analog gauges	Shows information in a continuous form, often a dial; often considered the opposite of digital gauges.
Ape hangers	Very high handlebars. Usually found on choppers.
Aperture	An opening, hole or port.
Apex	The vertex or tightest point of a curve.
API	American Petroleum Institute.
ASE	National Institute for Automotive Service Excellence.

Aspect ratio	The ratio of the height of the wall of a tire to the width of the tread expressed as a percent. Section height divided by section width equals aspect ratio.
Backfire	Explosion of fuel in the intake manifold or carburetor, but often used to describe explosion of unburned fuel in exhaust system.
BDC	Bottom dead center.
Bead	Edge or lip of a tire.
Bearing	Load supporting part designed to accept the wear and punishment of moving parts while protecting more valuable parts. Two types: roller ball and metal collar cap type.
Beemer	BMW motorcycle (Bimmer is a BMW automobile).
Belt drive	Final drive (sometimes also the cam drive) using a fabric belt to provide power to the rear wheel.
Bias ply	Tire design where cords run the length of the tire.
Black ice	Ice that cannot be seen on the road surface.
Blacklist	Insurance companies' list of motorcycles that they do not want to insure because of performance reputation.
Blip	Quick throttle burst.
Block	Basic engine frame containing one or more cylinders.
Blow-by	Exploded fuel and gases forced past the piston rings into the crankcase.
Blower	Supercharger. Mechanical pump driven by the engine to push more air past the carburetors.
BMW	Bavarian Motor Works.
Boost	The amount of pressure applied by the supercharger or turbocharger.
Bore	The interior diameter of a cylinder.
Brake cylinder	Cylinder with movable piston which forces brake shoes or pads against the braking surface, usually a drum or disc (rotor).
Breaker points	Points faced with silver, platinum or tungsten which interrupt the primary circuit in the distributor to induce a high-tension current in the ignition.
Brushes	Conducting material which contact commutator of an electric motor or generator.
BSA	British Small Arms. English motorcycle maker until the 1970s.
Buddy pegs	Footpegs for motorcycle passengers.
Bushing	A removable liner for a bearing.

Caliper	Non-rotating components of disc brake that straddles disc and contains hydraulic components.
Calipers	Devices for measuring inside or outside distances and thicknesses.
Camber	Inward or outward tilt of a wheel. Also convex curvature of the road surface.
Cam shaft	The shaft with cam lobes used to open and close valves.
Capacitor	A device for storing or collecting a surge of electrical current. Also called a condenser.
Carburetor	Mechanism for mixing fuel and air and controlling the amount entering the combustion chamber.
Caster	Forward tilt of steering axis that tends to stabilize the steering.
Catalytic converter	Exhaust device to reduce pollution emissions recently used on two-stroke motorcycles.
CC	Cubic centimeters.
Center of gravity	The point in or near a body where the force of gravity appears to act. If a body is balanced at any point on the vertical line through its center of gravity, it will remain balanced. The center of an object's mass.
Chicane	A series of "esses" or turns on a racetrack.
Choke	Air restriction device to enrich the fuel mixture with more gasoline.
Chopper	Term originated from owners removing, or "chopping," features from the motorcycle and adding their own customized detailing. Now refers to a motorcycle with heavily raked front forks, highrise handlebars and an increased angle of frame to fork head.
Clutch	Device to engage and disengage engine power to drive train.
Coil	Transformer in ignition circuit to step up voltage to spark plugs.
Compression ratio	Amount of compression of the fuel:air mixture in a piston, usually about 9:1.
Compression release	Used in two-stroke engines, the compression release opens an extra valve to prevent compression and increase engine drag.
Condenser	See capacitor.
Connecting rod	Rod connecting piston to crankshaft.
Counter steer	Action of moving the wheel to the opposite direction desired in a turn.
Counterweight	Rotating shaft used to offset vibration. Sometimes called counterbalance or countershaft.
Cradle frame	Frame design where the bottom tubes "cradle" or embrace the engine.
Crankcase	External housing for the crankshaft.

Crankshaft	Rotating part of engine to which connecting rods are attached.
Crotch rocket	Small, fast motorcycle.
Cruiser	Factory made descendants of customized choppers offering a classic look. Characterized by low seat, swept-back look, lots of power with a strong exhaust note, lots of chrome.
Cylinder	Parallel-sided circular cavity, usually housing a piston.
Cylinder sleeve	Liner for a cylinder.
Dampen	The act of eliminating, or device used to eliminate (damp), unwanted oscillations and unwanted energy.
Damper	Device for controlling unwanted movement or absorbing unwanted energy.
DC	Direct current.
Deflector piston	Piston designed for two-stroke engines to channel fresh fuel up to the head forcing burnt fuel out the exhaust ports.
Desmodronic	Ducati-designed valve opening and closing system that does not rely on springs. Design offers better high r.p.m. valve control.
Detailing	In-depth cleaning, polishing, waxing and other maintenance to make a motorcycle look great.
Dieseling	Ignition in a gasoline engine of the fuel vapor by means other than the spark plug. Also called preignition or run-on.
Disc brake	Brake that utilizes friction pads held in a caliper on either side of a rotating disc.
Displacement	Engine capacity measured in cubic inches or cubic centimeters.
Distributor	An electrical circuit breaker often consisting of points, timing advance device, condenser and cam used to direct high-tension current to spark plugs at the proper timing. Often replaced with electronic ignition.
Dive	Tendency of front suspension to compress during hard braking.
DOHC	Dual overhead cam.
DOHV	Double overhead valves.
Drag	The resistance of the air to forward motion. A flat disc moving broadside along its axis has a nominal rating of 1.00.
Drum brake	Brake design with brake shoes forced out against a rotating drum.
Dry sump	Lubrication system in four-stroke engines in which the oil is carried in a separate container. Oil drains into the sump and is pumped into the separate container, keeping the sump "dry."

Dual-purpose bike	Designed for most types of terrain, the name describes a bike that has off-road capabilities with street legal accessories.
Duck	Ducati.
Dynamite	Slang for instantly applying a system to full force (e.g., "I dynamited my brakes").
Electrolyte	Battery acid.
Electronic ignition	Computer-controlled method to convey high-tension current to spark plugs.
Enduro	Strictly interpreting FIM regulations, an enduro bike is a trials bike. Common use of the term describes bikes used in enduro racing, which is off-road trail riding competition.
Fatigue	Tendency of material to fail under repeated use.
FIM	Federation Internationale Motocyclist. International governing body of motorcycle sport.
Final drive	Mechanism that delivers power to the rear wheel, usually chain, shaft or belt.
Fins	Heat sinks on an air-cooled engine.
Fishtail	Rear wheel swinging from side to side caused by increased rolling resistance of the rear tire (often caused by over braking, flat tire or frozen drive train).
Flashover	Generally an unwanted electrical discharge through the air to the ground.
Flathead	Early head design where the valves resided in the block so the head only covered the block and held the spark plug. Also called L-Head or side-valve.
Flat spot	Term refers to the condition where opening the throttle results in a reduction in speed or power output caused by incorrect fuel mixture.
Fly wheel	Rotating weight used to damp engine vibration or to improve smooth operation of the engine between power strokes.
Footprint	Contact patch of tire with road surface.
Four-stroke	Engine with the common induction, compression, power, exhaust stroke sequence. Designed by Dr. Nicolas Otto in 1876.
Freightliner	Big truck.
Fuel injection	Replaces carburetors. Uses small nozzles, called injectors, supplied fuel by an injector pump, to inject fuel into the intake manifold.
Gearbox	Transmission housing.
Goose	Moto Guzzi.
Ground	The earth pole of a battery, usually negative on most motorcycles.

Hairpin turn	A decreasing radius turn. Turn that gets progressively "tighter."
Head	Also called cylinder head. This piece covers the top of the cylinder and often houses valves, rockers and overhead cams.
Head gasket	Gasket between the cylinder head and the block or piston cylinder.
Heat sink	A device to channel heat away from a heat source.
Hog	Nickname for Harley-Davidson motorcycles.
Horsepower	One horsepower is the force necessary to lift 550 pounds one foot in one second.
Hurt Report	1981 study by University of Southern California of 3,600 motorcycle traffic accidents.
Husky	Husqvarna.
Hydrometer	Device to measure the charge in a lead acid battery.
Hydroplane	A highly dangerous situation in which the tires lose contact with the road surface and actually lift on top of a shallow film of water.
Hypoid gears	Paired beveled gears with spirally or nonradially cut teeth mated so that the pinion does not intersect the axis of the gear used in transmissions and final drives.
Identification numbers	Factory stamped frame and engine numbers used to identify the motorcycle.
Idiot light	Control panel indicator light that warns of a problem situation. Commonly called an idiot light because it neither warns you before the problem develops, nor tells you what the problem is after the bike is disabled.
Impeller	Device that assists the movement of fluid.
Injector	Mechanism to squirt fuel or lubrication where required.
Jet	Precisely drilled opening in carburetor through which fuel passes into the air stream. More generally, any hole used to control the passage of gas or fluid.
Knucklehead	Slang for Harley-Davidson engine produced between 1936 and 1947. Name comes from the valve covers that look like the knuckles of a clinched fist (or so the legend goes).
Line	Path selected by the motorcycle rider to take through a turn.
Low-side	A type of motorcycle crash that involves laying the "low side" of the bike too low in a turn, resulting in loss of traction and grounding the bike.
Lug	Operating engine at lower than normal r.p.m.s.
Magneto	Self-contained device that can be easily driven by an engine to produce ignition spark.

Manifold	Pipes that supply fuel to and channel exhaust from the head.
Master cylinder	Forces hydraulic fluid to the brake cylinder, activating the brakes.
Minibike	A miniature version of a motorcycle.
Monocoque chassis	Steel pressings welded together, providing structural equivalent of a frame and body work. Unitized frame structure with stressed sheet metal panels.
Moped	A motorized bicycle, often with pedals still attached for human power assistance, usually legally defined in states and provinces as having fewer than 50cc and cannot be capable of propelling the moped over 30 m.p.h. on level ground.
Motocross bike	Motorcycles designed for closed course or cross-country competition. These bikes are generally more technologically advanced than their off-road siblings.
M.P.G.	Miles per gallon.
Muffler	Exhaust device that cools exhaust gases, quiets exhaust noise and provides pressure to improve engine performance.
Nut cracker	Slang for motorcycle fuel tank cap hinged closest to the front of the bike, so named for the tendency of the cap to flip open in a collision while the rider slides up the tank.
Octane rating	Indicates the ability of a fuel to resist early detonation called knock.
Off-camber turn	Turn that is banked higher on the inside than on the outside.
Off-road bike	Term for a motorcycle designed specifically for off-road use.
OHC	Overhead cam.
OHV	Overhead valve.
Oil bath	Lubrication by complete submergence into oil.
Oil-cooler	Engine cooling system where the engine's oil is sent through an external radiator to help remove heat from the engine.
Overdrive	Transmission gear such that one revolution of the engine produces more than one revolution of the driveshaft. A gear ratio of less than 1:1.
Oversquare	Cylinder diameter (bore) greater than stroke. Also called short stroke.
Pancake engine	Horizontally opposed engine.
Panhead	Slang for Harley-Davidson engine produced between 1948 and 1965. Named after the valve covers that look like small turkey roasting pans.
PCV	Positive crank ventilation. Vents crankcase vapors into the intake manifold to control pollution.
Petcock	Fuel valve.

Play the clutch	Use of partially engaged clutch.
Positive camber turn	Turn that is banked such that the outside of the turn is higher than the inside of the turn. Properly banked speedways and freeways have positive camber turns.
Power band	Range of r.p.m. where an engine produces the most power.
Power plant	The engine.
Power train	Components that deliver rotary motion from the engine to the drive wheels (transmission, clutch, primary and secondary drives).
PSI	Pounds per square inch.
Pushrod	In overhead valve engines, rods from the camshaft to the rockers, activating the valves.
Radial	Tire design where the cords of the tire run from the left side of the tire to the right side.
Radiator	In liquid-cooled engines, the heat sink where excess heat is purged into the environment.
Rake	Slope of the front forks.
Reciprocating weight	The total weight of all moving parts.
Redline	Indicates the maximum r.p.m.s an engine may run.
Relay	A light current electrical switch that triggers a heavier switch capable of carrying heavier current.
Repo artist	Business thug experienced at repossessing motorcycles for finance companies.
Retard	To set back the ignition timing before the piston reaches TDC.
Road crown	Arc of road, high at the middle line, to allow for water drainage.
Rodger Flannel	Boring. Dull. Desk job.
R.P.M.	Revolutions per minute.
SAE	Society of Automotive Engineers.
Scavenge	Clearing of exhaust fumes from a two-stroke engine.
Scooter	Motorcycle design where the tires are small and fat, the engine resides over the rear wheel permitting a sheltered driving platform for the rider's feet.
Seizure	The locking in place of moving parts due to overheating, lack of lubrication or opposing pressure. Also called freeze-up.
Sending unit	Electrical or mechanical device for sensing some physical property of the motorcycle's operating conditions. Also called a sensor unit.

Shaft drive	Direct connection method between transmission and rear wheel, as opposed to chain or belt final drive.
Shim	Small piece of metal used to set clearances between valves or other parts.
Shock absorber	Also known as damper, shocks absorb road surface vibration through hydraulic friction.
Shovelhead	Slang for Harley-Davidson engines produced between 1966 and 1984, so named because the shape of the head resembles a coal shovel.
Slave cylinder	Hydraulic cylinder activated by master cylinder, usually referring to clutch or brake cylinders.
Slick	Treadless tire.
SOHV	Single overhead valve.
Solenoid	A cylinder of wire magnetically controlling a free sliding metal core.
Spine frame	Main frame structure made up of two sheet steel pressings welded together along the center line. Also can be tubular construction. Often called a "T" or "7" frame as this describes the shape of the frame.
Sport bike	Motorcycle offering the high performance characterized by leading edge engine design, heavily applied racing technology, radical aerodynamic styling, low handlebars, high-performance tires and suspension, big disc brakes.
Sport touring bike	Sport touring bikes offer more comfort than a sport bike and more speed than a touring bike.
Standard bike	Term for a basic, universal, multipurpose motorcycle design.
Stroker	Two-stroke engine.
Sump	Oil reservoir that either scavenges free draining engine oil or separately holds oil.
Tappet	Device to self-adjust valve clearances.
T-bone	Common crash condition where a car turns in front of a motorcycle and the connecting vehicles are perpendicular—hence "T-bone."
TDC	Top dead center. The point at which a piston is at its highest position (and therefore point of greatest compression) within the cylinder.
Thermostat	Controls engine temperatures by preventing coolant flow when the engine is cold and permitting flow when the engine warms.
Torque	Measure of force producing torsion and rotation around an axis. A measurement of engine power described as the ability to turn or twist. Maximum torque is produced when an engine is operating at maximum combustion efficiency.

Touring bike	Luxurious motorcycle with many comforts and amenities for long-range travel.
Transfer port	Two-stroke fresh fuel port between crankcase and cylinder.
Trials bikes	For competition over radical, rough terrain. Trials motorcycles are designed to be extremely light, minimalist off-road specialties with low gear rations, high ground clearance and control layout suited for a standing rider.
Turbocharger	Arguably a more efficient variation of the supercharger. Impellers in the exhaust are turned by the exhaust gases, which powers impellers in the air intake forcing more air past the carburetors.
Two-stroke	Mechanically simple, light and powerful, two-stroke engines combine the exhaust and intake strokes, making every other stroke a power stroke.
Undersquare	Stroke greater than "bore."
Unsprung weight	Part of the motorcycle below or not supported by the suspension.
V	An engine designed in a "V" configuration.
Valve	Control gate that allows or prevents passage of fluid or gas.
Vapor lock	Condition where fluid expansion into a vapor state prevents a system from working, traditionally the fuel delivery system.
Vespa	Italian scooter manufacturer.
V^2 Evolution	Name for Harley-Davidson engine introduced in 1984.
VIN	Vehicle identification number.
Viscosity	Measurement of the thickness or denseness of a fluid.
Voltage regulator	Controls the output from the generator.
Wankel	A rotary engine using a triangular rotor creates three chambers, each performing the same cycles as a four-stroke engine.
Water jacket	Passages between cylinder walls through which coolant circulates.
Wear bar	Raised ridge in tire tread to indicate when tire needs replacement.
Wheelbase	Measurement from the center of the front wheel to the center of the rear wheel.
Wheelie	Running the motorcycle on the rear wheel only.

Page numbers in *italics* indicate illustrations. The letter *t* following a page number denotes a table.

riders
average, profile of, 216
beginning
decision to begin, 2–3
entry level bikes for, 27, 28
female, 218
good Harley-Davidson
for, 117
used motorcycles and,
109–110
female, 216–230
anatomical differences
and, 217–218
as beginning rider, 218
and bike ergonomics,
218–222
and biking equipment,
221–222
and cold weather, 223
custom-fitting of bikes for,
221–222
and fallen bikes, raising
of, 223–224
male attitudes toward,
225–226
outfitting of, 218–222
profile of, 217
and protective clothing,
221
and purchase of bike,
225–226
and safety, 223, 224–225
top bike models for,
226–230
and weight of bike,
220–221
judgment of, evaluating, 4–5
riding
decision to begin, 2–3
dissuading children from,
2–14
physics of, and safety, 164
preparation for, 167–176
safe strategies for, 176–184

rights
of consumer, under warran-
tee, 90–91
of motorcyclists on road,
233–234
rims, design of, 61
road conditions, and braking distances, 182
road hazards
animals as, 188–189
elderly drivers as, 188, 233,
236
night riding and, 185
swerving to avoid, 180
road service insurance, 85
road surface
oil on, 183
paying attention to, 5
roller chains, 206
RON See Research Octane
Number
rotary engines, 45–46, 46, 49,
51, 51–52
r.p.m.s
and break-in period, 145
and power, 63–64
ruts, in trail riding, 193

S
SAE See Society of Automotive
Engineers
safety See also accidents
and automobiles, 231–232
and bike weight, 220–221
and carrying loads, 173–174
classes in, 14, 164
and insurance, 85
locating, 168
comfort and, 173
and emergency maneuvers,
180–181
and evasive action, 5–6, 234
car-drivers' awareness of,
234

fatigue and, 189, 196
and female riders, 223,
224–225
and group riding, 190,
190–191
horror stories and, 12–13
inexperience and, 234–235
insurance, safety courses
and, 85
knowledge necessary to attain, 7–13, 167–176
maximization of, 176–184
for new riders, 13–14
and mopeds, 40
Motorcycle Safety Founda-
tion, 168
safety courses given by, 85
night riding and, 185
and oil on road, 183
and packing loads, 173–174
and passengers, 174–175
and physics of riding,
164–167
and preride inspection,
175–176
and scooters, 40–41
and visibility, 5, 232
sand, in trail riding, 193
scanning of road, and safety, 177
scooters, 40–42
seasonal maintenance, 160–163
seat(s)
customization of, for female
riders, 222
height of, and female riders,
219
senior citizens, as hazard, 188,
233, 236
service departments, evaluation
of, 81–82
sex, and motorcycles, 11
sharing road with motorcycles,
231–236